# Eternal light and earthly concerns

Manchester University Press

# artes liberales

Series Editors

*Carrie E. Beneš, T. J. H. McCarthy, Stephen Mossman and Jochen Schenk*

Artes Liberales aims to promote the study of the Middle Ages – broadly defined in geography and chronology – from a perspective that transcends modern disciplinary divisions. It seeks to publish scholarship of the highest quality that is interdisciplinary in topic or approach, integrating elements such as history, art history, musicology, literature, religion, political thought, philosophy and science. The series particularly seeks to support research based on the study of original manuscripts and archival sources, and to provide a recognised venue for increased exposure for scholars at all career stages around the world.

*Previously published*

Writing the Welsh borderlands in Anglo-Saxon England
*Lindy Brady*

Justice and mercy: Moral theology and the exercise of law in twelfth-century England
*Philippa Byrne*

Emotional monasticism: Affective piety in the eleventh-century monastery of John of Fécamp
*Lauren Mancia*

# Eternal light and earthly concerns

## Belief and the shaping of medieval society

Paul Fouracre

Manchester University Press

Copyright © Paul Fouracre 2021

The right of Paul Fouracre to be identified as the author of this work has been asserted by him in accordance with the Copyright, Designs and Patents Act 1988.

Published by Manchester University Press
Oxford Road, Manchester M13 9PL

www.manchesteruniversitypress.co.uk

British Library Cataloguing-in-Publication Data
A catalogue record for this book is available from the British Library

ISBN    978 1 7849 9301 6    hardback
ISBN    978 1 5261 6720 0    paperback

First published 2021
Paperback published 2023

The publisher has no responsibility for the persistence or accuracy of URLs for any external or third-party internet websites referred to in this book, and does not guarantee that any content on such websites is, or will remain, accurate or appropriate.

Typeset by
Servis Filmsetting Ltd, Stockport, Cheshire
Printed in Great Britain by
TJ Books, Ltd

# Contents

| | |
|---|---|
| *List of figures* | *page* vi |
| *Preface* | vii |
| Introduction | 1 |
| 1  Beginnings | 18 |
| 2  Consolidation of provision: elite practice | 50 |
| 3  Light and power: the 'Carolingian moment' | 78 |
| 4  Lighting, lords and peasants in post-Carolingian Europe | 107 |
| 5  Lights and social formation in the central Middle Ages | 154 |
| 6  Lights in the later Middle Ages: from devotion to destruction | 181 |
| Conclusions | 204 |
| *Bibliography* | 214 |
| *Index* | 231 |

# Figures

1. Simple terracotta lamp from the early Christian period, to be placed on or by a martyr's tomb. Illustration from H. R. d'Allemagne, *Histoire du luminaire depuis l'époque romaine jusqu'au xix siècle* (Paris, 1899), p. 58. Reproduced with acknowledgement to ETH-Bibliothek Zürich — page 23
2. Approximate location of properties from which the Emperor Constantine was said to have assigned revenues for churches in Rome — 27
3. Depiction of hanging oil lamps taken from the 'Vivian Bible' of 845. Illustration from H. R. d'Allemagne, *Histoire du luminaire depuis l'époque romaine jusqu'au xix siècle* (Paris, 1899), p. 70. Reproduced with acknowledgement to ETH-Bibliothek Zürich — 111
4. Location of the monasteries which produced the major polyptychs — 112
5. The Bellagio peninsula and the Limonta estate c. 880, following R. Balzaretti, *The Lands of Saint Ambrose: Monks and Society in Early Medieval Milan* (Turnhout, 2019), p. 424 — 126
6. Northern Spain c. 950, following W. Davies, *Windows on Justice in Northern Iberia 800–1000* (London and New York, 2016), p. 165 — 132
7. Illustration from the foundation charter of the confraternity of Saint Martin of Canigou, reproduced from L. Blancard, 'Role de la confrérie de Saint-Marin de Canigou', *Bibliothèque de l'École des chartes* 42 (1881) — 144
8. *The Presentation in the Temple*, copy of Cort's engraving after Frederico Zuccaro, 1568, © The Trustees of the British Museum 1874,0613.664 — 191
9. The Archbishop of Canterbury lights a candle in memory of Diana, Princess of Wales, PIC MIKE GIMES/PA Archives/PA Image — 212

# Preface

This book has been a very long time in the making. An anonymous reader for Manchester University Press opened their report on the work: 'We have all been waiting many years for this book and I am very pleased to see it finished at last.' Fair comment: twenty-five years *is* a long time, even in academic study. I first wrote about the subject of lights in a paper published in 1995. Studying royal charters of immunity from Merovingian Francia I noticed that when a church was granted this privilege, one that in effect saved it a lot of money, the ruler said that the proceeds should go towards the cost of maintaining lights that would burn day and night in the church. This phrase had always been dismissed as empty, that is, a mere formula or flourish tacked on to the meat of the privilege at the end of the document. I decided to take the phrase more seriously, not least because my work on hagiography had shown me several instances in which writers from churches and monasteries had both stressed the importance of keeping such a light burning and commented on the difficulty of doing so. Soon I was able to contextualise that importance and to see why it was difficult to keep the lights burning, this being down to a shortage of olive oil which was the preferred fuel for them. I was thus able to understand why rulers who wished to demonstrate their piety should have been willing to help privileged religious institutions get their hands on the oil they needed. A positive reaction to that initial paper encouraged me to follow the theme through in order to investigate what the social and economic consequences of providing for the lights might have been over the longer term.

As the study unfolded, I came to realise that, if it were to be at all comprehensive and comparative, I would have to look at all of Western Europe and to follow the subject right through the Middle Ages. That is

## Preface

just the kind of situation in which a subject goes on to the back burner while more circumscribed projects with more pressing deadlines take precedence. It was thus not until 2012 that I got down to write about lights in earnest. That I could so and was able to venture beyond my areas of expertise in early medieval history was due in large part to the kindness of colleagues, first at Goldsmiths College and then at the University of Manchester. Colleagues were always ready to discuss the subject and to give me the benefit of their own specialist knowledge. A host of others supplied me with material and answered my questions. Wendy Davies, Stephen Mossman, Jinty Nelson and Susan Reynolds read every chapter in draft and the writing was much improved when I responded to their comments. I am indebted to their careful and critical reading. Without their help this work would have been very much the poorer and riddled with careless errors. I could scarcely have tackled the later Middle Ages without the help of Stephen Mossman. My work on Spain would have been a generation out of date without the guidance of Wendy Davies, and the late Susan Reynolds was indefatigable in her pursuit of clarity, and firm (but still friendly) in her struggle to stop me overusing the first person plural. Jinty Nelson has helped me with every piece I have written since she began to supervise my PhD study in 1976, and my career simply would not have happened without her care. We have become comrades in arms as historians, and the best of friends. I am fortunate to count two of the other readers as good friends too, and the third is much missed.

Ross Balzaretti, Marios Costambeys, John Gillingham and Chris Wickham all read individual draft chapters and gave invaluable advice. I salute their expertise and thank them. Georg Christ, Ann Christys, Katy Cubitt, Roy Flechner, Marci Freedman, Caroline Goodson, Nick Higham, David Killingray, Stuart Pracy, Brigitte Resl, Philip Rössner, Rachel Stone, Orri Vesteinsson, Jennifer Ward, Andrew Weir, Mark Whelan and Ian Wood all sent me material and drew my attention to important works I would otherwise have missed. I thank them all. Generations of students have also taught me that nothing is self-evident when it is new to the reader. The errors and misunderstandings that surely remain in this work are all my own. Gratitude is also due to Meredith Carroll and her colleagues at Manchester University Press for their patient encouragement and professionalism. I was delighted when MUP agreed to publish this work, for, besides admiring MUP for its publication record on subjects medieval, I wished the study to reflect my time at Manchester. Manchester has a bee as its city symbol, and it is fitting that a work that celebrates the producers of wax for the lights should emanate from the city.

## Preface

Finally I must thank family and friends who were kind enough not to ask how the book was going every time they met me. My wife Joanna has been especially supportive and patient, despite living with the lights for over half of our marriage. It is to her that I dedicate this book.

# Introduction

In the year 1203 Bishop Jon of Gardar in Greenland met up with Bishop Páll of Skalholt in Iceland. Together they consecrated a great amount of chrism. Bishop Jon then taught his colleague how to make wine out of crowberries, the 'wine' being for use in the celebration of the Eucharist. Unfortunately the next summer there were hardly any berries to be found on Iceland.[1] Nevertheless the practice of making berry-wine grew, until the Papacy got wind of it, that is. In May 1237 Pope Gregory IX wrote to Sigurðr, archbishop of Niðaros (modern-day Trondheim) in Norway. Gregory was responding to Sigurðr who had apparently asked whether his suffragan bishops, that is, the bishops of the North Atlantic lands, might be allowed to celebrate the mass without using bread and wine. Gregory's answer was unhelpful. Though he recognised that there were in this region dire shortages of bread and wine which limited the celebration of the Eucharist, it was not allowable to substitute some made-up confection for the bread, and beer or other drink for the wine. Only bread made from wheat and wine made from grapes would do, for it was these, and only these, substances which Christ had said were his body and blood.[2] It is no surprise, then, to read in the Icelandic Annals for the years 1326 and 1350 that a scarcity of wine meant that the celebration of mass was severely restricted across the island.[3]

Christianity was, of course, a religion that had its origins in the Eastern Mediterranean. The Last Supper, with its bread and wine, had been a Mediterranean meal, and after the supper Christ and his disciples went out into an olive grove (the Mount of Olives). Miracles featured wine, parables pictured vineyards, and references to olives, to oil and to oil lamps are frequent in both Old and New Testaments. But when beliefs and practices that had evolved in the Mediterranean environment spread beyond the

Mediterranean to lands without olives and without vines, no allowance was made. Iceland did not even have the bees to make the wax that could be used instead of olive oil in religious ceremonies that required the burning of lights, and chrism could not be mixed without olive oil. Icelanders did, as we have just seen, talk about substituting local products such as beer for wine, and whale oil for wax and olive oil, but they still imported these southern products, probably in small quantities, though at great cost and at great inconvenience.[4]

Icelanders had famously decided to convert to Christianity at a single meeting in the year 999. Supporting the new religion may have been a burden on a very poor society, but garnering and husbanding the resources for that support had the effect of accelerating social differentiation. Chieftains who owned churches and who were often priests themselves could now support their social power with a degree of regular income. As Orri Vesteinsson has shown, not only did the institution of the tithe guarantee that income but the charitable element of tithe also had the effect of stabilising the payment of rent. The parish now supported the poor who were thus prevented from becoming so destitute that they could no longer pay rent. Tithe therefore had the effect of redistributing wealth from the wealthier to the poorer rent payers.[5] Church owners provided the wax and other materials for their churches, but, given the advantages in status and income that such ownership brought, this must have been a price worth paying. A similar picture of conversion and accelerated social differentiation can be seen in Russia, another area remote from the Mediterranean (though not quite as remote as Iceland) that converted to Christianity relatively late and rather rapidly. The archaeology of amphorae shows a great increase in the importation of wine from Byzantium to Novgorod and Kiev after conversion in the late tenth century. The wine, and some oil, found its way into the store houses of the elite, the *boyars*, who controlled its further distribution to churches of which they were the patrons.[6] Again, association with and control of churches (and monasteries) bolstered their power. As in Iceland there were worries about supplies. In the late eleventh century the Monastery of the Caves in Kiev was in danger of failing to provide wine for the liturgy and had to be rescued by the local big men. Another time they considered making oil from the seeds of flax to burn in the monastery's lamps, but after much prayer a rich man miraculously appeared with a barrel of 'proper oil' and the day was saved.[7]

It is striking that, despite being on the periphery of Christendom in the high Middle Ages, Iceland and Russia still strove to follow beliefs and implement practices that had originated in a very different and distant environment. In the case of thirteenth-century Iceland, at least, the evidence is that people took the popes very seriously when they tried to police those practices. That they did so is testament to a strong sense of religious conformity that was common to all of Europe. One element of that conformity, namely the provision of lighting for churches, is the subject of this book. By the seventh century it was well established that churches should have lamps or candles burning in them at all times, or at least during the times of the major Christian festivals. Soon it would be a requirement to have a certain number of candles burning during the mass. At the same time a separate but widespread development was the provision of ever-burning lights to commemorate individuals. Oil for the lamps was often scarce away from the Mediterranean, and wax for the candles was still relatively expensive. The miraculous replenishment of supplies, as just seen in relation to the Monastery of the Caves in Kiev, is a fairly common trope in hagiography across Europe and attests to the difficulty of meeting the needs of lighting. The ways and means of doing so differed across time and across space and had more or less important historical consequences. In some areas in the early Middle Ages the need to provide lighting can be said to have called certain dedicated forms of social organisation into being. In others the provision goes almost without mention. Though the practice generally begins in contexts of increasing social differentiation, by the end of the Middle Ages it can be associated with the undermining of traditional hierarchies. Again, Iceland makes the point: initially church owners provided wax for services, but by the mid-thirteenth century lighting dues were introduced which were paid by all tithe payers. This had an unintended consequence: it loosened ties between owners and churches and strengthened ties between church and congregation, which in turn helped the development of parishes.[8]

It would be foolish to claim that the provision of lighting for churches was of central importance to the religious economy, let alone crucial to economic and social activity more generally. If we reduce to essentials the contribution of the early medieval Church to economic development, as Jean-Pierre Devroey has done for the Carolingian Church, then this lies in the stimulus given to agrarian production.[9] Lighting should not be discussed in isolation, for there was a constant need to provide other elements deemed necessary for worship: wine, as we have already seen, but also books, vestments, utensils and, above all, buildings. Nevertheless, even if they were not of determinant economic importance, the ways in which these needs were provided for constitute very important evidence for our understanding of the material consequences of belief. It is at the very root of that cultural history without which our social and economic history must fall short in explaining behaviour and meaning.[10] More than any other element, the provision of light lies at the heart of the relationship between belief and the material world. I will not, however, discuss lighting in terms of the general illumination of the church. That form of lighting was utilitarian and not explicitly associated with the spirit. It did not carry the moral freight that lighting on the altar or before shrines did. Providing for the lighting of the body of the church was subsumed into the everyday costs of a running an institution, and thus does not stand out in the record. The cost of general illumination was ultimately covered by the tithe but is generally not itemised in church accounts. Using wax or oil to provide illumination in general would have been very expensive.

Nor was this illumination necessarily fuelled by wax or oil. In modern times providing illumination was more a civic good than a religious duty, but to provide light was always a good thing to do. A modern example can be taken from the church of Kirk Maughold on the Isle of Man, otherwise known for the collection of early medieval inscribed stones in its graveyard. Inside the church an inscription reads: 'To the Glory of God. The Electric Lighting in this Church is Dedicated in Memory of Those Who Gave Their Lives in the World War 1939–1945. Their Names are on the War Memorial'. The dedication is placed in a religious setting, but the memorial itself is civic and secular. This is a rather neat illustration of the way in which light would lose its spiritual charge in some post-medieval societies, and I will have something to say on that.

By contrast, lights of wax and oil on the altar, before shrines and at graves symbolised eternity, hence the desire to have lamps or candles burning all the time, and hence its importance in commemoration. An ever-burning light is what was called in German *ewiges Licht*, 'eternal light'. In Latin, the burning was said to occur *perpetualiter*. The material provided was thus visibly consumed and converted into something which rose heavenwards to eternity. Since that material (oil and wax) was relatively scarce, and expensive, its provision was prestigious and noteworthy. That is to say, it is well represented in the written record, and its history can thus be tracked across the entire Middle Ages. And since the provision was bound up with prestige, and the social and institutional privilege that came with prestige, its history reflects on development in a wide range of spheres. For example, it can be observed to have been important in acculturation within Christendom, as practices originally the preserve of the elite became more widespread as more people could afford to take part in them, thereby reinforcing their rising status. Of this the consequences

*Introduction*

included growing social diversity and, for some, increasing wealth. Finally, and importantly, as hinted earlier, the track is uneven, sometimes almost invisible. These gaps in our knowledge are of interest in themselves. In what contexts, and at what times, was provision of light apparently *not* recorded? Why did such provision have marked social consequences in one society but not in another? There is here an entry into comparative history at the level of widespread social practice. The provision of lighting was only one part of the cost of the liturgy, and the liturgy's overall cost was undoubtedly relatively small in comparison to the combined costs of, say, lordship, kingship or warfare. At the same time it was a requirement universally recognised. The provision of lighting is therefore a subject of great historical importance because it tells us much about how a common belief was translated into practice differently in different environments, and about what that practice can tell us about its otherwise unrecorded practitioners. It is, moreover, important to note that providing light, both for the liturgy and for commemoration, was in principle and practice not gendered. The subject thus has the capacity to tell us something about how women could contribute to religious life in a way that improved their social standing.

In order to cover what is a historical millennium and most of a continent, this study of lighting provision will of necessity be somewhat broad-brush. It will have more to say about the earlier part of this period than about later medieval provision, because it is in the earlier period that we first encounter the translation of belief into practice. Further, very little has been written about the earlier period in this respect, whereas the more plentiful records of lighting in the later Middle Ages have attracted considerable attention, especially in relation to religious guilds which were dedicated to its provision. After introducing the sources in which references to lighting are to be found, and after briefly discussing previous work on the subject, I will turn to the establishment of the belief that lights should be burned in every church. I will then look at the translation of that belief into practice against the background of a marked decline in olive oil production in the Mediterranean lands from the late fourth century onwards and the related incorporation of the Church as a lead player in the political economy. This will take us above all into Frankish territory where the means of provision found their strongest institutional form. We can then follow that thread through to the end of the Carolingian period, before cutting back to compare provision in Italy and Spain. Next we must consider the rise of the so-called *Zensualität* in Germany. This was a whole class of people ostensibly organised to pay tribute in wax to the Church. Why this class did not materialise in neighbouring West Frankish (i.e. French) lands is an intriguing question. We must then also compare the situation in late Anglo-Saxon England, a society from which there is only one single reference to an individual donating the means of provision of light to a church. How can this striking silence be explained? And why in England should the situation have been so sharply reversed after 1066? We can then move forward in time to the twelfth century when provision started to mushroom in the hands of dedicated associations (guilds and confraternities), and also became urbanised. I will finish with revolts against lighting practices. This was during the early Reformation, a time when lamps were seen as wasteful consumers of resources that could be better used elsewhere. For just as belief called the practice into being, a change in belief in some regions brought it to a sudden and even violent end. In parts of Germany, for example, lamps were smashed as *Ölgötzen* – 'oil guzzling idols'.

First, the sources. Lights, and the provision of lights, are mentioned in dispositive, normative, discursive and narrative sources, which is to say that references crop up in a very wide range of records, a fact that of itself is an indication of the perceived importance of the practice. The main group of dispositive records consists of charters which record gifts to churches and monasteries which were made in order to pay for lights. These documents survive either as original sheets of parchment, or more commonly as copies made by ecclesiastical institutions and archived in cartularies. The numbers of surviving charters rises as the medieval period progresses, as we see in England following the Norman Conquest. Their overall numbers have never been estimated, but it has been suggested for England at least that by the end of the Middle Ages charters were being produced in the millions. Generally speaking, the survival of charters depended upon the fate of the institutions which kept them. The rate of survival is thus relatively high in Italy, France and Germany where certain institutions were founded in the early Middle Ages and survived for several centuries, sometimes even down to the modern day.[11] These long runs are essential for the historian keen to identify changing patterns of donation. A case in point would be the Italian monastery of Farfa in Lazio which has an uninterrupted run of charters that starts in the year 705 and ends in 1120. In this cartulary, which was put together by the Farfa monk Gregory di Catino in the early twelfth century, there are no fewer than 1,323 charters.[12] In Spain, by contrast, the survivals from the Visigothic period are negligible. From Anglo-Saxon England survivals are relatively few: in all around sixteen hundred documents.[13] Thus for the equivalent period, Farfa alone has about two-thirds the number of charters that survive from Anglo-Saxon England in its entirety. The number from West Francia for the period before 1000 has been estimated by Nicolas Perreaux as 11,353, of which about 10 per cent are the original documents. In terms of this kind of record, then, some regions are very much better documented than others, and in some regions the frequency of references to lighting provision is much higher than in others. In the Farfa collection, for example, about 7 per cent of charters refer either to lighting or to olives or wax. That percentage is closely matched in runs of royal charters surviving from Francia in the ninth century: 8 per cent of the surviving charters from the reign of Lothar II (ruled 855–69), and 7.7 per cent of those of Charles the Bald (ruled 838–77) were concerned with lighting.[14] In England pre 1066, as just noted, only one document (a will from the year 995) ever makes mention of provision for lights.[15] There are thus plentiful records from some societies and hardly any from others. Such a difference in rates of reference is a major problem. Charters record instances of provision as opposed to discussions about providing, but where we find such discussion without the charter records of provision we may suspect that it is different habits in recording and differential rates of survival rather than differences in practice that are responsible.

One way to check whether the practice was in fact being carried out but not recorded in charters, or perhaps recorded in charters that have not survived, is to look for references in normative sources. Included in this category are 'formularies'. Formularies are collections of forms (*formulae*) to be used in the drawing up of charters. They are normative in that they set out the 'correct' way of doing this. Although formularies can also contain much that is outdated and sometimes seem to provide forms for the kinds of thing that never had taken and never would take place, a strong case can be made for seeing them as generally reflecting, and even facilitating, social and legal practice.[16] If *formulae* concerned with lighting do reflect what people were doing, or at least meant to be doing, it must be suspected that where there is a form for a charter detailing provision of lights, but no surviving charters in that form, the practice did take place. From Visigothic Spain, for example, there is a *formula* for drawing up a charter in which provision for lighting is made, but no actual charters which do this. Since the phrases used in the *formula* turn up several centuries later when the charters making provision first appear, we might infer that what we are then seeing is the first surviving record of what was a centuries-old practice. It could, of course, be the case that in Spain the practice was discontinued and then reinvented, with those drawing up charters looking to the ancient *formula* to see how to make provision, although this seems unlikely given the continuity of practice in other regions of Europe. Here, the subject is important in thinking about the wider question of continuity in relation to how Christian society developed in late ninth- and tenth-century northern Spain (at least as seen through the lens of the newly founded monasteries there).

More explicitly normative are the law and legislation which underpinned the dispositive force of charters. This material can be just as anachronistic and implausible as some elements in the formularies, and in addition it can be intentionally idealistic and imperialistic.[17] It can nevertheless reveal common concerns and these have important bearings on the issue of continuity. Also of great interest is the relationship between the secular and the sacred when both call for the needs of the Church to be provided for. Was it envisaged that people could simply be ordered to provide? Or was this a matter of religious exhortation? Alongside the law codes and the legislation of particular rulers, we have a raft of normative material produced by the Church. This consists of the rulings of church councils, episcopal orders and statutes, and the customs of religious houses. It is in these sources that we find the specifications for lighting rituals, that is, detailed liturgical arrangements. These are important for judging the place of lighting in the wider liturgical context. Further to be included amongst the normative material from the Church in the Carolingian period are the estate surveys known as polyptychs, which made inventories of church lands within the framework of norms. These date from the end of the eighth century to the late tenth century. They sometimes list tributes to be paid for lighting to the church in question and they provide invaluable information about the kind of people who paid. For actual accounts (what was paid rather than what was supposed to be paid) we have to go to the twelfth century and beyond, the period in which we also meet the regulations of guilds and confraternities dedicated to lighting. It is from the regulations and financial accounts of this later period that can be demonstrated the massive extent to which the number and range of people making provision, and thus the practice itself, had grown. Set against the norms for the earlier period which established the obligation to provide, the later growth raises very interesting questions of why interest in the provision increased when it did, and in particular, of what factors limited its growth at earlier times.

Discussions about the meaning of lighting and of its importance in worship preceded the laying down of norms. There is a range of discursive writing here, and lights are a subject that people returned to again and again in theological tracts, sermons and letters. A good example of this kind of discussion would be Saint Aldhelm's thoughts on the nature of bees, for this is relevant to the question of lighting materials because it

## Introduction

impacts on the question of the purity of wax.[18] The whole of this study is in effect sandwiched between two periods of lively discussions about the use of lights. The first, in the fourth century, concluded that their use was appropriate, efficacious and desirable. The second, in the sixteenth century, came to the conclusion that it was useless, inappropriate and undesirable to burn material in order to gain access to eternity. Narrative, our final category of sources, is informed by all the others, for it constructs practice on the basis of opinion, and according to norms about transaction with the holy. As was seen earlier with the story from the Monastery of the Caves, narrative can also reflect the conditions in which needs were met. There is indeed a significant corpus of miracle stories that revolve around the scarcity of lighting materials. Other stories relate the miraculous properties of such materials, and yet others speak of lighting in the context of venerating particular saints. Hagiography provided a kind of running commentary on the history of provision, for, if light signifies eternity, then it is only to be expected that it should be close at hand to the miraculous. Non-hagiographic narrative is useful where it mentions the materials and the conditions of trade. This, unfortunately, occurs seldom. For trade, especially in the earlier period, we must make use of archaeology, and further on the material side there is the art-historical evidence of lamps, candelabra and chandeliers. For the overall setting we must draw on architectural history.

We have seen that references to lighting are scattered across a wide variety of sources, and also that the records have a regional and chronological patchiness. It may be this unevenness that partly explains why the historical significance of the provision of lighting has not until very recently been subjected to sustained investigation, even though every church was in principle required to burn lights. It is nevertheless curious that historians have ignored, or somehow not seen, references to the provision for lighting even when they have commented on other ways in which particular churches or monasteries were provided for. Nicholas Schroeder, for example, has recently written at length about how the monks of the twin monasteries of Stavelot-Malmedy (in present-day Belgium) were supplied with what they needed and about how the peasants on the monasteries' estates were organised.[19] He did not mention lights as a need to be met, nor the peasants known as *censuales* (the peasants organised to pay dues often earmarked for the lights: this is the class of people referred to as the *Zensualität* in German-language studies) even though many of the monasteries' charters refer either to the lights or to the *censuales*. One charter that the author refers to, from the year 1153, announces as a general principle that the rent payed by the *censuales* must go towards the provision of lights and for the roof of a church.[20] From another Stavelot-Malmedy charter, issued in the year 1087, in which two peasants were given to the monasteries, Schroeder actually quotes the phrase that this was *ad lumine* ('for the light', i.e. to provide for the light).[21] One presumes that at some stage he must have transcribed this phrase from the document, but that he did not see it as significant, or in effect did not see it at all. The connection between provision and social formation has more generally been overlooked, perhaps because historians concerned with social development and the political economy are generally not interested in the liturgy, whilst those who concentrate on the detail of liturgical practice often do not think about the social and economic consequences of that practice. The two should of course be brought together because of the well-evidenced belief that enabling worship by providing the physical means was an act of social charity (i.e. the giving of alms) as well as a religious duty.[22] All Christians were in theory required to bring offerings to the mass, and the range of such offerings very much reflects what local communities could produce from the field.[23] Marc Bloch in his massively influential survey *Feudal Society* noted that the 'wretched' lighting of the Middle Ages must have made for poor living conditions, but he did not go on to consider how this gloomy situation had the effect of making light a focus of religious practice and led to the privileging of those who could provide the light.[24] This omission is slightly surprising because Bloch was keenly aware of environmental factors and he was very interested in a class of people, the *colliberti*, who were distinguished by the payment of tribute which was sometimes dedicated to lighting.[25] He noted that their tribute was often paid in wax, and that they paid 4 pence a year as *chevage*, 4 pence being for long the price of a pound of wax, but Bloch was apparently not interested in what the wax was used for.[26] We might see here a reflection of the anti-clericalism and French republicanism of the *Annales* school of History of which Bloch was a leading proponent.

In more modern surveys of the development of early medieval Europe, which include surveys of the Church, the subject of lighting hardly registers against the main concerns such as fiscal decline, agrarian development, and political and social reorientation, as well as the rise to power of the Church. In his magisterial *Framing the Early Middle Ages*, Chris Wickham was careful to chart the history of olive oil production in the various Mediterranean regions, because that history tells us much about the decline of inter-regional trade networks which marked the transition from the ancient to the medieval worlds.[27] He never asks what the oil might have been used for, and he never mentions the rise of wax production

*Introduction*

which resulted as a consequence of the oil shortage. To be fair, it was not Wickham's brief and certainly not his wish to write a cultural history of Catholic Christianity, yet an investigation of the way in which emerging elites consolidated their hold over others by providing the material means for worship and commemoration would have given him further insight into the construction of power in a world in which the elite could no longer fund their privilege from direct taxation.[28] Michael McCormick's *Origins of the European Economy* does mention olive oil.[29] For McCormick, as for Wickham, olive oil production and trade works as a barometer of the state of the later Roman Mediterranean economy, but again there is no discussion of what the oil was for, or of how people adjusted to its disappearance. In McCormick's thinking the 'economy' equates largely to Mediterranean trade. He is not concerned with agrarian production except where and when specialised products came to be traded. He is not interested in the political economy or in the Church's role in it. Despite McCormick's earlier interest in the liturgy, the materialisation of belief and its consequences have no place in his work on the economy.

We can find more about the consumption of oil and wine in specialist studies that focus on the part these two commodities played beyond trade in both daily life and religious culture. It is very useful, for example, to think about the alimentary use of oil in southern Europe.[30] This may help us understand why, in some areas where small olive groves were ubiquitous and oil relatively plentiful, there are so few grants for lighting. In parts of Italy and Spain a church with a dozen or so olive trees on its lands would have had sufficient oil for all of its needs. Seminal for an understanding of this small-scale production and use of both oil and wine is a paper by A. I. Pini published in the *Settimane di Spoleto* series in 1990 following a conference on the plant environment in the early Middle Ages.[31] This was succeeded in 2006 by another Spoleto conference concentrated solely on oil and wine.[32] The 32 papers in this impressive collection are concerned as much with the use of oil as they are with its production, and their authors are thus very much alive to the religious and cultural significance of both oil and wine. But in working out from the evidence for production and use in the Mediterranean zone (and above all in Italy), they hardly consider what happened in regions without ready access to these materials. This leaves Europe north of the Alps largely out of the picture, whereas it is in precisely these regions that the interplay of rising demand and growing shortage had palpable historical consequences.[33] It is interesting to note a significant degree of overlap in the 32 papers, as well as frequent reference back to Pini's original survey. Repetition here has the effect of establishing a canon of primary sources and secondary works which is very useful indeed in setting out what is immediately knowable about the subject. It is, however, rather disappointing when it is a matter of suggesting further lines of inquiry or in dealing with the essential problem of how societies from very different ecological zones met the material needs of a religion that had developed in the Mediterranean environment.

Following through on the use as opposed to the production and trading of oil, one might have expected lighting to have featured in Julia Smith's *Europe after Rome* which is a cultural history that does focus on the material production of cultural life. But Smith is primarily interested in the lived experience and the construction of cultural identity in the various regions of Europe.[34] In this big picture there is no room for a detailed examination of religious practice, although the fact that that practice is not gendered is of great relevance to that picture. More surprisingly, two recent big surveys of the Church, Susan Wood's *The Proprietary Church in the Medieval West* and John Blair's *The Church in Anglo-Saxon Society*, likewise have little to say on the subject.[35] In Blair's case, this is no doubt because he is following the lie of the Anglo-Saxon evidence, and as we have already seen this scarcely makes reference to lighting. Though Wood's work is monumental, it is very tightly focused on questions of church ownership rather than on religious practice. In a section which deals with church income, dues for lighting are not distinguished from the body of miscellaneous 'offerings' and *altaria* which went to meet a church's needs.[36] Likewise she does not ask whether a proportion of the tithe went towards the lights. Her concern is to investigate who had control over this income, rather than what it was used for. Finally, we have another monumental work, Robert Bartlett's *Why Can the Dead Do Such Great Things?*, published in 2013.[37] Bartlett surveys the cult of saints across the entire medieval period in both East and West, but his treatment of gifts to the saints is fleeting, and references to burning lights at shrines are curiously only incidental. He is not interested in the wider phenomenon of commemoration, although at the end of the work he does acknowledge that the latter may have been as important in terms of resources as the material dedicated to the cult of the saints.[38]

There are nevertheless a few works which do concentrate on lighting. In 1802 the scholar Fanciulli published a brilliant monograph on lighting and hanging lamps.[39] He noted the scriptural origins of lighting practices and importantly he listed all the gifts of lamps in the *Liber Pontificalis*, the collection of papal biographies from the early Middle Ages. Using conciliar sources, hagiography and letters, Fanciulli was able to describe the origins and spread of lighting rituals, and he had a keen eye for gifts

*Introduction*

of oil and grants towards the cost of lighting. His work is, however, rarely cited. This may be because it is short, written in Latin and concentrates only on Rome and the Papacy in the period up to the end of Lombard rule in Italy. More widely cited is H. R. d'Allemagne's *Histoire du luminaire depuis l'époque romaine jusqu'au xix siècle*, published in 1891.[40] D'Allemagne explained the origins of the use of lighting in religious practice, but for our purposes his account is of limited use. This is because he had little to say on the early Middle Ages, with the bulk of the work focusing on the late and post-medieval periods. Secondly, he was more interested in the technicalities and paraphernalia of lighting (above all in lamps and candelabra) than in how lighting materials were provided. A much more comprehensive, although relatively brief, account came in 1959 with D. R. Dendy's seminal work *The Use of Lights in Christian Worship*.[41] Dendy was not concerned with how the light was provided, but his account of how early Christians had misgivings about using light to signify the holy, and then of how the rituals spread, is concise, clear and well supported. He covered the entire medieval period and was able to include a postscript on the return of antipathy towards the practice in the Reformation. He is particularly helpful in demonstrating how lighting dedicated to the saints was far more important in material terms than the lighting used in services for the whole congregation.[42] The subject finally received an in-depth, all-round treatment in Catherine Vincent's *Fiat lux. Lumière et luminaires dans la vie religieuse du XIIe au XVIe siècle*.[43] Vincent tackled both the provision and the practice. She drew on Dendy for the origins and spread, and on d'Allemagne for the technical aspects. Using later medieval church accounts which detail the provision of wax and the cost of services as well as the duties of those concerned with lighting, she was able to quantify the phenomenon in a way that no previous scholar had even come close to doing. She could also detail the activities of guilds and confraternities dedicated to lighting so that we can have some impression of the relative social importance of the practice, at least for the period 1300–1500. Yet Vincent's work has by no means exhausted the subject, not least because she is another who seems not to have noticed the non-gendered aspect. As the title of her book indicates, she is primarily interested in the later medieval period, and the bulk of her material comes from France. The fifteenth-century financial accounts of the cathedrals of Paris and Rouen have pride of place as documentary sources, and, although she does draw on some English and Italian material, it is above all France that is made to stand for Europe as a whole.[44] The great omission here is Germany, arguably where provision had the greatest social and political consequences, first in the formation of the *Zensualität* and then in the rise of the *Zeche*, urban associations dedicated to providing lights which became nodal points of religious revolution. This means Vincent's work lacks the comparative element that the present study is seeking to supply. Drawn quite naturally to rich sources that have the detail to present to us the phenomenon at the height of its importance, Vincent is less aware of regional differences and of lacunae in the evidence. Her focus on the later part of the medieval period is entirely sensible, for this is where the richest evidence is to be found. But a consequence of that chronological focus is that the earlier (and much longer) period seems to serve only as a kind of prologue to the main event. Vincent is clear on how lighting practices developed in the early Middle Ages, and she rarely misses a reference to lighting in the period before 1200, but she explains how the practice came into being in order to show how it then 'took off' after 1200. Whereas for Vincent as a late medievalist the 'taking off' and subsequent high point of the use of lights in religious worship is the main concern, for the early medievalist the task is to understand why it took so long to take off after being established at the very beginning of the medieval period. Concentrating on this task draws us in to thinking more carefully about the historical contexts in which the practice developed. It requires us to put the phenomenon of lighting and the provision of lighting into fresh perspective. I will begin this by looking at how eternal light first entered religious practice in a newly Christian Western Europe.

## Notes

1 *Pals saga biskups*, ch. 9, *Izlenzk fornrit* XVI, ed. Asdis Egilsdottir (Reykjavik, 2002), p. 311. I owe this and the following Icelandic references to Orri Vesteinsson, who kindly translated this passage for me. See also B. Gellinger, *Icelandic Enterprise. Commerce and Economy in the Middle Ages* (South Carolina, 1981), p. 16.
2 *Diplomatarium Islandicum I*, ed. J. Sigurdsson (Copenhagen, 1857–1876), no. 131, p. 514.
3 *Islandske annaler indtil 1578*, ed. G. Storm (Chria, 1888), pp. 346, 335, 396. But note that in some years (e.g. 1389) wine was plentiful: p. 416. In the fifteenth century the Saxons had better luck when they asked Pope Nicholas V if they might be allowed to substitute butter for oil in the baking of Advent *Stollen*, for they could not get hold of olive oil, and the rape seed oil they were using tasted unpleasant. After forty years of deliberation, in 1490 the Papacy finally agreed to the change to butter.
4 The late eleventh-century collection of Icelandic laws known as *Grágás* ('Grey Goose') stipulated that the products most essential for import to Iceland were

grain, linen, timber, wax and tar: *Grágás: Elzta lögbók Íslendiga. Útgefin eptir skinnbókini í bókasafni konungs*, 2 vols, ed. V. Finsen (Copenhagen, 1852, repr. Reykjavik, 1945), 1b, 123–5, see Gellinger, *Icelandic Enterprise*, pp. 14–15. In 1200, for instance, a ship from the Orkneys carried grain to Iceland. The cargo also included 5.4 kg of wax (a tiny quantity in comparison to amounts used by churches in continental Europe where it was not unusual for individuals to donate their body weight in wax to the church). Wine generally came to Iceland via Norway. Occasionally, as in 1247, it was gifted in some quantity, the provision of wine being one way of establishing overlordship: *Thordar saga kakala*, ch. 48, *Sturlunga saga*, ed. Jon Johannesson, Magnus Finnbogason and Kristjan Eldjarn (Reykjavik, 1946), p. 84. According to one manuscript of a letter of 1277, wax might also be the subject of gift, but again in very small quantities (one pound from the king of Norway to a bishop): *Islenzk fornrit* XVII, ed. Gudrun Asa Grimsdottir (Reykjavik, 1998), p. 65.

5 O. Vesteinsson, *The Christianization of Iceland* (Oxford, 2000), pp. 78–84, 111. Tithe was established by law in 1097. On poor relief, *Gragas* 1b 1–28, 2 103–51.

6 T. S. Noonan and R. K. Kovalev, 'Prayer, Illumination and Good Times: the Export of Byzantine Wine and Oil to the North of Russia in Pre-Mongol Times', *Byzantium and the North (Acta Byzantina Fennica)* 8 (1997), 73–96, and T. S. Noonan and R. K. Kovalev, 'Wine and Oil for All the Rus! The Importation of Byzantine Wine and Olive Oil to Kievan Rus', *Byzantium and the North (Acta Byzantina Fennica)* 9 (1999), 118–52.

7 *The Paterik of the Kievan Caves Monastery*, trans. M. Heppell (Harvard Library of Early Ukrainian Literature, English Translations 1) (Cambridge, Mass., 1989), pp. 68–9. It is interesting to note that oil was considered so vital in a region that exported wax to Byzantium, and which would later export wax to England: see below, Chapter 6.

8 Vesteinsson, *Christianization*, pp. 110–11.

9 P. Devroey, 'Réflexions sur l'économie des premiers temps carolingiens (768–877)', *Francia* 13 (1986), 475–88. It is a theme than underpins several of the articles reprinted in the collection P. Devroey, *Études sur le grand domaine carolingien* (Aldershot, 1993).

10 Walter Benjamin, *The Arcades Project*, trans. H. Elland and K. McLaughlin (Cambridge, Mass., 1999).

11 For the effect of this clustering of documents around particularly long-lived institutions, see P. Fouracre, 'Francia and the History of Medieval Europe', *Haskins Society Journal* 23 (2011, pub. 2014), 1–21.

12 *Il Regesto di Farfa compilato da Gregorio di Catino*, 5 vols, ed. I. Giorgi and V. Balzani (Rome, 1879–1914).

13 This number is taken from P. Sawyer, *Anglo-Saxon Charters. An Annotated List and Bibliography* (London, 1968).

14 See below, Chapter 3.

15  *Anglo-Saxon Wills*, ed. and trans. D. Whitelock (Cambridge, 1930), no. 16(1).
16  The case is made in A. Rio, *Legal Practice and the Written Word in the Early Middle Ages. Frankish Formulae c. 500–1000* (Cambridge, 2009).
17  P. Wormald, 'Lex Scripta and Verbum Regis: legislation and Germanic kingship from Euric to Cnut', in P. Sawyer and I. Wood (eds), *Early Medieval Kingship* (Leeds, 1977), pp. 105–38.
18  A. Cassiday, 'Saint Aldhelm's Bees (De virginitate prosa, cc. iv–vi): Some Observations on Literary Tradition', *Anglo-Saxon England* 33 (2004), 1–22.
19  N. Schroeder, *Les hommes et la terre de Saint Remacle. Histoire sociale et économique de l'abbaye de Stavelot-Malmedy VIIe–XIVe siècles* (Brussels, 2015), pp. xx, 219–88. I am grateful to Wendy Davies for drawing my attention to this work.
20  *Recueil des chartes de l'abbaye de Stavelot-Malmedy*, ed. J. Halkin and C. Roland, 2 vols (Brussels, 1909), no. 244, pp. 467–9.
21  *Stavelot-Malmedy*, no. 116, p. 240.
22  On the development of donations and the theology of alms giving, Ph. Jobert, *La notion de donation: convergences: 630–750* (Paris, 1977).
23  D. Ganz, 'Giving to God in the mass. The experience of the offertory', in W. Davies and P. Fouracre (eds), *The Languages of Gift* (Cambridge, 2010), pp. 18–32, esp. p. 28.
24  M. Bloch, *Feudal Society*, trans. L. Manyon (London, 1961), p. 72.
25  M. Bloch, 'Les *colliberti*. Étude sur la formation de la classe servile', *Revue Historique* 57 (1928), pp. 1–48, 225–63, repr. M. Bloch, *Mélanges historiques I* (Paris, 1963), pp. 385–451.
26  Bloch, 'Les *colliberti*', *Mélanges I*, p. 401 for *chevage*, p. 426 for tribute.
27  C. Wickham, *Framing the Early Middle Ages. Europe and the Mediterranean, 400–800* (Oxford, 2005). Of the 34 references to olive oil production, the bulk come in part IV of the work (pp. 591–824), the three chapters of which deal with exchange networks.
28  For the development of this line of thinking, P. Fouracre, '"Framing" and lighting: another angle on transition', in R. Balzaretti, J. Barrow and P. Skinner (eds), *Italy and Early Medieval Europe. Papers for Chris Wickham* (Oxford, 2018), pp. 305–14.
29  M. McCormick, *Origins of the European Economy. Communications and Commerce AD 300–900* (Cambridge, 2001). There are 13 references to oil, and just one to wax. No connection is made between the decline of the Mediterranean oil trade and the rise of wax production north of the Alps.
30  A. J. Grieco, 'Olive tree cultivation and the alimentary use of olive oil in late medieval Italy (ca. 1300–1500)', in M. C. Amouretti and J.-P. Brun (eds), *La production du vin et d'huile en Mediterranée (Bulletin de Correspondance Hellénique*, Supplement 27, Paris, 1993), pp. 297–306.
31  A. I. Pini, 'Vite et olivo nell'alto Medioevo', in *L'Ambiente Vegetale nell'alto Medioevo* (Settimane di Spoleto 37, 1990), 329–70.
32  *Olio e Vino nell'alto Medioevo* (Settimane di Spoleto 54, 2007).

*Introduction*

33 Several of the papers rather lazily refer to a single paper to cover areas north of the Alps: P. Fouracre, 'Eternal light and earthly needs: practical aspects of the development of Frankish immunities', in W. Davies and P. Fouracre (eds), *Property and Power in the Early Middle Ages* (Cambridge, 1995), pp. 53–81.
34 J. M. H. Smith, *Europe after Rome. A New Cultural History 500–1000* (Oxford, 2005).
35 J. Blair, *The Church in Anglo-Saxon Society* (Oxford, 2005); S. Wood, *The Proprietary Church in the Medieval West* (Oxford, 2006).
36 Wood, *Proprietary Church*, pp. 459–518.
37 R. Bartlett, *Why Can the Dead Do Such Great Things?* (Princeton, 2013).
38 Bartlett, *Why Can the Dead Do Such Great Things?*, p. 633: 'It is an open question whether the amount of effort put into the commemoration of the (non-saintly) dead, and the investment it represented, was greater than that dedicated to the cult of the saints'.
39 L. Fanciulli, *De Lucernis sive Lampadibus Pensilibus* (Macerate, 1802).
40 H. R. d'Allemagne, *Histoire du luminaire depuis l'époque romaine jusqu'au xix siècle* (Paris, 1891).
41 D. R. Dendy, *The Use of Lights in Christian Worship* (London, 1959).
42 Dendy, *Use of Lights*, p. 69.
43 C. Vincent, *Fiat Lux. Lumière et luminaires dans la vie religieuse du XIIe au XVIe siècle* (Paris, 2004).
44 The index to *Fiat Lux* has 23 references to England and 13 to Italy, but only four to Germany and one to Spain.

# 1

## Beginnings

The burning of lights in Christian worship has its origins in Scripture. Honouring the saints with lights, and using lights to commemorate the dead more generally, were, however, practices arguably imported into Christianity from the funerary customs of the ancient world. The veneration of light is in fact common in religions across the world in which light symbolises good and darkness is associated with evil, or light with life and darkness with death. In Hinduism, for example, light represents divinity and the gods of heaven, whereas darkness portends the presence of demons. Light is even hidden in sound. Chanting and lighting propitiate God and protect from evil. Lamps and lights thus play an important part in the ritual of Hindu worship, and one of the most important Hindu festivals is a festival of light, *Diwali*. In ways that have striking parallels in the Christian world, in Hinduism the provision of material for lighting, that is, the lamps and the fuel, could have significant social and economic consequences. In Andhra Pradesh in south-east India in the central Middle Ages merchants donated lamps and cattle to temples, the cattle providing the *ghee* (clarified butter) which fuelled the lamps. Fifty cows were apparently needed to produce enough *ghee* to keep each lamp perpetually alight, and the cattle-herding which the provision required was a factor in bringing local hunter-gatherers into the pastoral economy.[1] Again with strong parallels in medieval Christian societies, the endowment of Hindu temples served to legitimise the status and authority of rulers and elites. In the southern Coromandel (a region roughly corresponding to modern Tamil Nadu) merchants identified themselves with local communities by donating to temples, and, as in Andhra Pradesh, they gave the livestock that would produce *ghee*. The military also donated treasures from conquests and raids, and this had the effect of pumping money into the local economy through

*Beginnings*

the temples. Local assemblies managed this wealth and made decisions about the allocation of temple income to provide for the lamps.[2] Lighting for religious purposes was thus integral to social and economic organisation. This book, which is about the material consequences of belief, could in fact have been written about religions other than Christianity, but my aim is to deal specifically with Christianity in order to show the impact the provision of lighting had upon the development of West European societies. The reason for doing that is that the social and economic effects of putting this particular belief into practice are an important factor in development, but one that has hardly been recognised.

In this chapter I will look at both the scriptural and the customary origins of the use of lights in the Christian Church, noting how and why that use was contested before it became fully established in the fifth century. I will then follow the spread of lighting practices against the background of economic changes at the end of the Roman period, for these changes would restrict the means by which many Europeans could provide for the lights. Here we will start with the situation in Rome before moving into other areas. Let me begin with Scripture, namely the Mosaic books in the Old Testament. The subject of light in worship is introduced in Exodus 27:20–1 (and repeated in Leviticus 24:2), in which God instructs the children of Israel to bring the purest olive oil so that the lamp before the tabernacle might burn at all times. Aaron, the brother of Moses, and the sons of Aaron were charged with collecting the oil and maintaining the flame. This charge would remain amongst the Israelites for all time.[3] In Judaism keeping a flame burning before the tabernacle became essential practice, and down to the present synagogues have a perpetual light in the form of a flame in front of the ark in which the scrolls of the Torah are kept. In Judaism it was essential to have lamps of sufficient capacity to burn throughout the Sabbath, for tending them would have counted as work. Several of these 'Sabbath lamps' have been found in Britain from the period prior to the expulsion of the Jews in 1290.[4] Following Leviticus, there was also concern to ensure the purity of the oil used. The Babylonian Talmud said that three grades of oil could be extracted from the olives. Only the first pressing could be used for the lamps as this contained the least sediment. The olives should not be milled as this process in particular produced sediment.[5] Where the oil came from, how it was distributed, and whether there was a shortage in northern Europe, we cannot tell. The original 'shortage miracle' was of course the miraculous replenishment of the lamps of the menorah, an episode of the Maccabean revolt when one day's oil burned for eight days.[6] Despite the fact that the celebration of this miracle evolved into the Hanukkah festival, which is a festival of light, miraculous replenishment does not occur again. The lamps, the oil and the lighting would nevertheless be mentioned fairly frequently in the Torah, namely in the Books of Exodus, Leviticus, Numbers and Deuteronomy, less so in subsequent books, and but rarely in the New Testament. In the latter, light is much more a metaphor for the Truth than it is a matter of paraphernalia and practice, although the two, oil for lamps and truth-metaphor, do come together in the parable of the wise and the foolish virgins (Matthew 25).

Islam is more in step with the New Testament here in taking a metaphorical approach to light. In the *sura* 'Light' in the Qur'ān (24; 34–6), 'Allah is the light of heavens and the earth. His light may be compared to a niche that enshrines a lamp, the lamp within is a crystal of star-like brilliance.' It is envisaged that this lamp is lit 'from a blessed olive tree'.[7] But although such lamps were to be found in 'temples' (i.e. mosques), this was not an injunction that lights should burn there at all times. It did not require a light for a mosque to be a place of worship, and lights did not *have* to be fuelled by olive oil. And later, when Islam spread to regions in which there were few or no olives, to Egypt for example, no effort seems to have been made to import olive oil. Lamps were indeed important in Islam, and providing for the lights was, as will be shown in a later chapter, a duty of the faithful, but in general lighting in mosques was of a utilitarian rather than symbolic nature.[8] Evening prayers required the mosque to be illuminated, and lamps were needed for those wishing to read the *hadīth*, the collected sayings of the Prophet. The Qur'ān notably incorporates elements of the Mosaic books of the Old Testament, but these borrowings are not detailed enough to include many of its injunctions, and in general the Qur'ān inclines towards the interplay of the metaphorical and the literal, rather than towards the symbolic. There is a contrast here with Christianity in which what is symbolic in Scripture is sometimes built up into sacramental practice.

Altogether there are over two hundred references to oil, lamps and lights across the Old and New Testaments. Perhaps the most startling of the references to keeping a flame burning on the altar (specified in Leviticus 6:12 as a fire of wood kindled from the embers of the previous day) comes in Leviticus 10:1–2, 6 (and repeated in Numbers 3:4), where Nadat and Abiu, two sons of Aaron, let the fire go out, and then kindled it afresh, thus offering, 'strange fire' to the Lord, and so they failed in their charge. As a punishment they were incinerated and God told Aaron's family not to mourn them. This reference we see picked up in Francia at the Council of Aachen, held in the year 836. There, the fire for the burnt offering was changed to the flame of the lamp, and the passage was used to upbraid a wayward king who was in danger of extinguishing the flame of the faith by allowing the Church to be despoiled of its property.⁹

In the early Christian church there was some reluctance to incorporate the burning of lights into worship. At a stage when doctrine was still inchoate there was uncertainty about how to read the Old Testament, and over whether the books inherited from the Jews had been superseded by the oral testimony to Christ. Saint Paul had been hostile to the Old Law, emphasising the novelty of Christian truth. The Gnostics tended to pick and choose texts, Jewish or otherwise, according to their insight, and this meant on occasion disregarding Mosaic precept in favour of a newly revealed Truth. Writing in about the year 144 Marcion went further in insisting on a complete discontinuity with the Jewish tradition. Struck by stories such as that of the fatal punishment of Nadat and Abiu, Marcion argued that the God of the Jewish scriptures was so malignant and spiteful that he was unworthy to be the father of Jesus. The Old Testament should thus be rejected in its entirety. It was Origen, writing at the very beginning of the third century in reaction to the Gnostics and in particular to refute Marcion, who would argue that the Old Testament should be read in the light of the New. That is to say, the Gospel embraced the Law and the Prophets as Moses and the Prophets were filled with Christ's spirit.[10] Origen's line of thought won the day and opened the way for an acceptance of Mosaic precepts, and to a Judaising tendency in the development of ritual: as can be seen at the Council of Aachen, the duties of the Christian priesthood would draw inspiration from the charges laid upon the sons of Aaron.[11]

The theological bar to the use of light in worship may have been broken, but there remained unease with the pagan connotations of the association between light and veneration.[12] 'Pagans' (undifferentiated in Christian sources) had used torches in processions, lit lamps at the doors to their houses, and burned candles and lamps at tombs, both in funeral ceremonies and for commemoration. The sacred person of the emperor was represented as flanked by torches in the *Notitia Dignitatum*, and there was a recognised group of torchbearers (*lampadarii*) who accompanied the imperial family.[13] Origen's contemporary Tertullian voiced concern about how Christians should deal with such aspects of pagan behaviour and custom. More Christians, he said, were lighting lamps outside their doors than pagans. It is the pagans, who have no light, i.e. truth, who need lamps, not the Christians who follow 'the light of the world' (i.e. Christ).[14] Christians cannot join in the festivities for Caesar, but should remain loyal. They are in fact more loyal than the hypocrites who hang bright lamps high in the halls yet plot against the authority of the emperor.[15] Tertullian seems to have been reacting against a rising tide of accommodation to existing Graeco-Roman customs that, in hindsight, looks inevitable as the numbers of Christians grew. This can be seen in terms of political rhetoric in which light had been a metaphor for power, giving a cosmic character to the power of the Roman emperor. Eusebius of Caesarea, in a eulogy to the Emperor Constantine, continued the ancient rhetoric, but made the emperor the 'light of justice' whose power continued to light the world, but that power now came from his position as envoy of heaven. This line of thinking would culminate in the representation of Charlemagne (d. 814) as the 'beacon of Europe', his very name *Carolus* being said to mean 'dear light' (*cara lux*).[16] Once Christianity became the religion of the Empire and bishops became local leaders in social and political as well as religious terms, Christian practice was 'Romanised' to an even greater degree, and commemorative light, not seen in Scripture, became completely normal. Providing for the lights was now both socially and religiously prestigious. The Emperor Constantine, as we shall see, led the way in his lavish generosity to the churches of Rome. There were, however, still misgivings. For example, the Council of Elvira, held near Grenada in Spain in about the year 306 (and the first church council for which the canons survive) stated that 'Candles are not to be burned in a cemetery during the day, for this practice disturbs the spirits of the saints. Those that do not observe this will be excommunicated.'[17]

What could not be harmful, and was indeed positively efficacious, was the burning of lights, day and night, before the tombs of the martyrs. Martyrs were Christians who died for their faith, and the obvious Christ analogy here made them the most powerful liminal figures imaginable to Christians. Their suffering and ultimate sacrifice ensured that they were in heaven and God revealed their presence there, that is, their sanctity, by performing miracles through them, usually around their tombs and at their shrines. Saints were thus perceived to be a conduit for supernatural power, and the cult of the saints grew rapidly and massively as people sought proximity to and benefit from that power by honouring the saints with gifts to their shrines.[18] Such veneration included maintaining perpetual light before their tombs.

There is a description of a richly illuminated shrine in the poems of Paulinus, bishop of Nola in Italy (d. 431). His poems were written at the end of the fourth and at the beginning of the fifth century in honour of Saint Felix of Nola, believed to have been a martyr who had died in about the year 250.[19] According to Paul, Felix's shrine was 'crowned with crowds

*Beginnings*

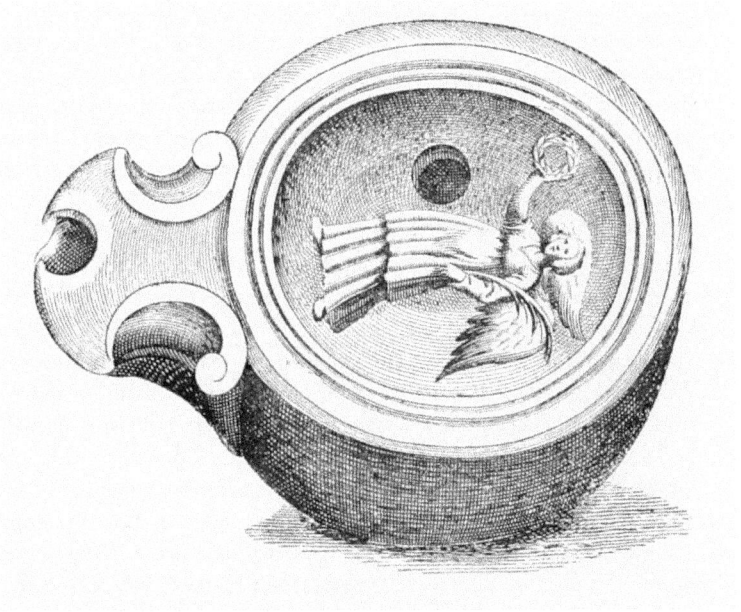

1 Simple terracotta lamp from the early Christian period, to be placed on or by a matyr's tomb. Note that the angel is holding a martryr's crown

of lanterns. The fragrant lamps burn with waxed wicks of paper, and are ablaze night and day so that the night shines with the brightness of day, and the day too is bright with heavenly glory, gleaming the more since its light is redoubled by the countless lamps.'[20] Light shines incessantly at Felix's tomb: 'proof that the dead martyr lives'.[21] In another poem Paul tells of a thief in the night who extinguishes the lights of a hanging candelabra in order to go about his business. He is not worried that putting out the lights will attract attention, because they often died down when the oil ran out.[22] It would thus seem that a century after the Council of Elvira the desire to honour the martyrs meant that the practice of burning lights in the daytime as well as night, thus 'perpetually', had become widespread. But it was not accepted everywhere. From about the year 406 there is a fierce diatribe from Saint Jerome attacking one Vigilantius who had apparently been critical of the veneration of the saints. What Vigilantius actually said to Jerome, with whom he had been staying in Bethlehem in Palestine, can only be reconstructed from Jerome's attack, but it included criticism of belief in the efficacy of saints' relics, and also it ridiculed the lighting of candles at shrines in the daytime.[23] It is intriguing to note that Vigilantius had been a protégé of Paulinus of Nola, for both came from Aquitaine, and that, when he returned from Palestine, Vigilantius was bearing a letter from Jerome to Paulinus. One wonders what Paulinus thought of his protégé, or Vigilantius of his erstwhile patron. Be that as it may, Vigilantius's apparent attack on perpetual light and the practices developing at shrines is the last we see for the next thousand years.

Paradoxically, although martyrdom was perceived to be the result of the persecution of Christians by the pagan Roman authorities, the cult of the saints became one of the chief avenues through which Roman traditions entered into Christian religious practice. Whereas Tertullian had, for instance, railed against Christians fixing laurel wreaths to their doors, a martyr would nevertheless soon be termed a 'champion of Christ' and his or her death would earn them a 'crown' (*corona*), which could be conceived as the laurels with which the champion athlete was honoured. After the end of the age of persecution when sanctity was extended to heroes of the faith who had not actually died for it, and this meant above all to bishops, the qualities of the male saint would come to include the civic virtues (including nobility) of the ideal Roman citizen (women, of course, were not citizens).[24] Burning light before the saint's shrine was arguably another import from ancient tradition. It would be extended to non-saints for the purpose of commemoration, as lights were placed at tombs as a symbol of life and reverence for the departed. Light symbolised eternity and burning oil or wax to produce it might ease the passage of the deceased into heaven, though for this post-Scriptural development there was no theological justification, and observation that the practice had no basis in Scripture would be 'weaponised' by the early Protestant reformers a thousand years later.[25] It is not, however, clear exactly how and when this idea was extended to non-saints, though the practice was clearly in place by the time that Charlemagne (768–814) made provision for a perpetual light to burn before the tomb of his late wife Hildegard.[26] For the purposes of this study these developments are of great importance on three counts, all related. First, sanctity had to be attested in writing and it is in the written record of a cult (the Saint's Life and miracle stories) that evidence of lighting before shrines is to be found. Second, the spread of saints' cults across Europe and through its various social hierarchies means that it is possible to see something of the wider social contexts in which light was provided. Third, the practice of commemorative lighting moved down the social scale as groups newly organised for this purpose come into view at the end of the early Middle Ages.

The extraordinarily lavish provision made for lighting by the Emperor Constantine (306–37) set an example that would inspire rulers in later centuries. The lavishness of the provision also allows a glimpse of a time at which oil was plentiful throughout the Mediterranean, and at which a Roman emperor could mobilise resources for giving to the Church from every region around the shores of the Mediterranean sea. In the year 313, following his conversion to Christianity, Constantine founded a basilica and neighbouring baptistery in honour of Saint John on the Lateran at Rome. He massively endowed his new foundations, assigning to them revenues from the Italian estates of his defeated rival Maxentius. In addition he and his family built and endowed Saint Peter's in Rome, giving to it revenues from estates in the east which had been taken from another opponent, Licinius. Constantine also founded and endowed six more churches in Rome, plus churches in Ostia, Albanum, Capua and Naples.[27] All this is known from the *Liber Pontificalis* (the 'Book of Pontiffs').[28] This work is a series of papal biographies which begins with the first pope, Saint Peter, and runs up to the year 891. The section which includes Constantine's gifts is the biography of Pope Silvester (314–35) and it was composed in the form we have it before the year 546.[29] Despite the later date of final composition, it is believed that the account of Constantine's donations is likely to be accurate where his basilica is concerned, although some donations to other churches may represent gifts from the emperor's family up to death of his son Constantius in 361.[30] The *Liber Pontificalis* would be widely circulated in the Middle Ages, becoming the essential source for the early history of the Papacy. The partnership between Silvester and Constantine would be held up as a model to later rulers, and from the Church's point of view the highlight of the relationship between pope and emperor was Constantine's generosity to the Papacy. The history of that generosity would in turn lead to the production of the infamous 'Donation of Constantine', a mid-eighth-century forgery in which Constantine supposedly gave to the Papacy not only authority over all Western lands but also massive estates in Asia, Palestine, Greece, Africa and Italy, a distribution which very much follows the pattern of estates given by Constantine to his new foundations as recorded in the in the *Liber Pontificalis*.[31] Another lesson to be learned here was that when the first Christian emperor founded and built churches he was concerned to provide them with the wherewithal for lighting, again on a massive scale. 'Giving for the lights' would later be repeated in the 'Donation of Constantine' as the essential reason for the ruler's hoped-for generosity to the Papacy.

The total revenue of the estates assigned to all of these churches was a staggering 30,493 *solidi* each year. Of this amount 4,390 *solidi* annually were provided to maintain the lights in Constantine's new Lateran basilica.[32] As well as providing the resource to fill the lamps, Constantine donated the lamps themselves. There were huge numbers of them, mostly made of gold or silver. The lights for the new basilica included 230 lamps known as 'dolphins' arranged in chandeliers, 70 other chandeliers, 40 silver lights, 50 silver candlesticks and, in front of the altars, seven brass candelabra, each ten feet tall.[33]

Other foundations were similarly furnished with lamps, chandeliers and candlesticks, though not on quite the same scale. The crypt which housed the tomb of Saint Laurence, however, must have been brilliantly lit: it was given a gold lantern with 20 wicks, a chandelier with 50 dolphins, two massive bronze candelabra and other six-wick silver lanterns.[34] Most of these lights would have burned olive oil, but some burned nard oil, a rare and expensive perfumed oil known from Scripture, too expensive to be used for lighting anywhere else. Some of the estate revenues listed amongst Constantine's donations were in kind: for example, of nard oil itself, balsam, spices, saffron, storax (a kind of perfume), or stacte (sweet spice for incense).[35] These were rare products, perhaps not readily available for cash. Olive oil, by contrast, was easily available, and this could explain why all the resources dedicated to the basilican lights were expressed in cash. The only time olive oil is mentioned is in the gift to the baptistery of revenue amounting to 810 *solidi* from 'the estate of Walzarus, an oil plantation, territory of Numidia'. Likewise there were no gifts in kind of grain or wine, both products which were also needed for worship. All three were staples.

At its height the Roman Empire produced and consumed massive amounts of oil. It has been calculated that up to 20 litres per inhabitant were consumed per annum and between 500,000 and one million tonnes were produced annually from the fruit of up to 700 million olive trees.[36] Museums across Europe and the Middle East are awash with examples of small terracotta oil lamps from the Roman period that indicate everyday use throughout society. There are also some metal lamps of very similar design which suggest that richer people used more durable and more expensive versions of the basic lamp.[37] The areas of greatest oil production were Tripolitania and Numidia (present day Libya and Tunisia), although oil was produced throughout the Mediterranean zone. This is the setting for Constantine's gifts for lighting – one of the estates he granted was, remember, an olive oil plantation in Numidia which supplied a substantial revenue. It was a world in which the Mediterranean was united around the needs of imperial power and for the purposes of trade: the revenues from a bakery in Antioch (Syria) could, for example, be assigned to Saint Peter's in Rome[38]. When the estates given by Constantine are plotted on a map we get a picture of a single Mediterranean political economy.

Over the next century this picture would change dramatically. As imperial power declined and instability grew, the Mediterranean network broke down, to be replaced first by regional networks and then by local trade. This is a complex and contested subject, for it is part of the wider debate about the decline of Roman power in which it is impossible to separate cause and effect in the progressive dislocation not only of the Mediterranean economy but also of trading and taxation throughout the Roman Empire.[39] This is not the place to enter into that debate, but it can be noted that there is consensus that the production of and trade in olive oil was a clear casualty of the breakdown. It is clear because olive oil had to be carried long distances in ceramic containers (*amphorae*) and it is the archaeology of these (known as 'Red African Slipware') which is used as strong evidence for the economic downturn as the shrinking distribution

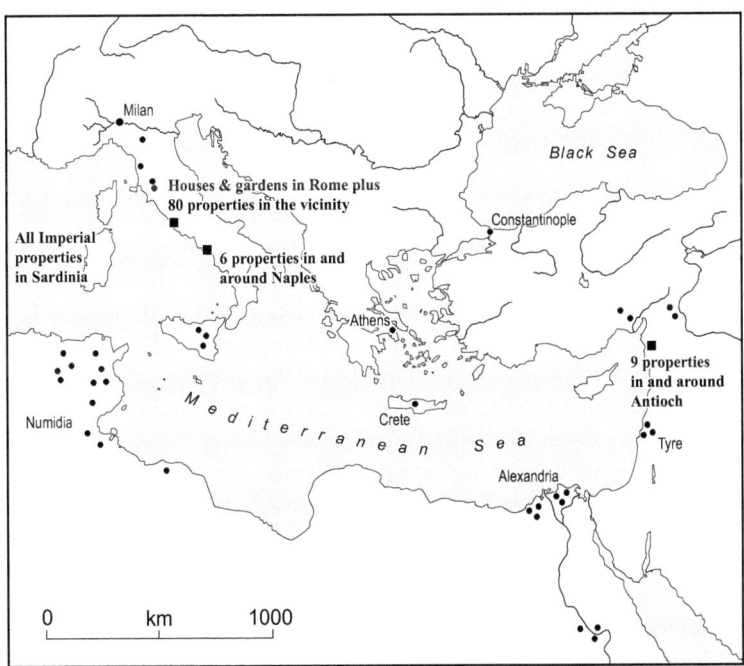

2 Approximate location of properties from which the Emperor Constantine was said to have assigned revenues for churches in Rome

of *amphorae* marks the breakdown of the wider networks.[40] Likewise, the once ubiquitous terracotta oil lamps fade from the archaeological record.

By the time that North Africa was occupied by the Arabs at the end of the seventh century, oil production had all but disappeared from Tripolitania and Numidia. The last ceramic evidence indicating imports into Gaul comes from the mid-seventh century. In Italy and Provence oil production had by then become very localised.[41] Southern Spain may have produced more, but was not visibly exporting it.[42] Oil now had no apparent alimentary use, and it has been remarked that all that kept production going was ecclesiastical demand.[43] This would in fact lead to a spread of olive culture northwards to the Italian lakes area in order to satisfy demand from the great northern Italian and Frankish churches.[44] Warfare and instability had compounded the earlier breakdown of the Mediterranean trading and taxation networks, so that conditions for the large-scale production of oil were never re-established.[45] We can get some impression of the consequences of instability from two later passages in the *Liber Pontificalis* which tell us what happened to some of the things that Constantine had given to his foundations. One was a silver *fastigium* with which Constantine had furnished his basilica.[46] This was a highly decorated canopy from which lights were suspended. We are told that its weight in silver was 2,215 lb. The biography of Pope Xystus (who was in office from 432 to 440) then says that, at this pope's request, the Emperor Valentinian had another silver *fastigium* made for the Constantinian basilica because the other one had been removed by the barbarians. The new one weighed 1610 lb.[47] We are not told who these barbarians were, but Alaric's Visigoths who famously sacked Rome in 410 seem to be the likely candidates. Later, in the biography of Pope Leo I ('the Great', 440–61) we learn that Leo had six silver water jars melted down. Three of these jars had been given by Constantine to Saint Peter's, Saint Paul's and the basilica respectively, each of them weighing 100 lb. The silver was needed to replace all the consecrated vessels from the Roman *tituli* (lesser churches or 'parish' churches).[48] The *tituli* had been despoiled during 'the Vandal disaster', this presumably being the Vandal sack of Rome in the year 455.

Constantine's generosity had been so lavish that later donations seemed meagre by comparison. The *Liber Pontificalis* also has less on gifts as it becomes more narrative in content. The popes had to deal with warfare and devastation in the mid-sixth century and then in the seventh and eighth with factional strife and doctrinal dispute, as well as with the complexities of Rome's relations with the Byzantines, the Lombards and the Franks. The papal biographies thus become more political in tone, and some are even critical of their subjects. Gifts get smaller and gifts of revenues disappear from the text after the mid-eighth century. More and more donations are of textiles, and from the early eighth century onwards, rather than foundation and endowment, the authors of the *Liber Pontificalis* mention the repair of churches: by then some of the Constantinian foundations were in a sorry state. Nevertheless, Constantine's Lateran basilica itself, as well as Saint Peter's and Saint Paul's Without the Walls, were very large buildings which required considerable resources to maintain their lights, and we continue to hear of gifts of lamps and chandeliers, and of the means of providing for them.[49] Two major gifts for provision reveal the importance attached to their lighting and also show how the popes themselves provided for it out of the papal patrimony.

The first of these grants is from the year 604. It comes in a letter from Pope Gregory ('the Great', 580–604) in which he instructs his official, Felix, to oversee the transfer of a large estate of the Appian Patrimony into the possession of the church of Saint Paul's Without the Walls.[50] Having heard of the inadequacy of lighting in Saint Paul's, Gregory was granting the land to provide for the lamps. This would honour Saint Paul who 'had filled the whole world with the light of his preaching'. This was a large estate made up of ten farms (*fundi* and *villae*) and other smaller properties were attached to it as well. Felix was to remove the records of the estate from the papal inventory, transfer them to Saint Paul's Without the Walls and to deposit a record of the order in the papal archives. Not only this, but the entire letter was copied in an inscription in stone and was displayed in the portico of Saint Paul's (where it can still be seen), making this the only surviving contemporary copy of one of Gregory's letters.

This remarkable inscription has recently been analysed by Jo Story.[51] She compares it to a second inscription set up in Saint Peter's in which Pope Gregory II (715–31) gave to the apostles Saint Peter and Saint Paul more lands to the east of Rome. This grant was made up of two blocks of land that comprised 43 farms. Listed are 55 olive groves on the farms and the purpose of the grant was to enable lights to be lit in Saint Paul's and Saint Peter's The two grants share the same formula here – they are made 'to make appropriate arrangements for the lights'.[52] Story argues that the two donations have such strong parallels that the later inscription must have been made with the earlier one in mind.[53] She also notes important differences between the two. Whereas the grant of 604 gave land the revenue from which would go to the lights, in the early eighth-century donation the lights would be fed from the olives grown on the land. She concludes that the differences mark the final breakdown of the trading networks that had enabled the importation of oil. In 604 it was possible to assign cash to buy oil that may have been produced at some distance from Rome. By the time of Gregory II, argues Story, oil had to be sourced locally, here from estates run by the Church, because no other source was available.[54] This may not have been entirely the case, for the author of the 'Life of Zacharias' says that not long after this Pope Zacharias (741–52) 'set aside 20lb of gold for the annual purchase of oil, so that the lights of the Apostles [i.e. Saint Peter and Saint Paul] would benefit from the revenue'.[55] This seems to be an enormous sum but it is tiny compared with Constantine's gifts: the gold ornaments that he gave to his Lateran basilica alone weighed in at 335 lb.[56] It is also in the 'Life of Zacharias' that we first meet the term *domuscultae* in relation to papal estates. These were lands farmed directly by dependants of the Church. They could not be leased out, and they may have acquired a military function too.[57] The consolidation of estates into *domuscultae* may support Story's argument that from the eighth century onwards the Papacy began to take produce in kind from its estates, though this need not mean that they could not draw on cash too, either from income from their estates or from reserves: Zacharias's gold could conceivably have come from dethesaurisation (Leo I, remember, had melted down six silver water jars). Famously, King Offa of Mercia in England (757–96) began the practice of sending of gold worth about 240 *solidi* to Rome each year (a payment that would evolve into the so-called 'Peter's Pence') for alms to the poor and for the maintenance of the lights.[58]

It is clear, then, that the great Roman basilicas were lavishly provided with lights from the time of their foundation, and that the continued provision for the lighting was a major concern to which substantial resources were devoted. The following rather charming passage, originally from a ninth-century Arab source, alludes to the insatiable demand for oil in Rome, and also to the difficulties of getting hold of the oil locally:

> In the middle of the city is the great church [Saint Peter's, presumably], two farsahk long, with 360 doors; in the middle of the church is a tower standing 10 cubits in the air, crowned with a dome of lead. Atop the cupola is a bronze simulacrum of a starling; at the time of the olive harvest, the wind, passing through the simulacrum of the starling, makes it cry. This convokes all the starlings of the city, each with an olive in its beak, and they throw the olives on the tower. The olives are collected and pressed, and enough oil is made for the lights of the church until the same season of the next year.[59]

In the three centuries after these churches were founded, the production and distribution of olive oil declined to the point at which this essential product was no longer imported from North Africa. Thereafter provision for the major Roman churches was made from oil produced in the locality of Rome, this also being a time in which the Papacy lost control over its more distant estates in Sicily. But since there were no more grand inscriptions and by no means all grants for lighting were recorded in the *Liber Pontificalis*, it is hard to assess the scale of provision. Compared to the time of Constantine, the resources devoted to lighting certainly declined, but it is much less certain that in terms of proportion to total wealth and income such resources got smaller. On the other hand, the Papacy may have been disproportionately rich in precious metals, in terms both of church treasure and income. The fact that cash (or gold) could still be assigned to lighting in the eighth century suggests that there was still a market in oil, even if this was a local market and a fraction of the size of the market in the ancient world. This observation is important because, as we shall see, churches outside the area of olive cultivation, and that is most of Western Europe, would have to rely on the purchase of oil produced far away and which was scarce and expensive. These conditions would privilege cash-rich institutions beyond Italy. It is to them that I now turn.

The first reference to the provision for lighting outside Italy comes from the will of Perpetuus, bishop of Tours (460–91). Perpetuus was another bishop of senatorial stock and had widespread landholdings across several regions. In 475 he bequeathed his land to the church of Tours, with the income going largely to provide alms.[60] But he also stipulated that revenue from the land be assigned to purchase oil 'for lighting the tomb of the Lord Martin perpetually'. Of how this revenue was collected, and who paid it, the will says nothing. The earliest estate-accounting documents to survive from early medieval Western Europe are in fact those of Saint Martin's.[61] They show agents collecting renders in kind from named peasants, but these records were made nearly two centuries after the will of Perpetuus. How, or even whether, these later dues were turned into cash we cannot tell, though we do know that Saint Martin's became one of the cash-rich institutions just referred to. Nor can it be seen where the oil that Perpetuus wished to be purchased was actually bought, although, from later Tours evidence which will be considered shortly, a fair guess would be that it was purchased in Marseilles. Saint Martin's tomb, in the monastery of his name, was a major shrine that would gain exceptionally large privileges under the patronage of the Merovingian and the Carolingian kings of Francia.[62] That, basically, is why there is so much later evidence from the monastery. Its almost continuous record over the next millennium acts as a kind of *vade mecum* to Frankish, and then French, and even European history.[63] As will be shown, the kings too would provide for Saint Martin's lights, and we shall revisit the monastery several times over the course of this study.

In addition to the documentary record, there is a great deal of narrative evidence from Saint Martin's. For the century after the death of Perpetuus this comes from the works of Bishop Gregory of Tours (573–94).[64] The veneration of Saint Martin, and an insistence on a personal association with the saint, was the key to Gregory's hold over the diocese of Tours where he was something of an outsider.[65] In his *Liber de virtutibus sancti Martini* ('Book of the miracles of Saint Martin') Gregory recounts 207 miracles performed through the saint, most of them at his shrine, but some elsewhere through contact relics (objects or material associated with the saint or saint's tomb). The great majority of these are healing miracles, and the accounts are repetitive to the point of tedium. But by the same token they give us a picture of the shrine as a busy healing centre, frequented by all social classes, many of the visitors being poor or even slaves (*servi*). Oil plays a significant part in the healing: in Graeco-Roman culture and in Scripture it had always had healing properties attributed to it, but now it received an extra charge through contact with the saints, and the main point of contact were the lamps burning before the saints' shrines.[66] Healing miracles thus provide much evidence for the use of lights. Brought to the shrine and mixed with dust from the tomb, a small amount of oil increased miraculously and healed many people. Sprinkled over fields it could even keep storms away.[67] Oil taken from a lamp that hung beneath a portrait of the saint in Ravenna cured two people of blindness.[68] Oil taken from the lamps before the shrine cured cattle plague.[69] In another of his works, 'The Glory of the Martyrs', Gregory tells of how the divine power of the Holy Cross relic was manifested by the overflowing of oil.[70] He himself witnessed a lamp before the relic that burned continuously but each hour produced four times as much oil as had originally filled it. In India, he tells us, there is a lamp marking the first burial place of Saint Thomas that burns perpetually without ever being tended.[71] To Gregory oil was at once a mysterious substance and a very generally recognised conduit for the supernatural. Oil lamps were important objects and their proximity to shrines put them close to the miraculous. That miracles should involve an increase of this substance suggests that it was precious, and one is led to conclude (although Gregory never spells it out) that it was in short supply by the mid-sixth century. It is no surprise, therefore, that Gregory also tells of miracles involving wax. This too was used for lighting and it too acquired healing properties when it had been in contact with the holy. Gregory refers to votive wax candles, and in one instance to a gift of wax for lighting: a beekeeper had lost control over a swarm of bees. He called upon Saint Martin who guided the swarm back to him. In return he vowed to send all the wax that the swarm produced 'for the lights in your church'.[72] After 'two or three years' he had accumulated 200 lb of wax, which he had to bury because of some sort of disorder in the region. When his servant was sent to dig it up he asked Saint Martin to cure him of kidney pain when he uncovered the wax. Saint Martin duly obliged.[73]

These miracles (which could be multiplied from other sources) are important in showing that from an early date all social classes participated in the veneration of the saints, and this in turn indicates that the use of lights in veneration had meaning and impact across the social spectrum. We also learn that there was no gender difference in attendance at the shrines and women benefited from the supernatural power of the saint just as much as men did. Our beekeeper's generosity suggests that people outside the elite were prepared to provide for the lights. In as much as provision was made from the income of estates, and if we read back from the later Tours accounting-documents, we can infer that peasants provided for the lights from their labours. As intimated earlier, oil (though not necessarily for these lights) was imported into Marseilles, though it is not clear where it came from beyond a tantalising 'overseas'.[74] In his historical writings Gregory tells of the theft of 70 jars of oil and fish sauce which had just been shipped into the port in *navibus transmarinis*.[75] An archdeacon, one Vigilius, was accused of responsibility for the theft and the story is about how he cleared his name. No more about Vigilius is known, but he seems to have been an outsider as he was invited by the bishop of Marseilles to join in the celebration of the Christmas mass. He could conceivably have been Gregory's archdeacon sent to purchase oil. The point for present purposes is that the theft of these 70 jars (which Gregory called *orcae*, 'big jars') was seen as a major crime. Later in the work Gregory insults his enemy, Felix bishop of Nantes, who had written him offensive letters. Telling Felix that the only thing that limits his unpleasant verbosity is a shortage of papyrus, he exclaims, 'If only you had been bishop of Marseilles then there would have been no more ships bringing in oil and other wares, but just papyrus which would have given you greater opportunity to scribble your infamous calumnies attacking good men'.[76] The term for wares – *species* – suggests goods of great value, and the term 'other' includes the oil in this category.

The evidence from Gregory of Tours therefore shows that the burning of lights, fuelled both by oil and by wax, was a normal part of the display at the shrine of the saint. This gives us practical examples of the kind of display that we met in the poems of Paulinus of Nola, who, incidentally, was also thought to have been a devotee of Martin.[77] And from Gregory it can be seen that that this culture had a wide appeal, so that it can be inferred that many people were involved in a form of support which was expensive and likely to have involved cash. But Saint Martin's was a shrine of exceptional renown and attraction, at least according to Gregory. Was it only major shrines that kept lights burning all the time, or was it expected that all churches should do this, and all Christians provide for the lights? For evidence here we have to turn to Spain and to conciliar material. The first Council of Braga (now in northern Portugal) held in 561 stipulated that the income from church lands be divided into three equal parts. One should go to the bishop, the second to the clergy and the third part should pay for the repair of churches and for the lights (*luminaria*). For this part the *archipresbyter* or the *archidiaconus* should account to the bishop.[78] In the second Council of Braga, held 11 years later, it was ruled that when bishops toured their dioceses they could take two *solidi* from each church. They could not, however, take anything from the third part of the offerings that the *populus* made to the parish churches, for this part was reserved for the lights and for the repair of the churches. If the bishop took anything from this fund, then churches would be deprived of light and holy shelter (*tecta*, literally, 'roofs').[79] Bishops should not charge for the consecration of a church if its founders were poor, but every bishop should remember that they should not consecrate a church before they had seen a charter (document) that detailed its endowment. For it was a serious matter to consecrate a church if it did not have the wherewithal to provide lights or for the upkeep of those who served there.[80] A council held at Toledo in 597 decreed that a church should be served by a priest, but, if unable to afford a priest, it should have a deacon. If the income (*census*) was even smaller, then the church should have a doorkeeper (*ostiarius*, lowest grade of church officer) chosen by a priest who will keep the inside of the church nice (*nitor*) and each night light the lamps before the relics of the saints.[81]

This evidence from late sixth-century Spain indicates strongly that lights were indeed required to burn in all churches, even in the poorest of them. It is striking that maintenance of the lights seems to be a priority for resources and that up to a third of income should be dedicated to them alongside maintenance of the fabric of the church. That it was envisaged that some churches would not be able to afford a priest suggests that their congregations were poor, and that the charge upon them was significant. It is, however, hard to assess the social and economic ramifications of the norms set out in these councils. Were the demands at all practical and were they indeed put into practice? There is little case material with which to answer these questions. There are very few charters from Visigothic Spain and narrative material is thin. A handful of charters or fragments of charters also survive on slates recovered from a quarry and they date to the end of the sixth century and the beginning of the seventh century.[82] Four of them mention olives or oil. In one of them, a fragment, *mancipia* (un-free people or slaves on an estate) were said to have to have defrauded an owner over the collection of olives.[83] This fragment invites comparison with a well-known case from ninth- and tenth-century Italy in which peasants protested against having to collect olives.[84] Such work was apparently regarded an onerous. Four very early charters (sixth century) have recently been identified as coming from the monastery of San Martin de Asán in the foothills of the Pyrenees.[85] The earliest of these is from the year 522. It is a grant of land to the monastery and olive trees are mentioned in the description of the land. This is also the case from a grant of 576. Then in 586 King Reccared made a grant to Asán *pro luminaribus*. So, three out of four documents in this tiny corpus made reference either to olives or to lights. It is interesting to note that the cult of Saint Martin was involved, given Gregory of Tours's accounts of lights before shrines and images associated with Martin. Taking the charters together with the evidence from the slates there is therefore some indication that olives were being cultivated for ecclesiastical use in Spain, with rulers in the vanguard. Had we more evidence from Spain, it would be a fair guess to say that it would very much resemble Francia or Italy in the way in which provision was made for the lights.

From Spain there is a small corpus of hagiography (tiny in comparison with that from Francia), but nothing like the hundreds of miracle stories that are to found in the works of Gregory of Tours: early Spanish saint's lives are long on asceticism and conflict but short on miracles.[86] Though only one lighting miracle is mentioned, it is interestingly one that suggests a shortage of oil: in the 'Life of Saint Aemilian' we hear that the light before his tomb went out for lack of oil.[87] When the night vigils began it was found to have been replenished and was burning. The oil from the lamp then 'produced further wonders'. This 'Life', which was written by Braulio of Saragossa between 631 and 645, is the only one to have a set of post-mortem healing miracles, albeit there are only four of them. It has been suggested that Braulio wrote it partly to provide 'a Gothic parallel to Martin'. This might explain why it has these post-mortem miracles, and why one of them is a lighting miracle.[88] As is often the case, the reasons for recording miracle stories could be more complicated than first meets the eye.

Only one text gets us any further with the question of whether the conciliar decrees on lighting were put into practice. This not a case study but a model for drawing up a document in which a grant for lights is made. It comes from a collection of *formulae* in all probability made in the later Visigothic period, although the text survives only in a twelfth-century edition.[89] It is addressed to the patron saint of a church. Since wealth on this earth is as nothing compared with the favour that might accrue in heaven, it reads, the donor wishes to provide for the lights of a church and for alms for the poor and to give to those who daily serve the church. They give all they have in territory X in place X along with slaves (*mancipiis*) named as follows: X, and X with wife and children, and with buildings, vines, woods, meadows, pasture, marshes and water and channelled water and all the rights over that place. It recaps that this is for those who serve 'your glory' and for the lights of your church and for provisions for the poor. It is to last for all time.[90] The wording of this model document is very similar to that of Frankish grants of property to the Church. It could have been influenced by Frankish examples, or vice versa, or both could have a common origin. The latter seems most likely, especially for the so-called 'appurtenance clause' in which what we might term the 'fixtures and fittings' (including people) of the land are described. That way of describing the land is to be found in late Roman law. We may therefore be seeing here a documentary tradition that goes back at least to the time of the Councils of Braga, which would give a context in which to read those conciliar decrees. If so, it is significant that slaves (*mancipia*) are given along with the land, for this indicates that, when church income is spoken of, it could well have been produced by persons who were in effect owned by the church. In later chapters it will be seen that such people could form a distinctive group in society, for the wider social ramifications of provision for lighting begin to be revealed from the later ninth century onwards. Here there is a hint that there may have been such people in Visigothic Spain, but this is a tenuous conclusion that rests on too many guesses and too few texts. There is a particular problem with Spain as the record, always meagre, goes virtually silent after the Arab conquest of 711 until it reappears in the late ninth century. Then grants for lighting can be seen again, but whether this indicates a continuous tradition of provision or a new beginning is strictly not possible to say. That discussion we will revisit in a later chapter.

Finally, let us look at the appearance of lights in churches in early Anglo-Saxon England where there are references to the use of lights in religious commentaries and in poetic representation. There are, however, no documents recording gifts for lights, nor do lamps feature in any hagiographic narratives. How the Anglo-Saxons were converted to Christianity is a complex story but one which came to privilege a narrative of conversion by missionaries from Rome. Part of that narrative was the development of a cult around Pope Gregory the Great who was said to have first despatched missionaries to England.[91] We have already seen that cult building under Pope Gregory II who imitated his namesake in erecting an inscription which celebrated his own gift of lighting provision to the churches of Saint Peter and Saint Paul's Without the Walls in Rome. By then, Anglo-Saxons had been visiting Rome for several decades, and in 668 Canterbury had received an archbishop, Theodore, who was appointed by the pope and came to England from Rome.[92] Leading Anglo-Saxon churchmen were familiar with the Roman churches and must have seen the sumptuous lights in Saint Paul's and Saint Peter's, just as they would have seen the inscriptions of the first and then the second Gregory.[93] King Offa instituted an annual gift to Rome for those lights, and in addition Anglo-Saxon pilgrims with sufficient means gave churches in Rome hanging bowls, which may have been used as lamps, or lamp components.[94] It is reasonable to assume, therefore, that any Anglo-Saxon who had knowledge of Rome would have been familiar with the idea that a major church should demonstrate its importance in the magnificence of its lights. This is certainly the case with Bede, who imagined such a church in his work *De Temporum Ratione*, written in 725. 'You will', he wrote, 'enter some great building, surely a church of unusual length and breadth, filled with an immense supply of burning lanterns in honour of the martyr whose day it is'.[95] Something similar appears in an early ninth-century poem, Æthelwulf's *De Abbatibus*, which describes three churches of an abbey that was a dependant of Lindisfarne. In one of them, dedicated to the Virgin Mary, the poet asks 'who should number all the lights throughout that church, which shine in the church and overhead to our true delight?' In a second church which is imaginary (it is seen in a vision), 'In all the *porticus* bright waxen lights were burning, honouring altars with flaming donations'. And elsewhere in the monastery, 'men wished to hang up numerous bowls, which would give soft light'.[96] The latter would seem to refer to the hanging bowls mentioned above in written evidence but also well attested in the archaeology of the early Anglo-Saxon period. Æthelwulf's lines have been taken, reasonably enough, to show that some at least of these hanging bowls were used in lighting.[97]

From such slender evidence very little can be said about the use of lights in England at this date, and we remain completely ignorant about how they were provided for. Brilliant lighting could be imagined, and was understood as something wonderful. One suspects, however, that it remained largely imaginary because oil was very difficult to obtain. There is a letter written by Alcuin of York that strongly suggests this. It was written in the late eighth century while Alcuin was in Francia and it was addressed to an abbot Colcu in England. Alcuin says that he has sent Colcu some oil 'which is scarcely now to be found in Britain'. Colcu is to send it out amongst the bishops of various places to be used 'in the service and honour of God'.[98] Much later, as will be shown, texts from Anglo-Saxon England mention only the use of wax for lighting, and oil seems to have been reserved for making up the chrism required in the liturgy of baptism, which was used in much smaller quantities than lighting fuel. At that later date the oil was very firmly under the control of the bishop who gave out the chrism. Although wax would come to be hallowed across Europe, compared to olive oil it is actually a much less efficient fuel for lighting. Oil generates less smoke (particulates) than wax. According to Benjamin Graham, it was 'by far the cleanest-burning lamp fuel available to early medieval Europeans', and it burned at about one-third the rate of wax.[99] It was thus far more useful when it came to maintaining a light throughout the night, as the ancient Israelites had found. The superiority of olive oil over wax in this respect suggests that the switch from the one to the other was indeed caused by a shortage of oil. It was the availability of wax that gave it the edge. A hallowing of wax followed. Perhaps significant in this context is the fact that an early treatise that celebrates the qualities of bees comes from England, the area in which oil was simply unavailable. The treatise is by Aldhelm (d. 709) and is part of his work *De Virginitate*. Building on a comparison between monks and bees that comes from the 'Life of Saint Antony', Aldhelm makes the analogy between the extraction of honey from the flower and spiritual truth from Scripture.[100] By inference this hallows wax, which was no doubt the normal lighting fuel in Aldhelm's time. A more explicit hallowing of wax comes in a comparison between Christ's sacrifice on the cross and the burning of the paschal candle: both perished in order to provide light. Prayers that blessed the paschal candle in fact eulogised wax for its purity. Because it came from a virginal source (bees were believed to be virgins, and their reproduction was miraculous) wax could never be impure in a moral sense. On a prosaic level, candle wax was pure because it was refined by boiling, something which must have added to its value. The result was a bright white substance, a 'snow-white mystery' which poured out a torrent of virtue as it burned.[101] Given that wax was both a wonderful and a mysterious substance, and that it could be gathered in the field, as it were, one can understand why people were keen to provide it and to share in the virtue that it provided. Bees, the providers of the wax, were thus seen as virtuous animals. The idea that they were hard workers in a good cause has come down to the present day. Manchester's town symbol is a bee which signifies the busy and hard-working character of the town. It comes as a surprise, therefore, to learn that bees have not always been valued in this way. In Zoroastrian culture in pre-Islamic Iran (Persia) bees were regarded as evil creatures, and wax and honey were spurned as fuel and food.[102] The reason for this antipathy towards bees was that the Asvin gods who were believed to have given honey to the bees had fallen and had become demonic, and honey had become demonic along with them So, as in the West, belief had material consequence as the Zoroastrians were denied an important resource: in both cases it cost to believe. In the event this refusal to touch the produce of bees disappeared in Iran after its conquest by Islamic forces, although it did linger on in the areas of western India to which Zoroastrian refugees moved.

In contrast to Aldhelm's reflections on the spiritual analogy between the beehive and the monastery, and in contrast to the hallowing of wax in the Easter litany, the early laws followed Roman tradition in treating bees as animals which were property subject to theft and capable of doing damage.[103] There is a mid-seventh-century Old Irish law tract, *Bechbretha*, on beekeeping. This has been associated with the growth of monasticism in Ireland. *Bechbretha*, however, has very little on honey, and in common with the continental, Anglo-Saxon and Welsh laws it is concerned only with the theft of bees and with the damage they might do.[104] Wax is not mentioned in any of this material. This might suggest that in the rural economy the production of honey was regarded as far more important that the gathering of its by-product, wax. Another way of looking at the silence on wax in these normative sources might be to think that at this early stage (seventh century) the Church was still rather thin on the ground. As yet it had made little impact on the relations between farmers which are the subject of much of the legal material.

There is from Anglo-Saxon England nothing to compare with the Visigothic formula just examined. That document allowed one to think that in Spain individuals gave land and people to provide for lights. As already noted, there are no surviving charters to show any Anglo-Saxon making such a donation, and no early will that shows us land being bequeathed for this purpose. In fact, across the entire Anglo-Saxon period there is only one document of any kind that makes reference to an individual donation for lighting.[105] This silence could be explained by the vagaries of the evidence: that is, grants for lighting were made but have not survived. On the other hand, charters in which land is given to the church have survived in considerable numbers. The lack of provision for lighting in them might otherwise be explained by differences in the form of charter: English charters stipulate what land is to be given, often with detailed boundary clauses, but, unlike continental charters or that Visigothic charter formula, they do not mention the people on the land or the revenues that might come from the land. What the recipient is to do with the gift is never spelled out, and this might conceal a range of purposes for which the donation was made. In this context it is not surprising that donation for lights is never mentioned. A third possibility is that such grants were never in fact made by individuals in England. This is conceivable if provision for lighting and other ecclesiastical needs came from charges laid on all people by rulers, bishops or other lords, in other words as a kind of tax. This seems to have been the case later with 'Peter's Pence' which was levied on households. Then, in the later tenth century we hear of 'wax-scot' and 'light-scot' which were general levies for the lights.[106] If it were the case that in the earlier period too provision was met by a charge on all those who paid dues, then, in terms of resources taken from producers, the cost of lights in Anglo-Saxon England may not have been very different from the cost in any other region, but the social consequences would have been different, in that discrete groups of providers would not have been created as they were in some continental regions. I will return to this issue when in a later chapter I examine the formation of such groups.

## Conclusion

This survey of how the growing Christian Church made use of lights has drawn upon a wide variety of evidence. It began with Scripture and then turned to the discursive material of early church thinkers. It looked at the evidence of donations in the 'Book of Pontiffs' and set this in the context of declining trade, for which the evidence was archaeological. Evidence for the use of lights at shrines, and for the healing property of oil, was taken from miracle stories and from poetry. Evidence of donation for lights was scarce, but, apart from the donations listed in the 'Book of the Pontiffs', donations were found in two papal charters, in one Will, and, from Spain, there was the formula for a charter of donation. Conciliar material from Spain provided the strongest indication that all churches, not just the major basilicas and shrines, were required to burn lights. It is striking that there are references to the use of lights across such a variety of sources and in every region that had an organised church by the year 700. It is the variety of reference that is the most persuasive evidence that the burning of lights in churches had become the norm. As the conciliar evidence put it, it was inconceivable that a church should not be provided with lights. At the same time, the evidence for shrinkage in the production and exchange of olive oil, the lighting fuel preferred in Scripture, is clear and consistent. Three observations are thus left to be taken forward into the next chapter of this study. The first is that lights had to be provided for, everywhere. Second is that provision was important enough a matter to require the dedication of resources. Land, people, money and other forms of income were dedicated, *pro concinnatione luminariorum* 'to arrange for the lights' as Gregory's charter put it. Third, the case of England suggests that, though every region shared the same idea about the importance of lights, these were not provided for in the same ways in all areas. It is not possible at this stage to determine what effect providing for the lights had upon social organisation and economic activity, though it has been established that in principle every church congregation should have been affected. For the poor churches envisaged in the Council of Toledo, the cost of lighting was no doubt low. It has been demonstrated that one litre of oil can give up to 250–300 hours of light, though this figure seems very high.[107] A small olive grove of, say, six trees would be sufficient to meet the needs of a church for one year. But as Alcuin's letter to Colcu suggests, even a litre of oil may have been hard to obtain in late eighth-century England. It is the interplay of demand and supply, shortage, necessity, religious practice, prestige and power that I shall consider in the next chapter.

## Notes

1 P. S. Kanaka Durgan and Y. A. Sudhakar Reddy, 'Kings, Temples and Legitimation of Autochthonous Communities', *Journal of the Economic and Social History of the Orient* 35 (1992), 145–66. I am grateful to Ian Wood for drawing my attention to this important paper.
2 Kanakalatha Mukund, *The Trading World of the Tamil Merchant* (Hyderabad and London, 1999), pp. 25–41.
3 *Praecipe filiis Israel ut afferant tibi oleum de arboribus olivarum purissimum, piloque contusum: ut ardeant lucerna semper in tabernaculo testimonii, extra velum quod oppansum est testimonio. Et collocabunt eam Aaron et filii eius, ut usque mane luceat coram Domino. Perpetuus erit cultus per successiones eorum a filiis Israel.*
4 E. J. Bose, 'A Medieval Lamp from Peter Street, Bristol', *Transactions of the Bristol and Gloucestershire Archaeological Society* 199 (2001), 179–82.
5 *Tractate Menachot* 86a, sefania.org/william-davidson-talmud.
6 I Maccabees 4:36–41 and II Maccabees 1:18–36 give the context but do not refer to the lighting miracle by name.

7 Translation from *The Koran*, trans. N. J. Dawood, *Penguin Classics*, 4th edn (Harmondsworth, 1974), p. 217.
8 *Encylopaedia of Islam* VI (Leiden, 1986), MASDJID (mosque), D, h 'lighting', pp. 665–6.
9 *MHG Concilia* II, ed. A. Werminghoff, *Concilia aevi Karolini* II i, ii (Hanover, 1906–8), no. 28, p. 739. The wood fire for burnt offerings is changed thus: *ignis perpetuus, id est luminaria*. For further discussion of this passage, see below Chapter 3, pp. 95–7.
10 This synopsis is taken from Frances M. Young, *Biblical Exegesis and the Formation of Christian Culture* (Cambridge, 1997), pp. 22–69. Origen, *De Principiis* IV, ch. 1, trans. J. Behr, *Origen on First Principles* (Oxford, 2017).
11 Isidore of Seville (d. 636), whose work was very influential amongst the Carolingians, set the pace in looking for Old Testament precedents for Christian ritual. See Isidore of Seville, *De Ecclesiasticis Officiis*, ed. C. Lawson, *Corpus Christianorum*, Series Latina 113 (Turnhout, 1989), II, v. *De Sacerdotibus*, pp. 56–64, which begins with the story of Aaron.
12 D. R. Dendy, *The Use of Lights in Christian Worship* (London, 1959), pp. 1–3; C. Vincent, *Fiat Lux. Lumière et luminaires dans la vie religieuse du XIIe au XVIe siècle* (Paris, 2004), pp. 26–9.
13 *Notitia Dignitatum: La Notitia Dignitatums. Nueva edición crítica y commentario histório* (Madrid, 2004), *Notitia Orientis* XI, 12, p. 195. R. Delmaire, *Les institutions du Bas-Empire romain, de Constantin à Justinien* (Paris, 1995), p. 79, and also S. MacCormack, *Art and Ceremony in Late Antiquity* (Berkeley, 1995).
14 Tertullian, *De Idolataria*, ed. and trans. with commentary J. Wascinc and J. M. C. Van Winden (Leiden, 1987), 15.1, 15.5, 15.10, pp. 51, 53, 55. The seminal text for the light metaphor is John 8:12: 'I am the light of the world'. For the later theological development of this theme, which encompasses the carrying of torches and candles in the ceremony of baptism, Gregory of Nazianzen, 'Oration on the Holy Lights', preached in 381, *Gregory of Nazianzen, Select Orations*, ed. C. Brown and J. Swallow, *Nicene and Post Nicene Fathers of the Christian Church*, vol. 7 (Grand Rapids, 1893), pp. 352–9.
15 Tertullian, *Apology*, trans. T. R. Glover (London, 1931), 35, pp. 161–5.
16 G. Bührer-Thierry, 'Lumière et pouvoir dans le haut moyen âge occidental. Célébration de pouvoir et metaphors lumineuses', *Mélanges de l'École Française de Rome. Moyen Age*, 116.2 (2004), 521–56. See also P. Fouracre, 'Lights, Power and the Moral Economy of Early Medieval Europe', *Early Medieval Europe* 28.3 (2020), 1–21.
17 Council of Elvira, ed. J. Vives, *Concilios Visigóticos et Hispano-Romanos* (Barcelona and Madrid, 1963), pp. 1–15, c. 34., p. 7.
18 The literature on this subject is vast since the cult of saints itself produced so much writing and was a mainstay of the written culture of the Middle Ages. In 1983 S. Wilson counted 1,300 titles dealing with the subject, but this is only a fraction of the present total: S. Wilson, 'Annotated bibliography', in S. Wilson

(ed.), *Saints and Their Cults. Studies in Religious Sociology Folklore and History* (Cambridge, 1983), pp. 309–417. For the most recent survey of the phenomenon of sanctity and cults (but which does not tackle the material basis that allowed them to function) see R. Bartlett, *Why Can the Dead Do Such Great Things?* (Princeton, 2013). For the generation of cults through writing, the classic work is H. Delehaye, *The Legends of the Saints*, 4th edn, trans. D. Attwater (London, 1962). For the early evidence for the setting of saints' tombs in buildings (which goes back to the mid-second century), see J. Crook, *The Architectural Setting of the Cult of Saints in the Early Christian West* (Oxford, 2000), esp. pp. 10–40.

19 *The Poems of Saint Paulinus of Nola*, trans. P. G Walsh (New York, 1975). See also Dennis E. Trout, *Paulinus of Nola. Life, Letters and Poems* (Berkeley, Los Angeles and London, 1999).

20 Paulinus, poem 14 (the third Natalicum, 397), lines 98ff.

21 Paulinus, poem 18 (the sixth Natalicum, 400), line 160.

22 Paulinus, poem 19, lines 457ff.

23 Jerome, *Contra Vigilantium*, PL 22, 339, cc. 4, 5, 7.

24 The seminal works which demonstrated how civic virtue was incorporated into the values of sanctity, with the opening of saints' lives coming to resemble the epitaph of the worthy citizen are M. Heinzelmann, 'Neue Aspekte der biographischen und hagiographischen Literatur in der Lateinischen Welt (1–6 Jahrhundert)', *Francia* 1 (1973), 27–44, and M. Heinzelmann, '"Sanctitas" und "Tugendadel": zur Konzeptionen von "Heilgikeit" in 5 und 10 Jahrhundert', *Francia* 5 (1977), 741–52. Paulinus of Nola provides a good example of a later Roman aristocratic (senatorial) figure who entered the Church, became a bishop and would be venerated as a saint. His poetry demonstrates his classical education.

25 Dendy, *Use of Lights*, pp. 92–7, was of the opinion that this came from pagan practice with lights lit at funerals and to honour gods and demi-gods. He noted that lamps burned perpetually before the statue of Athena in the Acropolis, with the lamps being filled with oil once a year. On the rejection of this belief in the sixteenth century, see below Chapter 6.

26 This grant was made in 783: *MGH Diplomata Karolinorum* I, ed. E. Mühlbacher (Hanover, 1906), no. 149.

27 The six churches in Rome are Saint Paul's Without the Walls, Santa Croce in Gerusalemme, S Agnese, plus a baptistery, unnamed here but possibly identified as S Constanza as it was where the emperor's sister Constantia was baptised, S Lorenzo Without the Walls, and SS Marcellino e Pietro.

28 This work is translated by R. Davis in three volumes: R. Davis, *The Lives of the Eighth-Century Popes (Liber Pontificalis): The Ancient Biographies of Nine Popes from AD 715 to AD 817* (Liverpool, 1992); R. Davis, *The Lives of the Ninth-Century Popes (Liber Pontificalis): The Ancient Biographies of Ten Popes from AD 817–891* Liverpool, 1995); R. Davis, *The Book of Pontiffs (Liber Pontificalis): The Ancient Biographies of the First Ninety Roman Bishops to AD 715* (Liverpool, 2nd rev. edn, 2000).

29 *The Book of Pontiffs* 34, pp. 14–27.
30 Davis, *The Book of Pontiffs*, pp. xxix–xxxi.
31 On the 'Donation of Constantine', see further below, p. 78.
32 *The Book of Pontiffs* 34.12, pp. 17–18. Fanciulli, *De Lucernis seu lampadibus pensilibus* (Macerate, 1802), p. 54, noted the scale of this provision. He also listed all the references to gifts of lamps in the *Liber Pontificalis*, pp. 37–40.
33 *The Book of Pontiffs* 34.9–11, pp. 16–17. On the variety of lamps listed in this source, H. Geertmans, 'L'illuminazione della basilica paleocristiana secondo il Liber Pontificalis', *Rivista di Archeologia Christiana* 64 (1988), 135–60.
34 *The Book of Pontiffs* 34.24, pp. 22–3.
35 See for example, *The Book of Pontiffs* 34.21, p. 21.
36 These are the calculations of H. Bresc, 'Mer morte et oliviers perdus. Repli et survie de l'olivaie Méditerranéenne (ive–xiie siècle)', in *Olio e vino nell'alto medioevo*, *Settimane di Spoleto* 54 (2007), 55–106, 58.
37 M. Xanthopoulou, 'Lampes en metal, lampes en terre cuite: vies parallèles', *Lychonological Acts 1* (2005), 303–6. Xanthopoulou's paper has very useful illustrations of a range of early terracotta lamps.
38 *The Book of Pontiffs* 34.19.
39 On this subject there is a vast literature. Recent big books indicative of the range of views in the English language are C. Wickham, *Framing the Early Middle Ages* (Oxford, 2005), P. Heather, *The Fall of the Roman Empire* (Basingstoke and Oxford, 2005), M. McCormick, *The Origins of the European Economy* (Cambridge, 2002) and G. Halsall, *The Barbarian Migrations* (Cambridge, 2007).
40 On circulation and transport, with 46 useful maps and illustrations, L. Ermine Pani and F. R. Stasolla, 'Le strade del vino e dell'olio: commercio, transporto e conversazione', *Settimane di Spoleto* 54, 539–97; on the breakdown of systems of exchange in the Western Mediterranean, the account of Wickham, *Framing*, pp. 693–759, is largely based on the ceramic evidence,
41 On Provence, and arguing that production was not increased there when it declined elsewhere, G. Comet, 'Le vin et l'huile en Provence médiévale, essai de bilan', in *L'Ambiente Vegetale nell'alto Medioevo*, *Settimane di Spoleto* 37 (1990), 343–58, at 343–4.
42 For a clear account of the decline, dealing with all areas, Bresc, 'Mer morte', 70–8. On Spain, though arguing from later evidence, L. Bolens, 'Al-Andalus: la vigne et l'olivier, un secteur de pointe (xe–xiiie siècles)', *Settimane di Spoleto* 37 (1990), 423–8.
43 A. J. Grieco, 'Olive tree cultivation and the alimentary use of olive oil in late medieval Italy', in M. C. Amouretti and J.-P. Brun (eds), *La production du vin et d'huile en Méditerranée* (Bulletin de Corrèspondance Hellénique, Supplément 26) (Paris, 1993), pp. 297–306. It was A. I. Pini who remarked that continued production was guaranteed by ecclesiastical demand: A. I. Pini, 'Vite e olivo nell'alto medioevo', *Settimane di Spoleto* 37 (1990), 329–70, at 339. In discussion,

at 381, it was pointed out, however, that this view may simply relate to the fact that the only documents to survive from the early period are of ecclesiastical provenance.

44 Grieco, 'Olive tree cultivation', 28–9, points out that it was not worth growing olives this far north in the Roman period when there were cheap imports from Africa, adding that a slight rise in temperature in the early Middle Ages might also have facilitated the move northwards.

45 For the post-Roman history of olive cultivation in general, seminal is A. I. Pini, 'La vite e olivo nell'Italia padana. Due collture specialiistiche del Medioevo', in V. Fumigalli and G. Rosetti (eds), *Medioevo rurale. Sulle trace della civiltà Contadina* (Bologna, 1980), pp. 119–38, followed by Bresc, 'Mer morte'.

46 *The Book of Pontiffs* 34.9, p. 16. The *fastigium* is the first thing on the list.

47 *The Book of Pontiffs* 46.1, p. 37.

48 *The Book of Pontiffs* 47.6, p. 39.

49 From the time of Gregory II (715–31) we see a new item in the lighting paraphernalia – *canistra*. These were silver drip-trays placed beneath the lamps, which might suggest that in order to economise greater care was being taken over the oil, or possibly wax: *The Lives of the Eighth-century Popes* 91.10, p. 9.

50 *Gregorii Magni, Opera Registrum Epistularum*, ed. D. Norberg, CCSL cxl–cxlA (Turnhout, 1982), *Ep* XIV.14, pp. 1086–7.

51 J. Story, 'Land and lights in early medieval Rome', in R. Balzaretti, J. Barrow and P. Skinner (eds), *Italy and Early Medieval Europe* (Oxford, 2018), pp. 315–38.

52 *Pro concinnatione luminariorum vestrorum*. This formula, which has scriptural resonance (cf. Exodus 25:6, Leviticus 24:2), would be common in grants for lighting elsewhere in Italy and in Francia.

53 Story, 'Land and lights'. She notes that the modelling of the second inscription on the first is further evidence that the cult of Gregory the Great was building up at this time. The two Latin texts and translations are published by Story in 'Lands and lights', pp. 335–8.

54 This argument was put forward at a conference held in honour of Chris Wickham and it follows his model for the breakdown of exchange networks. For argument that the history of lighting provision complicates Wickham's model, see P. Fouracre, '"Framing" and lighting: Another angle on transition' in R. Balzaretti, J. Barrow and P. Skinner (eds), *Italy and Early Medieval Europe* (Oxford, 2018), pp. 305–14, which began as another paper delivered at the same conference.

55 *The Book of Pontiffs* 93.19, p. 45.

56 *The Book of Pontiffs* 34.9, pp. 15–16.

57 Davis, *Lives of the Eighth-century Popes*, pp. 31–4; T. F. X. Noble, *The Republic of Saint Peter. The Birth of the Papal State 680–825* (Philadelphia, 1984), pp. 53–75.

58 The reference to Offa's instigation of the practice comes in a letter of Pope Leo III to Coenwulf, a later king of Mercia. It is translated in *English Historical Documents I*, ed. D. Whitelock (London, 1968), no. 205. On the evolution of

regular payments to Rome after Offa, R. Naismith and F. Tinti, 'The Origins of Peter's Pence', *English Historical Review* 134 (2019), 521–52.

59 Ibn Rustah, *al-Alāq al-nafīsa* (tenth-century), reporting the story of Harūn ibn Yahya (late ninth-century), in M. G. Stasolla, *Italia euro-mediterranea nel medioevo. Testimonianze de scrittore arabi* (Bologna, 1983), p. 220. I am grateful to Caroline Goodson for drawing my attention to this passage.

60 M. Bourasse, 'Le testament de S. Perpetue, évêque de Tours', *Bulletin de la Société Archéologique de Touraine* 2 (1871–73), 256.

61 S. Sato, 'The Merovingian Accounting Documents of Tours', *Early Medieval Europe* 9 (2000), 143–61.

62 That the Tours monastery became the premier site associated with Martin owed a great deal to Perpetuus's promotion of the cult there: R. van Dam, *Saints and Their Miracles in Late Antique Gaul* (Princeton, 1993), pp. 13–22.

63 For the role of the continuous record of Saint Martin's and other elite Frankish monastery in the construction of models of European history, P. Fouracre, 'Francia and the History of Medieval Europe', *The Haskins Society Journal* 23 (2011, pub. 2014), 1–22.

64 The two principal works of Gregory in which the cult features are *Decem Libri Historiarum*, ed. B. Krusch and W. Levison, *MGH Scriptores Rerum Merovingicarum* 1.i (Hanover and Leipzig, 1937–51), trans. L. Thorpe, *Gregory of Tours, The History of the Franks* (Harmondsworth, 1974), and *Libri de virtutibus sancti Martini episcopi*, ed. B. Krusch, *MGH SRM* 1 (Hanover and Leipzig, 1885), pp. 584–661, trans. van Dam. *Saints and Their Miracles*, pp. 199–303. As the best known, and most read, historian of the sixth century Gregory has attracted a great deal of scholarly attention, especially with regard to the *Decem Libri*. For a judicious analysis see M. Heinzelmann, *Gregory of Tours* (Cambridge, 2001).

65 For Gregory and his dependence on Saint Martin, van Dam, *Saints and Their Miracles*, pp. 62–81.

66 An example of the medicinal use of oil in the Bible is Luke 10:34, the parable of the Good Samaritan. On the history of healing miracles involving oil, and also wax, L. Canetti, '*Olea sanctorum*: reliquie e miracoli fra tardoantico e alto medieoevo', *Settimane di Spoleto* 54 (2007), 1335–415, esp. 1342–7 and 1409–15.

67 'Miracles of Saint Martin' 1.2, van Dam, pp. 203–4.

68 'Miracles of Saint Martin' 1.15, van Dam, p. 215.

69 'Miracles of Saint Martin' 3.18, van Dam, p. 267.

70 Gregory of Tours, *Liber in gloria martyrum*, ed. B. Krusch, *MGH SRM* 1, trans. R. van Dam, *Gregory of Tours. Glory of the Martyrs* (Liverpool, 1988), here 5, pp. 22–4.

71 *Glory of the Martyrs* 31, p. 51.

72 In this story the beekeeper kept the honey while reserving the wax. The standard observation is that 1 lb of wax is produced for every 6–10 lb of honey. If this ratio is applicable here, the amount of honey produced per annum would

have been between 666 and 1,000 lb. This suggests that he was relatively well off, but not rich.
73 'Miracles of Saint Martin' 4.15, van Dam, p. 291. Note that the wax was valuable enough to bury in this way.
74 For the role of Marseilles in the oil trade at this time, D. Claude, 'Der Handel im westlichen Mittelmeer während des Frühmittelalters', in K. Düwel, H. Jankhun, H. Siems and D. Timpe (eds), *Untersuchungen zu Handel und Verkehr der vor- und frühgeschichtlichen Zeit im Mittel- und Nordeuropa* (Göttingen, 1985), pp. 74–6.
75 Gregory, *Decem Libri Historiarum*! V, c. 23, pp. 177–8: *advenientibus at cataplum navibus transmarinis, Vigilii archidiaconis homines septuaginta vasa quas vulgo orcas vocant olei et liquaminisque furati sunt.*
76 Gregory, *Decem Libri Historiarum* V, c. 5, p. 200: *O si te habuisset Massilia sacerdotum! Numquam naves oleum aut reliquas species detulissent, nisi cartam tantum, quo maiorem opportunitatem scribendi ad bonos infamandos habere.*
77 Gregory was familiar with the works of Paulinus of Nola and believed that he was the author of a five-book verse account of the miracles of Saint Martin: 'Miracles of Saint Martin' 1.2, van Dam pp. 201–5. The author was in fact Paulinus of Périgueux. See van Dam, p. 201, n. 7.
78 Council of Braga I, *Concilios Visigóticos e Hispano-Romanos*, ed. J. Vives (Barcelona and Madrid, 1963), pp. 65–77, c. 7, p. 72.
79 Council of Braga II, *Concilios Visigóticos*, pp. 78–102, c. 2, pp. 81–2.
80 Counciil of Braga II, c. 5, p. 87.
81 Council of Toledo 597, *Concilios Visigóticos*, pp. 156–7, c. 1, p. 156.
82 *Las Pizzaras Visigodas*, ed. Isabel Velázquez Soriano (Madrid and Burgos, 2004).
83 *Las Pizzaras*, no. 103, p. 362.
84 This is the so-called 'Limonta case'. See below, Chapter 4.
85 G. Thomás-Faci and J. C. Martín-Iglesias, 'Cuatro documentos inéditos de San Martín de Asán (522–586), *Mittellateinisches Jahrbuch* 52 (2017), 261–86, charter texts at 277–85.
86 S. Castellanos, 'The Significance of Social Unanimity in a Visigothic Hagiography: Keys to an Ideological Screen', *Journal of Early Christian Studies* 11 (2003), 387–420.
87 'The Life of Saint Aemilian', trans. A. Fear, *Lives of the Visigothic Fathers* (Liverpool, 1997), pp. 15–43, c. 29, p. 41.
88 Fear, *Visigothic Fathers*, p. xxix. Aemilian lived in Cantabria, part of the former Suevic kingdom which was, according to Gregory of Tours, converted to Catholic orthodoxy through miracles performed by the relics of Saint Martin. The Franks and Visigoths were bitter rivals in Braulio's lifetime, hence the need to have an alternative cult to that of Martin in Cantabria.
89 *Formuale Visigothicae*, ed. K. Zeumer, *MGH Formulae Merowingici et Karolini Aevi* (Hanover, 1882–86), pp. 572–95, no. 8, p. 579.
90 Present opinion is that *formulae* such as this one do represent actual practice at the time they were produced or at the time of later copying: see A. Rio,

'Charters, law codes and formulae: the Franks between theory and practice', in P. Fouracre and D. Ganz (eds), *Frankland. The Franks and the World of the Early Middle Ages* (Manchester, 2008), pp. 7–27. But of course it not possible to demonstrate that the *formulae* do represent the documents that were in use when there are no surviving documents of that type.

91 A. Thacker, 'Memorialising Gregory the Great: the Origins and Transmission of a Papal Cult in the Seventh and Early Eighth Centuries', *Early Medieval Europe* 7 (1998), 59–85.

92 Chief amongst the visitors to Rome was Bishop Wilfrid who made three trips there over a 50-year period (the first being in 653) and was in close contact with the Papacy. For his career, and the effects of his Roman contacts upon it, see the essays in N. Higham (ed.), *Wilfrid. Abbot, Bishop, Saint* (Donington, 2013). It is interesting to note that Wilfrid's crypts in the churches at Ripon and Hexham were designed to maximise the effect of lighting. It may have been inspired by Roman crypts such as that of Saint Lawrence as well as the crypt under Saint Peter's.

93 On how the early Anglo-Saxon Church modelled itself on what pilgrims had seen in Rome, especially in terms of the liturgy, E. O'Carraragáin, *The City of Rome and the World of Bede*, Jarrow Lecture 1994. On Wilfrid and the Roman crypts, p. 7.

94 R. Gem, '*Gabatae Saxiscae*: Saxon bowls in the churches of Rome during the eighth and ninth centuries', in A. Reynolds and L. Webster (eds), *Early Medieval Art and Archaeology in the Northern World. Studies in Honour of James Graham-Campbell* (Leiden and Boston, 2013), pp. 87–110.

95 Bede, *The Reckoning of Time*, trans. F. Wallis (Liverpool, 1999), ch. 26.

96 H. M. Taylor, 'The Architectural Interest of Æthelwulf's *De Abbatibus*', *Anglo-Saxon England* 3 (1974), 163–7. These quotes are at 165, 166 and 167 respectively.

97 On the widespread use of hanging bowls, and with a good bibliography on the subject, N. Adams, 'Hanging basins and the wine-coloured sea. The wider context of early medieval hanging bowls', in A. Reynolds and L. Webster (eds), *Early Medieval Art and Archaeology in the Northern World. Studies in Honour of James Graham-Campbell* (Leiden and Boston, 2013), pp. 3–49.

98 *MGH Epistolae Merovingici et Karolini Aevi* IV, ed. E. Dümmler (Berlin, 1895), no. 7, pp. 31–3.

99 B. Graham, 'Olives and Lighting in Dark Age Europe', *Early Medieval Europe* 28.3 (2020), 344–66, at 351–2.

100 A. Cassiday, 'Saint Aldhelm's Bees (*De virginitate prosaic*, cc. iv–vi): Some Observations on a Literary Tradition', *Anglo-Saxon England* 33 (2004), 1–22. A close relationship between monks and bees, on both an allegorical and a practical level, is well attested throughout the Middle Ages and beyond. See the illustrated survey and exhibition catalogue by G. Schrott, *Mönche, Bienen, Bücher. Ein ertragreiche Symbiose* (Amberg, 2011).

## Beginnings

101 On wax on the paschal candle as a gift from God, Bührer-Thierry, 'Lumière et pouvoir', 529–31. On the Christ analogy, Schrott, *Mönche, Bücher, Biener*, p. 17, for the 'snow-white mystery' of wax and the prayer for the benediction of the paschal candle see, for example, the tenth-century Mozarabic antiphony from Léon in Spain: *Antifonario Visigotica Mozarabe de la Catedral de Léon*, ed. L. Brou and J. Vives (Barcelona and Madrid, 1959), pp. 280–3. This text is discussed in more detail below in Chapter 4.

102 Touraj Daryaee, 'Honey: a Demonic Food in Zoroastrian Iran?', *Studia Litteraria Universitatis Iagellonicae Cracoviensis*, Special Issue (2019), 53–7. I am grateful to Mark Whelan for this reference.

103 These are the law-codes of Francia (*Lex Salica* and *Lex Ripuaria*), Bavaria, Lombard Italy, Visigothic Spain, Anglo-Saxon England (the Laws of Alfred) and Wales.

104 *Bechbretha*, ed. and trans. T. Charles-Edwards and F. Kelly, *Early Irish Laws Series* 1 (Dublin, 1983). The editors think that the tract relates to the growth of beekeeping per se, rather than the growth of monasticism, pp. 38–49. I am grateful to Roy Flechner for drawing my attention to this material.

105 See above, p. 15.

106 See below, Chapter 4, pp. 120–2.

107 G. Archetti, 'Infundit vinum et oleum. Olio e vino nella traditzione monastica', *Settimane di Spoleto* 54, 1098–203, at 1110. Graham, 'Olives and Lighting', cites a much lower estimation of 134 hours per litre, still vastly superior to wax.

# 2

## Consolidation of provision: elite practice

The last chapter showed that by the late sixth century church councils were insisting that all churches should have provision for the burning of lights. In subsequent centuries this requirement would be repeatedly voiced in councils and in royal and episcopal legislation. Although it was possible to demonstrate the use of oil lamps and candles at saints' shrines in the three centuries after Constantine's conversion, there was very little case material to show how the lights were actually provided for. In the *Liber Pontificalis* there was, of course, much about donating lamps, and here and in two papal charters there are details about the resources dedicated to keeping those lamps filled. It is not, however, until the seventh century that such details are to be found outside Rome. This information comes from a will (the will of Bertramn of Le Mans who died in 623), from charters and from formularies: these make it possible to say something about the place of lighting in the wider economy. Although the formularies have models for charters that seem on a contextual basis to go back well into the sixth century, and Bertramn's will contains phrases that would later be found in charters, the first charters themselves survive only from the mid-seventh century in Francia, from the very end of the seventh century in northern Italy and from the late seventh century in England.[1] As noted in the last chapter, there are effectively no charters from Visigothic Spain, and charters from England have nothing to say on lighting. This means that our focus for the later seventh and early eighth centuries must be on the evidence from first Francia and then Italy, beginning with Frankish charters of immunity and with charters that exempted leading ecclesiastical institutions from toll charges.[2] These documents, which are privileges issued by kings, show the important contribution that rulers made to the provision of lighting, for the privileges not only enabled northern monasteries and bishops' churches to acquire cash but also helped their agents to travel to the south to spend that cash on the purchase of oil. The documents therefore have a strong association with lights, but their significance is usually understood in relation to a perceived decline in royal authority: by granting away their rights, kings, it has been said, were denuding themselves of the resources needed to govern effectively. This is particularly the case with immunities which transferred judicial rights from the king to the Church. I shall argue here that that understanding of immunities is misleading and unhelpful. It draws attention to the potential effects of granting immunity, whereas I shall concentrate on the purpose of granting them in the first place, for it is here that one can see how immunities, along with exemptions from toll, were designed to support the Church. I will then look at the situation in Italy in the early to mid-eighth century which presents a rather different picture. In Italy it is possible to see beyond kings to a wide range of people making provision for lights on a smaller scale and from locally produced oil rather than by the purchase of oil from distant sources. The Italian evidence helps to put the provision for lights into a wider social context. A similar approach works for Francia too, but only from a slightly later date. After an initial burst of grants in the eighth century there was an apparent decline in numbers of charters associated with lighting in Italy. There is also a decline in such grants from rulers in Francia. It is therefore necessary to think about why references to lighting in charters should apparently fall at a time that the use of lights in churches was spreading. First, however, I look at the will of Bertramn of Le Mans, which is of the early seventh century, thus coming at a point after the writings of Gregory of Tours but before the time in which immunities and toll privileges began to be issued. As a piece of evidence it is too chronologically isolated for it to be said that it links the two periods. Nevertheless it illuminates an early seventh-century Frankish world.

Bertramn was bishop of Le Mans and he died in 623. He had been a loyal supporter of King Clothar II in what had been very difficult times, and he was richly rewarded by Clothar when the latter gained control of all of Francia in 613. Bertramn's astonishing wealth is revealed in the will he drew up in 616.[3] Bertramn left estates over most of what is now France to various religious institutions and to his relatives. He freed slaves and gave them and other servants money and horses. Having given many *villae* to the churches of Le Mans, he asked the abbots of his diocese to take the tribute (*tributum* and *suffragium*) from these estates and to divide it in half. On the anniversary of his death the poor were to receive half of it in clothes and gold. The other half was to be used for perpetual lighting in the cathedral of Le Mans. In addition, the income from a tavern in Paris was to go towards the lighting, a detail which recalls the income from a bakery in Antioch that Constantine had once assigned to Saint Peter's in Rome.[4] Bertramn's will spelled out very clearly that the lights were to burn at all times: 'not a single hour of the night is to be without lights'. The Apostles were to be thus honoured 'for all time'. Bertramn had founded a *xendochium* (hospital) dedicated to Saint Martin and a *matricula* (a system whereby the officially listed poor – the *matricularii* – were given relief). For these, tribute was to be collected from yet more *villae* to pay for lights that would burn all night. Finally, he left money for a perpetual light to burn before his own tomb, as well as to pay for someone to maintain the tomb itself. In order to make sure that the lights were properly attended, Bertramn made it a condition of freeing his slaves that they become in effect servants to his memory: he wanted his memory to shine in the cathedral of Le Mans. His will is comparable to the late fifth-century will of Perpetuus, discussed in the last chapter. Both men gave *villae* from which *tributum* was raised in order to pay for lights. The freeing of slaves who would then tend the lights is first seen in Bertramn's will, but the provision appears as a normal practice in the late seventh-century *Formulary of Marculf* which presented a model form for a will: 'Let the freedmen and freed women whom we have freed or will want to free in the future for our salvation, and to whom we have given documents signed by our hand, know that they will owe service to our children, and let them take care to provide hosts and lights for our tomb, according to what is contained in these documents, both themselves and their offspring'.[5] The idea that the freed slave (and his or her offspring) owed a debt to the former master comes from late Roman law, and as will be seen in subsequent chapters of this work, that practice would later be source for those ecclesiastical tributaries known as *censuales* (the so-called *Zensualität*), although this was only one route to tributary status and a dedication to lighting. Others would arrive at this status as tenants of the Church. As with the earlier will, it is not possible to tell from the will of Bertramn exactly who, apart from the freed slaves, paid the *tributum*, but it can again be suggested that at this time cash could be raised from the land, for Bertramn certainly disposed of large amounts in cash, although his wealth was in land. Immunities, as we shall see shortly, were another means of raising cash from estates. Nor is it clear from this evidence whether oil or wax, or both, were used for lighting fuel. One can reason that it was oil given the stress on the perpetual burning of the light, and because, as I shall show, later seventh-century evidence makes it clear that the most prestigious religious institutions preferred to burn oil, scarce though this was becoming. What is different about Bertramn's will is that it provides the first reference to commemorative lighting in Francia. From a single reference it is impossible to tell whether this practice was widespread, and we must bear in mind that Bertramn was a very exceptional man, glorious (and perhaps vainglorious, if the preparations for his memorial are anything to go by) and very, very rich. The care taken to provide for his tomb and to celebrate the anniversary of his death suggests that he wished to be venerated in Le Mans after his death. In the event, it does not seem that he was. I now turn to the privileges which granted immunity and exemption from toll.

The immunity was a privilege granted to favoured ecclesiastical institutions by rulers. The privilege allowed the beneficiary certain rights of jurisdiction over their lands, and this meant that the recipient could keep the income from fines. The king's officials ('the public judges', which no doubt means 'counts') were forbidden to enter the lands to hear cases and levy fines. The beneficiary could also collect and enjoy certain other fiscal charges that lay upon the land and its inhabitants. The stated purpose of such grants was to provide lights for the church in question, and often (but not always) to furnish stipends for those who served the church, and (slightly less often) alms for the poor. Below are the terms of the basic privilege as set out in a model for an immunity in the *Formulary of Marculf*, which was most likely produced around the turn of the seventh century in, or in association with, the monastery of Saint Denis near Paris.[6] In this section it appears that a count is being addressed:

> We decree, therefore, that neither you nor your subordinates nor your successors nor any public judiciary power should ever presume to enter the villas of that church anywhere in our kingdom, whether those given by the generosity of the king or of private persons or those that are to be given at a later time, in order to hear disputes or collect fines from any legal cases or to demand lodgings or supplies or legal guarantors, but let whatever the fisc could have expected to obtain from there, whether from fines or from anything else, whether from free men or from servants of any other status who live within the fields and the boundaries or on the lands of the said church, benefit [this church] in perpetuity through its representatives, by our grant [and] for our future salvation, by [providing] lights for this church.[7]

The purpose of the grant was clearly to provide lights for the church. This aspect of the immunity has nevertheless been ignored until relatively recently, and the clause that said that lights should be provided was generally dismissed as an empty formula that had little historical significance compared with the banning of royal officials from lands granted immunity.[8] This argument must be reviewed in order to consider why there should be a connection between the grant of judicial exemptions and the provision of lighting. This will involve taking the immunity out of the teleological frame in which it has traditionally been considered, and thinking more precisely about the context in which the privilege came into being. It is important, moreover, to view immunities in conjunction with exemptions from toll for they had a common purpose. I will then return to the issues of demand, supply and the need for cash raised at the end of the last chapter.

The term 'immunity' (which is closely derived from the Latin word *immunitas* in all modern West European and Slavonic languages) has often had negative connotations when applied to the body politic. It can imply exemption from burdens and obligations shouldered by the mass of people, and one can see why such exemptions might be seen as harmful to the state, or to the community at large. This negative feeling about immunities, which was strong in the late nineteenth and early twentieth centuries, becomes somewhat anachronistic when applied to the early Middle Ages, a time in which states were configured very differently, that is, a time in which there were no states in the modern sense. But in the traditional view, the weakness (or even non-existence) of the early medieval state was perceived to have been the result of the dissolution of public authority in the post-Roman world. The dissolving of the public was put down to the incompetence of rulers and the greediness of the aristocracy, both parties being unable to resist the short-term, but short-sighted, advantage of giving away resources and appropriating them for 'private' use respectively. Public authority, faced with the loss of rights and resources, was thought by modern historians to have declined inexorably over the whole early medieval period, despite the valiant attempts of certain rulers, such as Charlemagne, to shore it up. The final result, in this view, was a complete breakdown of first royal and then comital authority (sometimes termed the 'feudal crisis', or the 'feudal revolution') which came about around the turn of the first millennium in West Francia (France), after which public authority and the rule of law were painfully built up again.[9] The granting of immunities plays an important part in this scenario.[10] The Merovingian rulers of Francia, who started the ball rolling here, have been seen as notoriously feckless and incompetent, and their magnates as particularly self-serving and greedy. It was allegedly thus a fateful move to ban judicial officials from entering the lands of an immunity, and just as unhelpful to give up revenues to people who were already privileged. The result, on this view, was nothing less than a privatisation of power. One can see why the lighting clause in immunities should have slipped out of view when the immunities themselves were considered in such dramatic terms.

Today, this line of reasoning about the significance of immunities seems misguided at several turns. A basic objection is that it imagines a dichotomy between the public and private that is ill-fitted to an early medieval context. Rather than seeing king and aristocracy as having opposing interests, we now tend to think of a strong social conservatism that put them in the same camp.[11] Nor, as suggested earlier, was there much of a 'state' to be weakened. Recent thinking has been that the closest the Franks came to creating a state was the way in which power and authority were legitimated and to some extent exercised through the Church.[12] Ian Wood goes further and sees the Church as determinant of social organisation: post-Roman Europe had become, he says, 'a Temple Society'.[13] It is therefore logical to reason that granting immunities to churches would have had the effect of strengthening, rather than weakening, 'the state'.[14] It is also the case that rulers did not entirely abandon immunities to the control of the beneficiaries, for they insisted that 'major crimes' committed in immunities should be dealt with by the local count.[15] In later centuries (from the tenth century onwards) when lords, both lay and ecclesiastical, did appropriate royal rights this was not on the basis of ancient immunities. Similarly, the distribution of immunities granted by the Merovingian and Carolingian rulers hardly maps on to the pattern of these later territorial lordships. In fact the establishment of territorial lordships in France comes at a time when immunities had in effect ceased to operate: rulers no longer had the power to guarantee the beneficiaries' income or protection. The argument that the granting of immunities weakened royal authority by giving rights and resources over to the aristocracy hangs on the conviction that lay magnates were granted the privilege. Every surviving immunity is, however, a grant to a church. There is evidence that immunities could in principle be granted to lay people, but no evidence that they actually were.[16] So why do immunities seem to have a particular association with the Church and with lighting? A large part of the answer is surely that the immunity was a source of cash. Let us look in more detail at the cash element and at how the money was spent.

The count and his underlings (his *iuniores*) were forbidden to enter the lands of an immunity to 'hear disputes or collect fines (*freta*) from any legal cases or to demand lodgings or supplies or legal guarantors'. Instead, whatever the fisc (*fiscus*) could have expected to get from fines or other charges on the land and the people on the land was to go to the church. Later confirmations of immunity added the term *redibuciones* to what the fisc gave over to the beneficiary. The word 'fisc' can refer to royal lands, and to income from land and people in general (including a proportion of judicial fines) that went to the king. Since the land in the immunity was said to have come to the church from unspecified sources (i.e. it was not all land that had been the king's), here the term 'fisc' would seem to refer to income. Historians are divided over what resources were available to the fisc, and in particular they disagree on the extent to which direct taxation survived in Merovingian Francia. One near contemporary saint's life, the *Vita Balthildis*, says Queen Balthild put an end to head tax, which must have been before the year 664 when she fell from power.[17] That she did do this is possibly supported by fact that in Francia the gold coinage in which the tax had been traditionally collected came to an end about ten years after the queen's fall: in the mid 670s there was an abrupt and near complete switch from a gold to a silver coinage.[18] Though one school of historians holds that the Roman head and land taxes did survive across the whole early medieval period, there is more general agreement that they disappeared, as the *Vita Balthildis* says they did, or at least that they atrophied in the hands of private landowners who took them over.[19] What was left was what we would term indirect taxation: tolls, fines and special payments, all of which are associated with cash, as well as various services such as forced labour, the building of shelters or the provision of accommodation. It was indirect taxation of this kind that was being remitted to the beneficiary of the privilege of immunity, and this seems to be what lay behind the grant of judicial rights to the immunist. Chief amongst these was the right to collect the *fretum*. This was a proportion (usually said to be one-third) of the composition fine paid to the ruler or to his or her representative the count for arranging the peace between a victim of a 'crime' and its perpetrator. Such compensation arrangements, the stuff of the law codes, were always expressed in cash amounts, as were other sorts of fine, such as the fine for breaking the terms of a gift to a church, the fine for non-performance of military duty or the 600 *solidi* fine that was later stipulated as the penalty for infringing an immunity. *Redibuciones* means simply 'payments', but, since the term is used for payments to the fisc from tolls, it too may have a cash association.[20] It is of course possible that what was expressed in amounts of cash was actually paid in kind: this is the case in tenth-century northern Spain where prices and fines were expressed in *solidi* (gold coin) in a society that shows no sign of having had a coinage. But there are coins from later seventh-century Francia: the *tremissis* which was worth a third of a gold *solidus*, and a growing number of silver *denarii* (pennies) which would soon become the sole currency. Even if some dues were indeed paid in kind, it can be accepted that the Frankish economy did have a monetary element at this time, and that there was some cash amongst the inhabitants of immunities, both free and un-free. It is this that the fisc 'could have expected to obtain', and which now went to the beneficiary, with fines being highlighted as the source of that income.

Where provision for lighting is mentioned in documents other than immunities, there is also an association with cash. King Theuderic III (d. 690) exempted Saint Denis from tolls throughout the kingdom, the savings to be spent on lights.[21] Then in 693 King Clovis III reiterated this exemption and confirmed the monastery's right to receive 100 *solidi* per annum from the revenues of Marseilles to be spent on whatever was available in the port.[22] The grant of the Marseilles revenues had originally been made by King Dagobert I who died in 639. The *Gesta Dagoberti*, which was put together some time before the year 835 but which was based on items in the Saint Denis archive, refers to this charter and tells us that the monastery was to spend the money on oil. The king's agents in the port were to buy the oil from ships as they came in (*secundum quod ordo cataboli esset*), and then they were to pass the oil over to the monastery's agents.[23] In a charter of 694 Saint Denis received land from the fisc in lieu both of this cash and of another 200 *solidi* it had been receiving from the fisc, but, in a confirmation of the 693 charter issued in 716, the 100 *solidi* from Marseilles figured once more.[24] It is interesting to see that land could be substituted for cash here, which might imply that revenue from land could come in the form of cash, or, if in kind, be converted into cash via market exchange. In privileges that granted exemptions from toll, or (rarely) income from toll, the same phrase occurs as in the immunitiy fourmula: 'whatever our fisc had been able to hope for' was now to go to the monastery, for the lights and for the maintenance of the monks. In addition to the toll exemptions there also survives one *tractoria*, a document of Roman origin which entitled the beneficiary (formerly officials travelling on behalf of the Roman emperor, but now churchmen hand in glove with the king) to receive supplies en route to their destination.[25] This benefit was granted to the monastery of Corbie in the year 716.[26] The destination of Corbie's agents was Marseilles. In addition to getting supplies for 15 carts and lodging on their journey, the agents were also to pick up 10,000 lb of oil from the royal depot of Fosses at the mouth of the Rhône, near Marseilles. Immunities, grants of toll and other payments evidently generated cash, and some at least of that cash was spent on oil imported into Marseilles. Further confirmation of the fact that leading ecclesiastical institutions were visiting Marseilles or other Mediterranean ports to buy oil for lighting comes from another model appended to the Marculf collection not long after the main body of the work was completed. This is called an 'immunity' but it is actually an exemption from tolls, and the privilege is directed towards a bishop rather than to a monastery.[27] The document addresses 'all agents in public service' who levy tolls. 'The travelling agents [of the bishop] should not pay any toll or charges to our fisc out of the carts with which [they go] every year to buy lights in Marseilles and in the other ports of our kingdom ...'. Again, 'any payment which our fisc could have expected out of these carts' is 'to provide for the lights of this holy place'. The model details the toll stations the bishop's agents were likely to pass through: Marseilles itself, Toulon, Fosses, Arles, Avignon, Soyons, Valence, Vienne, Lyons, Chalon 'and the other cities'. From this list it looks as if the agents were from a northern bishopric and it was envisaged that they would travel along the Rhône-Saone rivers. It is puzzling as to why, in this case, tolls would be levied on carts rather than boats. Perhaps the agents went downstream in boats, returning upstream by road. Finally, one reference to lighting provision does not involve cash. This comes from the *Vita Ansberti*, the 'Life' of Ansbert, bishop of Rouen 684–90. Though this work was not composed before the end of the eighth century, it is here thought to be reliably based on documents from the abbey of Saint Wandrille.[28] The *Vita Ansberti* tells us that King Theuderic III granted the estate of Donzère to Saint Wandrille. Saint Wandrille lies on the Seine downstream from Rouen, but Donzère is in Provence on the east bank of the Rhône (dep. Drôme). This distant property was to provide oil and other necessities for the monks.[29] Saint Wandrille sent down a party of monks who founded a monastery at Donzère and managed the estate directly. It was, we are told, very productive until the kingdom was divided (referring, no doubt, to the wars after 714), and the Arabs invaded Provence (which they did in alliance with local rebels in 732) as a result of which the area was depopulated. The passage suggests both that in the later seventh century oil was being produced in Provence for monasteries in the north of the Loire, and that that production came to an end when Provence fell into disorder in the mid-eighth century.

The evidence from late seventh- and early eighth-century Francia thus shows major ecclesiastical institutions (bishop's churches and monasteries) being given privileges of immunity, toll exemption, toll income and supplies all of which facilitated their purchase of oil for lighting. Nevertheless, caution is required before a general impression can be inferred from the evidence. Firstly, our documents largely concern institutions north of the River Loire. The south figures only as the destination of northern churchmen seeking oil. This is arguably due to the fact that royal documents survive from the north but not from the south of the Merovingian kingdom. There is a particular cluster of original documents which concern the monastery of Saint Denis near Paris: the Merovingian charters of Saint Denis famously survived the French Revolution. They were thrown on to the street when the Revolutionaries burned down the abbey, but gathered up by an antiquary. The importance of Saint Denis may therefore be exaggerated by this fortunate survival. Other monasteries, such as Corbie, Saint Wandrille and Saint Bertin may similarly be over-represented in the record, as Saint Martin's at Tours would be over the whole period. Second, it is not possible to see from the documents when the practice of privileging institutions in this way actually began, although Saint Denis's revenue from Marseilles was first granted by King Dagobert, who died in 639. Some of these monasteries, such as Saint Wandrille, Corbie, Stavelot-Malmédy or Jumièges, were foundations of the mid-seventh century. Others, such as Saint Germain-des-Prés in Paris, or Saint Calais near Le Mans, were much older, so there remains a possibility that they had received privileges at a much earlier date. A document from the year 693 for Saint Calais, for example, confirms the monastery's immunity which was said to have been first granted by the founder, King Guntramn.[30] He died in 593, and the document names five kings who confirmed the privilege over the next century. It tells us that these documents of confirmation were all examined in 693, which would suggest that Saint Calais did indeed have an immunity and confirmations that went back a century. It may be significant that the text of the Saint Calais immunity is the one least like the model from Marculf with which we began this discussion. It has no lighting clause: the privilege is given so that the monks may live in peace and pray for the well-being of the kingdom and the king. In this respect, the Saint Calais immunity has more similarities with immunities issued, or confirmed, by Carolingian rulers in the eighth and ninth centuries, for these too do not generally have a lighting clause, but do offer protection so that the beneficiary might 'live in peace'.

Although the uneven distribution of documents might well distort the picture, it is possible to reconstruct a plausible historical context in which immunities and toll privileges came to acquire a particular association with the provision of lighting, namely the need to provide cash for an expensive product available only at great distance. It looks as if that association could be lost as oil became even scarcer and wax tribute replaced the cash formerly needed to provide for the lights. At the same time, ecclesiastical institutions continued to build up their wealth in land until the value of the immunity lay less in the indirect taxation it offered than in the protection of landed assets: a key advantage of acquiring jurisdiction over land was that it allowed the beneficiary to hold inquests (the examination of sworn testimonies) through which they could recover estates that had been leased out and then in effect lost.[31] That immunities and toll exemptions may indeed have been multiplying from the mid-seventh century onwards is suggested in the *Vita Balthildis*. It tells us that the queen reformed the 'senior churches' of her kingdom. This must have been between 657 and 664. She regularised monastic life in them and gave the leading institutions immunity. These included Saint Denis, Saint Medard's at Soissons, Saint Martin's at Tours, Saint Germain-des-Prés as well as the churches at Sens and Orléans.[32] If this is trustworthy information (and the documents do support this), then it would seem that all the major ecclesiastical houses were acquiring immunities at this time. It is impossible to be sure of what was given away at this mid-seventh-century date, or earlier, because, with the exception of two heavily interpolated documents, nearly all Merovingian immunities come from the period 690–717.[33] If there was a spate of grants from the mid-seventh century onwards, this could explain why Marculf has a model for an immunity whereas the earlier *Formulary of Angers* does not, and why the form of immunity, as presented in Marculf, became common, or was already common, when the Marculf collection was put together. Toll exemptions follow the same pattern but the surviving documents start slightly earlier. The earliest document is from 661. It granted toll exemptions to the monks of Corbie as they made their way to Provence.[34]

It seems likely that three factors lay behind the association of immunities, tolls and the one surviving *tractoria* with lighting provision. First, there was, as noted, an increase in numbers of monasteries in the north in the mid-seventh century.[35] As with all churches, founders and donors were obliged to provide the means for worship and this included the provision of lighting. These were highly prestigious institutions and provision must have been on a scale that reflected their spiritual, social and political importance. They thus needed the means to go and get oil from Mediterranean ports, and this meant making sure that they had cash, and the privileges that facilitated the yearly run to the south where some of that cash was spent on oil. These favourable arrangements were extended to bishops as well as abbots. Second, the immunity reflects the way in which cash was generated through fines and tolls and other payments rather than through more direct taxation which had once been collected by the rulers and then directed to the church, as had perhaps been the case with 200 *solidi* that Saint Denis at one time received from the fisc. The third factor to take into account is the probability that there were decreasing amounts of cash available at a time when oil was becoming scarcer but demand from the growing number of privileged institutions was increasing. A conjunction of circumstances – the foundation of new institutions, the concentration on cash generation through fines and customary payments, and the interplay between rising demand and falling supply – could explain the development of privileges of immunity and toll exemption that designated lighting provision as a key part of the gift to the holy. The gradual disappearance of that conjunction could also explain why the lighting clause tended to drop out of immunity privileges in the eighth century when the purchase of oil for cash seems to have come to an end.

One consequence of privileging important churches when cash may have been in short supply is that favoured institutions became relatively cash-rich, and possibly much richer than other elements in society, although the evidence from non-ecclesiastical sources does not exist to make a comparison. It is clear, however, that Saint Denis was able to pay large cash fines on behalf of others. A charter of 694 refers to the monastery having paid a 600 *solidi* fine on behalf of a man called Ibbo who had failed to turn up for a military campaign when required to do so.[36] Saint Denis received land from Ibbo's family who presumably could not repay this amount. There is also a court case from 693 in which Saint Denis charged one Abbot Ermenoald with not making good on a pledge of 1,500 lb of oil and 100 barrels of 'good wine'. The pledge was made on behalf of 'Bishop Ansbert'. If this is Bishop Ansbert of Rouen who was deposed and imprisoned in 690, the pledge may have been used to secure a loan to pay a fine on Ansbert's behalf.[37] Saint Denis seems to have been accumulating cash over and beyond its needs, and was acting rather like a bank, increasing its assets as it did so. It is interesting to see oil being pledged as collateral, which could suggest that a few exceptionally privileged institutions were able to build up stocks of oil, although the thrust of the evidence is that it was at this time becoming even more scarce and expensive. Taking this into account, one could reason that privileges enabling institutions to collect cash to buy oil also had the effect of increasing their economic importance as well their spiritual prestige.

The *Vita Ansberti*, remember, said that the monastery of Saint Wandrille lost control of its oil-producing estate in Provence when the kingdom was divided and the area depopulated. It is known that Provence and Marseilles were of great importance to the Merovingian kings. Gold coins were minted there in their names long after this coinage had ceased elsewhere. The ruler of Provence, Antenor, attended the court of King Childebert III but was said to have rebelled after this king's death in 711. The area was apparently hostile to the family of Pippin and then of his son Charles Martel (both 'mayors of the palace', the effective leaders of the northern Franks), but contact with the north was resumed when that family was out of power from 714 to 717.[38] That was the window in which Saint Denis's receipt of 100 *solidi* per annum from the revenues of Marseilles was reconfirmed, and when there was confirmation of the toll privileges and *tractoria* that enabled Corbie to collect oil from Fosses. After this no northern monastery or bishopric received privileges in the south, although it must be said that there are very few royal charters of any kind for the period 718–51. Narrative sources say that Provence was again in revolt by 732 and that Arabs from Spain had moved into the area. Starting in 736 Charles Martel reconquered it, driving out the Arabs, but, as the *Vita Ansberti* indicates, by then Provence had been devastated.[39] The Will of Abbo (d. 739), ruler of Provence and an ally of Charles Martel, supports this picture in telling of how during the disorder peasants in the mountainous areas had slipped their bonds and abandoned the lands to which they were tied.[40] When the monastery of Saint Germain-des-Prés had a toll privilege confirmed in the year 779, Marseilles was no longer mentioned as the destination for monks seeking lighting provision, and when in the early ninth century the monasteries of Stavelot-Malmedy concocted a toll privilege that enabled the monks to seek lighting provision, and was supposedly issued by the monasteries' founder King Sigibert in 647 or 648, this was for toll exemptions on the River Loire.[41] Journeys to Marseilles to collect oil were now, it seems, beyond memory.

That there was indeed a shortage of oil is indicated in the hagiography of this period. The 'Life of Saint Philibert' (*Vita Filiberti*), composed around the middle of the eighth century, concerns the monastery of Jumièges, one of the mid-seventh-century foundations.[42] It lay on the banks of the Seine downstream from Rouen opposite Saint Wandrille, another foundation of the same period which had, as mentioned above, been given an estate in Provence. Jumièges apparently had no such property. The *Vita Filiberti* tells us that the monastery was down to its last half pound of oil which its steward wished to reserve for the healing of the sick. Saint Philibert, abbot of Jumièges, nevertheless told him to put the oil into the lamps, declaring that God would ensure that they had enough oil for a whole year. That evening a ship from Bordeaux arrived carrying oil that had been sent 'by friends'.[43] The cargo amounted to 40 *modii* (barrels) of oil, perhaps equivalent to a year's supply, though unfortunately it remains unclear how much a *modius* contained. This was surely less oil than would have been carried by the 15 carts for which Corbie was assigned supplies in 716, given that each cart must have carried more than three *modii*. However welcome, the amount of oil Jumièges received was modest. That the ship came from Bordeaux cannot indicate that the oil was produced in the south-west, for no olives can be grown in the Atlantic region of France. Given that the western sea route is involved here, one could imagine that the oil came from Spain, but there is no clear reference to oil coming from anywhere other than the ports at the base of the Rhône river system or from Provence. On another occasion when Jumièges was looking for lighting fuel, a whale was washed up near the monastery. From the blubber the monks made 30 *modii* of oil.[44] This is the only time we hear of whale oil being substituted for olive oil. Despite its availability in northern coastal areas, whale oil was clearly not a commonly accepted substitute, even though there is no evidence of its use being forbidden in the way that the Papacy was to stop the Icelanders substituting berry-juice for wine in the Eucharist.[45] The monks of Jumièges clearly preferred oil as the fuel for perpetual lighting, for otherwise they could surely have used wax, or, in extremis, tallow. That it continued to be a requirement for churches to have lights burning at all hours is confirmed by a rare vision-text composed in the time of King Theuderic III (d. 690). This is the *Visio Baronti*.[46] Barontus was a monk of the monastery of Longoretus (today Saint-Cyran-en-Brenne, dép. Indre). Apparently near to death, he had a vision in which he was taken by the archangel Raphael to the portals of heaven, fighting off demons en route and meeting various prominent churchmen who had been condemned for their sins, as well as fellow monks who had made it into heaven. One of the latter was a brother called Betolenus who told Barontus that he had been charged by Saint Peter with responsibility for the lights of churches throughout the world. Betolenus wanted to know why the lights in Barontus's monastery went out in the night and did not burn every hour of the day.[47]

Let us now turn to Italy, where a lack of contemporary hagiographical texts means that there are no 'shortage miracles' to compare with those said to have been experienced by the monks of Jumièges. But given that there are plenty of eighth-century Italian charters which mention olives in connection with lighting for churches, often in relation to fairly small parcels of land, it is likely that indigenous and local oil production meant that there was in fact no shortage of oil to an extent that required miraculous intervention. At the beginning of the eighth century the political make-up of Italy was rather more complex than that of the Frankish kingdom which was, in theory, united under a single king: hence the ability of Frankish rulers to issue charters that gave northern monasteries privileged access to the Mediterranean. Italy, by contrast, was divided between Byzantine enclaves around the Adriatic and, in the south, the Lombard principalities of Benevento and Spoleto, the kingdom of the Lombards in the north and, of course, the territory held by the Papacy. This was the complexity reflected from Rome's point of view in the thickening narrative of the *Liber Pontificalis*.[48] In other respects there was much similarity between Lombard Italy and Francia. In Italy as in Francia, head and land taxes had come to an end by the year 700 and rulers in both regions relied on a medley of indirect taxes and services, with judicial fines making up an important part of their revenue.[49] According to Lombard laws (but less clear in the charters) society was, as in Francia, divided into three groups: the free (in which landholders were distinguished from the landless), semi-free (the *aldii* or *aldiones*) and slaves (household slaves, the *servi ministeriales*, and field slaves, the *servi rustici*). The Lombard kings had the equivalent of the Frankish fisc, but in more Romano-Byzantine fashion it was termed the 'royal' or the 'sacred palace'. Lombard kings also gave churches immunities, but these were not named as such before the Franks conquered the region in 774. In 713, for instance, the Lombard king Liutprand (713–44) gave land to the monastery of S. Pietro in Ciel d'oro in the capital Pavia.[50] As well as forbidding archbishops and bishops to enter the monastery's lands, the S. Pietro grant stated that no judicial authority or secular officer (*nulla iudicaria potestas aut reipublicae minister*) was allowed to enter or take anything from the inhabitants. This no doubt meant that the monastery was able to keep the revenues that had once gone to the sacred palace, but this is not spelled out, and what the privilege was to be used for, other than for the general good of the monastery, is not specified. The differences between this and a Frankish immunity may lie in diplomatic form, but one suspects that such a monastery did not need cash to be earmarked for lighting.

In the early Middle Ages Italy had a stronger bureaucratic tradition than Francia, and as a result a wider range of people are visibly involved in transactions.[51] Italian charters reveal a variety of people, from rulers to lesser nobility or even peasants, giving gifts to a large range of churches, from major monasteries to the kind of small church needing basic support that was envisaged in the record of the Second Council of Braga.[52] It was seen in the last chapter that two inscriptions from Rome which record papal charters indicated that between 604 and 731 the provision of oil for lighting moved from cash purchases to production based on olives farmed on estates near Rome, although some exceptions to this pattern were noted.[53] The early eighth-century charters from a variety of locations in northern Italy strongly support this picture in that many of them show olive groves included in appurtenance clauses, that is as part of the facilities of lands given over the church. These gifts, and also sales, were often of small amounts of land and sometimes the number of olive trees was spelled out. In 718, for example, the monastery of Farfa in Lazio was sold a 'new olive grove' for 8 *solidi*, another grove that had 12 *olivas tallias* (pruned trees) for 12 *solidii*, plus another four trees for 4 *solidi*.[54] It may be significant here that a 'new' grove (*olivetum novellum*) featured, if this can be taken to indicate that local producers were stepping in to replace oil once imported from overseas, or perhaps that which had come from production centres elsewhere in Italy. That it was stated that some trees were pruned could refer to them being productive, unlike the new groves, for it takes up to ten years before olives can be harvested from newly planted trees and pruning is necessary to ensure steady levels of fruit production. According to this charter, each tree was valued at one *solidus*. This is a high value compared to stock, and to other kinds of tree. The comparatively high value of olive trees also features in Lombard legislation from the mid-seventh century: the *Edict of Rothari* (issued in 643) stated that, if anyone cut down an olive tree, they would have to pay 3 *solidi* in compensation, whereas the fine for cutting down any other kind of tree was only one *solidus*.[55] Olive trees were also more highly valued than other trees in Visigothic law.[56] This invites comparison between olive production in Spain and Italy, but, as already noted, there are no Visigothic charters that would allow the comparison to be taken further.

In the standard edition of charters from Lombard Italy (that is, from the Lombard kingdom before its destruction in the year 774) there are 293 documents.[57] These include gifts, sales, leases, exchanges and judgements, and, in most of these, olives, oil and lighting are of no concern. Nevertheless, no fewer than 51 of the charters, recording gifts to churches, do mention olives or oil or lighting, and sometimes all three together. Typical of simple appurtenance clauses that mention olives is the phrasing 'land, vines, meadows, cultivated and uncultivated, olive groves, woods, orchards'.[58] The amounts of land given could be small, such as 'half a *casa*'.[59] The term *casa* refers to a peasant holding, and it is sometimes coupled with the word *tributaria* which means that the inhabitants of the land owed some kind of rent or services. It can be specified that the tribute payers were part of the gift and that whatever they paid in dues was transferred to the recipient.[60] That such people were given along with the land indicates that they were not free landholders, and this is clear from the terminology occasionally used to describe them (the social terminology of the charters, it should be noted, does not generally match that seen in the Lombard laws). Rather than the *servi* or *aldii* of the laws, tribute payers who could be given along with land were, for instance, termed *coloni* or *Romani*, for some, at least, of those of 'Roman' descent had a subordinate status in Lombard territory. In a charter of 767 from Pistoia in Tuscany land was given to the church of Saint Peter and Saint Mary, but each of the *Romani* of one particular property were to pay tribute worth one *tremissis* in oil, wax or gold for the lighting (*luminaria*) of the church.[61] It is striking to see the juxtaposition of oil and wax here. When wax is mentioned this is usually in the context of tribute, which suggests production from the land that was given. That oil too could be produced on the local estate, rather than purchased with income from the land, is spelled out in just one charter: a document from Siena from the year 730 which is longer and more detailed than most.[62] The *gastaldius* (administrator of royal estates) of Siena made gifts for the foundation of a monastery and a church in Siena. These included an olive grove which was situated beneath the walls of the town and was located between another grove and the land of the sons of the late Auduale, plus a *petia* (small portion) of yet another grove. 'Of the oil now made on the estate', half was to go to the monastery and half to the church. The picture here is of a mosaic of small groves and parcels of land in the vicinity of the town and it confirms the impression of small-scale production for very local needs.[63] Where income dedicated to lighting was involved and no olive trees mentioned, one must assume that the source of oil was further away. Tributaries, as just noted, were a source of income. Another source was the annual rent paid in usufruct. This was when people gave land to the church but retained the use of the land for their lifetime, making a small annual payment which signified that they were now only the temporary holders of the land. That income, sometimes paid in wax, often went to pay for lighting.[64] This kind of arrangement was never very common in Italy, but as we shall see, it would become the bedrock of church–client relationships in Francia, where, unlike in Italy, the usufruct or beneficial tenancy was typically passed down the generations.[65]

Where the provision of lighting was designated as one, or the main, purpose of a gift it could be simply termed as being 'for the *luminaria*', that is, for lights for the church. This, for instance, was what the oil, wax or gold was to provide for the church of Saint Peter and Saint Mary in Pistoia, and the expression 'for the lights of Church X' is as it is in Frankish documents. It was on occasion spelled out that the lights should burn day and night.[66] We also see the provision of lights for particular saints' festivals, for instance in a charter for the church of Saint Martin's in Lucca where lights were provided for the festivals of the saints Peter, Martin and Quiricus.[67] But often the saints were not named, which could imply that the expression

*Consolidation of provision*

'lights for the saints of God' was a way of referring to the church as a whole rather than to particular shrines.[68] As indicated earlier, there are no narrative texts that might show lamps burning day and night before a shrine. Where perpetual light is more commonly seen in these charters is in the provision of commemorative lighting. Typical is the expression 'for lights and masses to be provided for myself and my parents' (or 'relatives').[69] In a fuller variant of this formula, *luminaria* are associated with the saving of the soul.[70] In the Farfa cartulary there is a series of seven charters issued from 745 to 750 in which the duke of Spoleto made such gifts for his salvation and for that of his ancestors, and, in one document, also for the Lombard king, Ratchis (744–9).[71] Such grants were not, however, restricted to the powerful.[72] Since they appear in a largely common form in the earliest charters from Lombard Italy it is likely that the practice of endowment for commemorative light was already established before the beginning of the eighth century when the run of surviving charters begins. In terms of record (but with the exception of the will of Bertramn of Le Mans) the practice is seen earlier in Italy than in Francia, where the earliest recorded grant of this nature (Bertramn's apart) comes from 783 when Charlemagne gave property on the River Moselle for an eternal light to be maintained before the tomb of his late wife Hildegard.[73] Whether the practice had existed earlier than this in Francia, as the will of Bertramn would suggest, or whether the Franks copied it from the Italians, perhaps after their conquest of the Lombard kingdom in 774, must remain an open question.

One thing the victorious Franks did take from northern Italy was the oil from the lakes region, as will be seen in more detail in the next chapter. As mentioned above, olive-growing in Italy moved northwards in the early Middle Ages.[74] In contrast to the very local production and use of oil that so many charters record, early documents from the lakes area refer to much larger (but still not very large) numbers of olive trees. In an exchange of 771, for instance, 159 trees near Lake Garda were acquired for the convent of the Lombard queen Anselperga.[75] In 756 the lady Walderata donated to the church of San Zeno in Campione (near Lake Lugano) a grove of six olive trees for lights for her deceased husband Arichis.[76] Walderata was part of a family who were patrons of San Zeno and seem to have risen socially along with increasing oil production on their lands.[77] In 777, not long after the Frankish conquest, and soon after Charlemagne had taken over Anselperga's convent and its olive trees, Toto of Campione founded a hospital (*xenodochium*) to be under the control of the basilica of Sant' Ambrogio (soon to become the monastery of Sant' Ambrogio) and the archbishop of Milan.[78] He gave to the hospital lands, un-free tenants (*massarii* and *aldiones*), and olive groves for his soul and for those of his relatives. The person in charge of the hospital, and the monastery of Saint Ambrogio, were each to receive out of this property 20 lb of oil a year for their *luminaria*. The church of Saint Zeno was to receive 200 lb of oil on the festival of the saint. And on this festival the head of the hospital, the poor for whom he cared and the priests who served there were all to eat at Saint Zeno's, and lights were to be kindled there, day and night. Four lamps were to burn through the night, and one through each day, but on Zeno's feast-day itself all the lamps were to be lit 'for the love of this saintly place and for our souls'. In addition, three other Milan churches were each to receive 10 lb of oil annually. Finally, Toto made all his male and female serfs into *aldiones*, that is, gave them a degree of freedom, but put them under the control of the hospital, to which each of them was to pay one *solidus* each year, and all his men who performed yearly works for him were now to be at the service of the hospital. Since the family's special saint was Zeno, this might suggest that the family were relative newcomers to Campione, for Zeno is the premier saint of Verona.[79] Their glory was reflected in the magnificence of his festival, and the family had the oil, and the wealth from oil, to put on a really impressive show which marked their rising status both in Campione itself where the festival was held and in Milan, where they were in effect deploying their resources around Campione to acquire influence.

Toto of Campione's charter is very unusual in specifying the amount of oil each institution was to receive, and what the details show is that the amounts were small – 270 lb of oil in total. This is a fraction of, say, the 10,000 lb that the monastery of Corbie was scheduled to pick up at the port of Fosses each year. The contrast lies in the difference between the royal privileges granted to a major Frankish monastery and the local arrangements of one Italian family of modest standing. The Corbie grant comes at the tail end of international oil imports, or possibly harks back to a time when those imports were the normal source of oil. Toto's grant, sixty years later, was made in the context of the local production of small amounts of oil. It may be that provisions for lighting, or at least the grants of olive groves, were frequently mentioned in early Italian charters because this was a period of transition to local production. There were, remember, references to 'new groves' at this time. After the turn of the eighth century olive groves tend to appear less frequently in appurtenance formulae. The formulae now included fruit and chestnut trees, and, for reasons that have never been explained, plantations of willow trees (*salicta*) become more prominent. The later charters were also much briefer when it came to stating the reasons for making a gift to a church, so that 'lighting clauses'

*Consolidation of provision*

become rarer. In the run of charters from Pistoia, for example, four charters from a total of 25 for the period 767–804 refer to olives, oil, wax or lighting. *Luminaria* do not feature again until the year 973, and this is in the ninety-first charter in the series.

## Conclusion

For the declining frequency of references to lighting in Italian charters a variety of explanations can be suggested, though not proved. Changes in diplomatic style meant that charters generally became shorter and more terse. There is less reflection on the spiritual motives for gifts, and so it is not surprising that we hear less about lighting. It is also very likely that we hear more about lighting when institutions were being founded and endowed, rather than when established institutions were simply being maintained. The phrase *concinnanda luminaria* found in some early charters conveys the meaning that 'lights should be arranged' for the church in question. Once these arrangements had been made, it may have been unnecessary to mention them again. As for the arrangements themselves, we have seen the donation of olive groves and giving of income from land and people, with groups of people, like the *Romani* in the Pistoia charter mentioned above, becoming hereditary payers of tribute to institutions. If these payments did indeed become hereditary, customary and largely uncontested, again they would not surface in documents. When they were contested, as we shall see in a later chapter in the context of oil production around Lake Como, they certainly did appear. Another factor in the relative decline in the frequency of references to lighting in charters is the rising number of leases as opposed to gifts. Leases, which started out as petitions to have usufruct of land given or sold, and which did occasionally specify that any rent should support the church, had by the tenth century become much shorter statements of agreements that contained no religious terms.[80] The numbers of charters referring to lighting may have declined as a proportion of all documents, but lighting concerns did continue to feature on a more occasional basis. Though after 800 we hear of it less, lighting provision, including provision for commemorative lighting, continued in Italy throughout the early medieval period. As shown in the last chapter, the idea that a church could not function properly without being able to maintain lights was well established by the eighth century. The early Italian charters reveal that all levels of society were involved in provision for lighting, and that people even of relatively modest status made provision for commemoration in this way. There is no reason why these practices should have declined, given that the same religious precepts and social and economic conditions remained in place. Understanding this continuity and widespread involvement is important, for otherwise it would be hard to comprehend how organisations dedicated to the provision of lighting mushroomed in Italy (and elsewhere) from the late tenth century onwards.

Whereas the evidence from Italy showed people of different social status making gifts for lighting, in Francia the early evidence was concerned with kings and with elite institutions. There was a particular seventh-century moment at which kings, and one queen, stepped in to guarantee that the most prestigious religious institutions (on whom those same rulers relied for support) could obtain supplies of oil. This was evident in privileges of immunity and toll exemption. These privileges ceased to contain a lighting clause when that moment had passed, that is to say, when there was no longer oil to be found in the Mediterranean ports or in Provence. Nevertheless, the terms of the immunity show that, as in Italy, a wide range of people could be involved in supplying the resources for lighting, whether or not this support was given voluntarily. It is also from this time (the mid- to later seventh century) that we have the first indications from accounting documents of how resources were gathered from peasants on church estates, so that it is at last possible to see something not only of how wealth could have been extracted from the countryside generally but also in particular of how demands to supply churches had an impact upon their tenants.[81] As in Italy, this is helpful in understanding how, later, groups and organisations dedicated to the provision of lighting could spring up in support of particular churches and saints, and to commemorate their own members. In contrast to Italy, however, commemorative lighting in Francia seems to have spread from the top down and (with the exception of Bertramn of Le Mans's arrangements) to have grown at a later date than in Italy. Again in contrast to Italy, in Francia charters which refer to lighting provision do not decline as a proportion of all charters in the ninth century. New churches and monasteries continued to be founded and endowed as the Franks under the Carolingians expanded into new areas such as northern Germany and also developed the ecclesiastical structures in areas long under their control: to reiterate, it was at the stage of endowment that lighting provision was likely to be mentioned. Secondly, at the beginning of the eighth century, Frankish churches began to lease out some of the lands they had accumulated in massive amounts over the previous two centuries. Unlike Italian leases, these Frankish usufruct arrangements (which would come to be known as *precaria*) did display religious terms, or connotations: the rent (*census*) paid for them was dedicated to churches, often being earmarked for lighting.[82] As *precaria* spread, lighting provision thus becomes more visible in the political economy. This phenomenon will be investigated in some detail in the next chapter, for it was through *census* payment that the provision of lighting can be seen to have had effects on the organisation of peasant society. I shall also look at how the Carolingian regimes in Francia managed support for the Church and reinforced (or possibly reinvigorated) scriptural precepts about the need to keep lights burning at all times before the tabernacle. But before turning to Carolingian developments, I want to register a familiar caveat about the dangers of overemphasing the importance of lighting. From the evidence reviewed thus far, the religious, social or economic importance of providing resources for lights cannot be quantified. Charters at this stage record a fairly restricted range of activities, all concerning the Church in one way or another. It is not possible to compare the resources dedicated to lighting with resource perception that lay outside the range recorded in charters. But it can at least be said that the provision of lighting was a distinctive element in a small proportion of charters. What the early charters show us is that the dedication of resources to lighting was firmly established on a wide scale in the seventh and early eighth centuries. That this had become a fixture, however small, of religious, social and economic life is what allows us to trace the provision and the providers over the centuries to come.

### Notes

1  An important question regarding the use of formularies as evidence is whether the models they set out reflect past or present social and legal practice, for there are no extant charters for many of the models, and the formularies themselves survive in manuscripts only from the eighth century onwards. Recent thinking is that they do reflect such practice, although this cannot be demonstrated where no charters survive, and copying models over centuries does seem to have led to a degree of anachronism. Where immunities are concerned, there are extant charters which in essentials do accord with the models. For a stalwart defence of the positive view of formularies as evidence for past practice, A. Rio, *Legal Practice and the Written Word in the Early Middle Ages. Frankish Formulae c. 500–1000* (Cambridge, 2009).

2  What follows builds on P. Fouracre, 'Eternal light and earthly needs: practical aspects of the development of Frankish immunities', in W. Davies and P. Fouracre (eds), *Property and Power in the Early Middle Ages* (Cambridge, 1995), pp. 53–81, repr. P. Fouracre, *Frankish History. Studies in the Construction of Power* (Farnham, 2013), no. XII. On immunities in the wider political-cultural frame,

B. Rosenwein, *Negotiating Space: Power, Restraint and Privileges of Immunity in Early Medieval Europe* (Manchester, 1999).
3   M. Weidmann, *Das Testament des Bischofs Bertramn von Le Mans von 27 März 616* (Mainz, 1986).
4   See above, Chapter 1.
5   *Formulary of Marculf* II, c. 17 (repeated in a model for manumission in Marculf II, c. 34), trans. A. Rio, *The Formularies of Angers and Marculf: Two Merovingian Legal Handbooks* (Liverpool, 2008), pp. 202, 216.
6   For the dating of the Marculf collection and its association with Saint Denis, Rio, *The Formularies of Angers and Marculf*, pp. 110–17. Rio translates and comments on the two formularies.
7   Marculf I, 3: Latin text, *Marculfi Formularum Libri Duo*, ed. A. Uddholm (Uppsala, 1962), pp. 34–6: ... *ut neque vos neque iuniores neque successores vestri nec nulla publica iudicaria potestas quoque tempore in villas ubicumque in regno nostro ipsius ecclesiae aut regia aut privatorum conlatas, aut qui inantea fuerint conlatas, ad audiendas altercationes ingredire aut freta de quaslibet causas exigere nec mansiones aut paratas vel fideiussores tollere non presumatis. Quicquid exinde aut de ingenuis aut de servientibus ceteris nacionibus, qui sunt infra agros vel finis – seo: super terras – predicte ecclesiae commanentes, fiscus aut de freta undecumque potuerat sperare, ex nostra indulgentia pro future salutae in luminaribus ipsius ecclesiae per manu agentum/eorum proficiat in perpetuum*, trans. Rio, pp. 134–6.
8   Fouracre, 'Eternal light', was the first paper to suggest otherwise.
9   The 'feudal crisis' model has been the subject of great debate between those who see a long-term development or process of evolution, and those who see a more sudden change resulting in the collapse of institutions. The debate was conducted in *Past and Present* beginning with a restatement of the 'crisis' model: T. Bisson, 'The Feudal Revolution', 142 (1994), 6–42, followed by discussion of the implications of this piece in 155 (1996) and 157 (1997). For a recent rethinking of the issues involved rebalancing changes and continuities from the Carolingian period, C. West, *Reframing the Feudal Revolution. Political and Social Transformation between Marne and Moselle c. 800 – c. 1100* (Cambridge, 2013).
10  For a clear account along these lines, M. Kroell, *L'immunité franque* (Paris, 1910). According to Kroell (at pp. 71–2), when the Merovingian kings granted immunities they had in effect 'introduced into the structure of the Frankish kingdom elements of decay which would act to bring about a slow but continuous weakening of the bonds which united the subjects to the public power'.
11  P. Fouracre, 'Cultural Conformity and Social Conservatism in Early Medieval Europe', *History Workshop Journal* 33 (1992), 152–61, repr. Fouracre, *Frankish History*, no. XIV.
12  A view often put forward, but strongly restated in M. de Jong, '"Ecclesia" and the early medieval polity', in S. Airlie, W. Pohl and H. Reimitz (eds), *Staat im frühen Mittelalter* (Vienna, 2006), pp. 113–32, and M. de Jong, 'The state of the Church: *ecclesia* and early-medieval state formation', in W. Pohl and V. Wieser

(eds), *Der frühmittelalterliche Staat. Europäische Perspectiven* (Vienna, 2009), pp. 242–54.

13  I. Wood, 'Creating a Temple Society in the Early Medieval West', 'Annual *Early Medieval Europe* Lecture', Leeds International Medieval Congress, 2019, *Early Medieval Europe* (forthcoming), and I. Wood, *The Transformation of the Roman West* (Leeds, 2018), pp. 110–11.

14  R. Kaiser makes this point in relation to bishops: R. Kaiser, 'Royauté et pouvoir épiscopale au Nord de la Gaule vii–ix siècles', in H. Atsma (ed.), *La Neustrie: les pays au nord de la Loire de 650 à 850*, Actes du colloque historique international (2 vols, Sigmaringen, 1989), I, pp. 143–60, at pp. 147–8.

15  Fouracre, 'Eternal light', pp. 63–4.

16  For discussion of the evidence for lay immunities, Fouracre, 'Eternal light', pp. 62–3.

17  *Vita Balthildis*, trans. with commentary P. Fouracre and R. Gerberding, *Late Merovingian France. History and Hagiography 640–720* (Manchester, 1996), pp. 95–132, ch. 6, p. 123.

18  For the switch from gold to silver coinage in the wider European context, P. Grierson and M. Blackburn, *Medieval European Coinage, I: The Early Middle Ages (5th to 10th Centuries)* (Cambridge, 1986).

19  The three positions can be represented by C. Wickham, *Framing the Early Middle Ages. Europe and the Mediterranean Economy, 400–800* (Oxford, 2005), pp. 107–15 (that Roman taxation did not survive in Merovingian Francia); J. Durliat, *Les finances publiques de Dioclétian aux Carolingiens* (Sigmaringen, 1990) and, with particular reference to immunities, E. Magnou-Nortier, 'Étude sur le privilège d'immunité du IVe au IXe siècle', *Revue Mabillon* 60 (1984), 465–512 (that Roman taxation survived more or less intact); W. Goffart, 'Old and New in Merovingian Taxation', *Past and Present* 96 (1982), 3–32 (that elements of Roman taxation did continue, but in the hands of landlords).

20  For example in a toll exemption for Saint Denis, issued between 679 and 690. The monastery was exempted from six kinds of dues and from any other payment (*qualibet redebicione*). What the monastery saved from this exemption was to go towards the lights. *MGH Diplomata Regum Francorum e stirpe Merovingicarum*, ed. T. Kölzer, *Die Urkunden der Merowinger* (Hanover, 2001), no. 123, pp. 313–14.

21  *MGH DM*, no. 123.

22  On this and other Merovingian toll exemptions, A. Stoclet, *Immunes ab omni teloneo. Étude de diplomatique, de philologie et d'histoire sur l'exemption de tonlieux au haut Moyen Age et spécialement sur la 'Praeceptio de navibus'* (Brussels and Rome, 1999), pp. 44–65. On Merovingian tolls more generally, F.-L. Ganshof, 'À propos du tonlieu sous les Mérovingiens', in *Studi in onore di Amintore di Fanfani* 1 (Milan, 1962), pp. 291–315. The 693 document is *MGH DM*, no. 138, pp. 348–50.

23  *Gesta Dagoberti I*, ed. B. Krusch, *MGH Scriptores Rerum Merovingicarum* II (Hanover, 1888), pp. 399–425, c. 18, pp. 406–7: *Nam et de proprio teloneo, quod ei*

*annis singulis ex Massilia solvebatur, centum solidos in luminaribus eiusdem ecclesiae* [i.e. Saint Denis] *eo tenore concessit, ut oleum exinde actores regi, secundum quod ordo cataboli esset, quasi ad opus regi studiose emergent et sic demum missis ispius loci annuatim traderent*.

24 *MGH DM*, no. 142, pp. 358–60, for the 694 grant, and *MGH DM*, no. 170, pp. 422–3, for the 716 confirmation. It is very unlikely that *solidi* (or thirds of a *solidus*, the *tremisses*) were being minted in northern Francia at this date, so that the *solidus* should be seen as a unit of account. Where that account was paid in cash, the coinage was the silver *denarii*.
25 On *tractoriae*, Stoclet, *Immunes ab omni teloneo*, pp. 55–63.
26 *MGH DM*, no. 171, pp. 424–6; Stoclet, *Immunes ab omni teloneo*, p. 58.
27 Marculf, Supplement 1, trans. Rio, pp. 230–1.
28 *Vita Ansberti*, ed. W. Levison, MGH SRM V (Hanover and Leipzig, 1910), pp. 618–43, see pp. 613–16, Levison's comments on the work's composition.
29 *Vita Ansberti*, c. 9, p. 625, *ut hoc praedium monachis in coenobio Fontanella* [Saint Wandrille] *morantibus luminaria ministraret ecclesiae in oleo et ceteris huius rei necessariis*.
30 *MHG DM*, no. 140, pp. 353–4.
31 W. Goffart, *The Le Mans Forgeries. A Chapter from the History of Church Property in the Ninth Century* (Cambridge, Mass., 1966), p. 16.
32 *Vita Balthildis*, c. 9, trans. Fouracre and Gerberding, pp. 125–6.
33 *MGH DM*, nos 99, p. 254 (issued some time 662–75), and 128, pp. 326–7 (issued in 685).
34 *MGH DM*, no. 96, p. 248.
35 The authoritative account of the growth of monasticism in seventh-century Francia is F. Prinz, *Frühes Mönchtum im Frankenreich* (Munich, 1965), though there has been much revision of Prinz's views of a monastic growth driven by Irish missionaries. See, for instance, I. Wood, 'A prelude to Columbanus: the monastic achievement in the Burgundian territories', in H. Clarke and M. Brennan (eds), *Columbanus and Merovingian Monasticism*, British Archaeological Reports, International series 113 (Oxford, 1981), pp. 3–32.
36 *MGH DM*, no. 143, pp. 361–2.
37 *MGH DM*, no. 137, pp. 347–8, discussion of the case in P. Fouracre, '"Placita" and the settlement of disputes in later Merovingian Francia', in W. Davies and P. Fouracre (eds), *The Settlement of Disputes in Early Medieval Europe* (Cambridge, 1986), pp. 23–43, at pp. 27–35, repr. Fouracre, *Frankish History*, no. X.
38 P. Geary, 'Die Provenz zur Zeit Karl Martells', in J. Jarnut, U. Nonn and M. Richter (eds), *Karl Martell in seiner Zeit*, Beihefte der *Francia* 37 (Sigmaringen, 1994), pp. 381–92; P. Fouracre, *The Age of Charles Martel* (Harlow, 2000), pp. 93–9.
39 P. Fouracre, *The Age of Charles Martel*, pp. 89–99.
40 The Will of Abbo is translated, with full discussion, by P. Geary, *Aristocracy in Provence: The Rhône Basin at the Dawn of the Carolingian Age* (Stuttgart, 1985), here p. 77.

*Consolidation of provision*

41 *MGH Diplomata Karolinorum* I, ed. E. Mühlbacher (Hanover, 1906), no. 122, pp. 170–2, for the 779 confirmation. The Stavelot-Malmedy toll privilege was regarded as genuine by its first modern editors: J. Halkin and C. Roland, *Recueil des chartes de l'abbaye de Stavelot-Malmédy* (Brussels, 1909), no. 4, pp. 12–14. If so this would make it the earliest surviving toll privilege in Francia, but Kölzer, the charter's most recent editor (*MGH DM*, no. 86, pp. 213–15) regarded it as *unecht* (not genuine) as it contains material that is clearly ninth-century, and, one might add, the fact that it does not envisage the monks travelling to the south is another indication that it is not from the mid-seventh century.

42 *Vita Filiberti*, ed. W. Levison, *MGH SRM* V (Hanover, 1910), pp. 583–612.

43 *Vita Filiberti*, c. 37, p. 602.

44 *Vita Filiberti*, c. 38, p. 602. This story, and the history of whaling in these waters, are discussed by L. Musset, 'Quelques notes sur les baleiniers Normands du Xe au XIIIe siècle', *Revue d'Histoire Economique et Social* 42 (1964), 147–61.

45 See above, Introduction.

46 *Visio Baronti*, ed. W. Levison, *MGH SRM* V, pp. 377–94.

47 *Visio Baronti*, c. 11, pp. 385–6. Betolenus was charged by Saint Peter with the *cura in toto mundo de luminaribus ecclesiarum*.

48 See above, Chapter 1, pp. 28–9.

49 Wickham, *Framing*, pp. 11–20; M. Costambeys, 'Settlement, Taxation and the Condition of the Peasantry in Post-Roman Central Italy', *Journal of Agrarian Change* 9 (2009), 92–119.

50 *Il Museo Diplomatico dell'Archivio di Stato di Milano*, ed. with facsimile A. Natale (Milan, c. 1970), no. 3 (no page numbers).

51 N. Everett, *Literacy in Lombard Italy c. 568–774* (Cambridge, 2003); C. Wickham, 'Lawyers' time: history and memory in tenth- and eleventh-century Italy', in H. Mayr-Harting and R. Moore (eds), *Studies in Medieval History Presented to R. H. C. Davis* (London, 1985), pp. 53–71.

52 See above, Chapter 1, p. 34. The range of people giving is clear, for instance in the cartulary of the monastery of Farfa in Lazio: *Il Regesto di Farfa compilato da Gregorio di Catino* 2, ed. I Giorgi and U. Balzani (Rome, 1879), no. 12 from a king, nos 9–16 from a duke, no. 39 from a peasant (*colonus*).

53 See above, Chapter 1, pp. 29–30.

54 *Farfa*, no. 3, p. 25. The smallest number of trees was three, in *Farfa* no. 7, pp. 27–8, from the year 740. The smaller numbers of trees were usually a factor of 12 (3, 4, 6, 8 or 12). Whether this numbering represented simple counting and was coincidental, or had religious significance, is unclear.

55 *Edictus Rothari*, ed. G. Pertz, *MGH Legum* III (Hanover, 1868), 300–3, p. 302, trans. K. Fischer-Drew, *The Lombard Law* (Philadelphia, 1973), pp. 111–12.

56 *Leges Visigothorum*, ed. K. Zeumer, *MGH Legum* I, I (Hanover and Leipzig, 1902), VIII.3, p. 321: compensation for an apple tree was 3 *solidi*, for an olive tree 5 *solidi* and for others 2 *solidi*.

57 *Codice Diplomatico Langobardo*, vols I and II, ed. L. Schiaparelli, *Fonti per la Storia d'Italia* 62 (Rome, 1929 and 1933). This collection is not exhaustive, nor does it include charters from elsewhere in Italy, but it is very useful for giving an impression of the overall picture. Here, where the charters have been consulted in other editions they will be cited accordingly.
58 *Terra, vinea, pratis, cultum et incultum, olivitis, silvis, vergariis*, for example in *Codice Diplomatico*, no. 42, pp. 144–5, from the year 728.
59 As in *Codice Diplomatico*, no. 42.
60 For example a gift to the church of Saint Maria in Lucca in 722 was of *duas casas tributarias cum familia eorum, vinea, olivitio, silva, peculiare prato*: *Codice Diplomatico*, no. 30, pp. 109–12, or *Farfa*, no. 7, pp. 27–8, two *coloni* were given to Farfa along with the land they held.
61 *Regesta Chartarum Pistorensium* (no editor given), *Fonti Storiche Pistoeisi* 2 (Pistoia, 1973), no. 11, pp. 12–13.
62 *Codice Diplomatico*, no. 50, pp. 165–71.
63 *Farfa*, no. 75, p. 79, from the year 770 provides another example of a grove beneath a town wall, that of Rieti in the duchy of Spoleto.
64 For examples, *Codice Diplomatico*, no. 94, pp. 272–4, the yearly rent for usufruct was 1 lb of wax; no. 171, pp. 129–31, an original charter from Pisa from 763 the terms of the usufruct are: *ut per uno quemquem anno dare diveas in ecclesia ipsa luminaria sol[i]do uno pro usufructum de ipsas ris*.
65 In Italy, leases were generally for fixed periods of time, in units of 30 years.
66 *Codice Diplomatico*, no. 173, pp. 134–5, a Lucca charter of 763 in which someone paid 200 *solidi* to become the priest of the church of Saint Genesius, promising to 'keep the law of the church' (despite the obvious simony here) and to 'kindle the lights, day and night, for all time'.
67 *Codice Diplomatico*, no. 35, pp. 125–6, from the year 724.
68 For examples, *Codice Diplomatico*, nos 67, pp. 209–11, 120, pp. 360–2 (note that this is a rare grant from a woman) and (vol. II) 145, pp. 53–4.
69 For example *Codice Diplomatico*, no. 190, pp. 176–8: the grant was *pro messa et luminaria mee vel parentorum meorum faciendum*.
70 For example *Codice Diplomatico*, no. 188, pp. 172–3: the gift was *pro anime mee remedio vel pro luminaribus meis*.
71 *Farfa*, nos 9–16. The formula here is *pro mercede et luminare animae nostrae*. It is not certain that the 'light of the soul' is not metaphorical, but in the opinion of Latinist colleagues, though grammatically awkward, it should be taken literally as a 'light for'. I am grateful to Tim Parkin and David Langslow for advice on this reading.
72 *Farfa*, no. 47, p. 53, provides an example of a small gift *pro luminare et remedio animae meae*.
73 *MGH Dip. Karol.* I, no. 149.
74 See above, p. 28.
75 A. Brugnoli, 'Del Mediterraneo all'Europa: l'olivocultura di frontier nell'alto

medioevo', *Settimane di Spoleto* 54 (2007), 107–54, on the Campione charters, and also on the area around Lake Garda, 133–5. The 771 exchange is in *Codice Diplomatico* II, no. 257, pp. 346–7.

76 *Codice Diplomatico*, no. 123, pp. 365–6.
77 G. Varani and A. Brugnoli, 'Olivi e olio nel patrimonio della famiglia di Totone di Campione', in S. Gasparri and C. La Rocca (eds), *Carte di famiglia. Strategie, rappresentazione e memoria del gruppo familiar di Totone di Campione (721–877)* (Rome, 2005), pp. 141–56.
78 This exceptionally interesting charter survives as an original in the archive of Milan: *Il Museo Diplomatico*, no. 25.
79 I am grateful to Ross Balzaretti for pointing this out to me (pers. comm.).
80 See for instance G. Zucchetti's discussion in *Liber largitorius vel notarius Parphanensis* I, ed. G. Zucchetti (Rome, 1913).
81 The accounting documents relate to the monastery of Saint Martin, Tours. For how they may have related to estate management, S. Sato, 'The Merovingian Accounting Documents of Tours', *Early Medieval Europe* 9 (2000), 143–61.
82 On the growth of *precaria*, I. Wood, 'Teutsind, Witlaic and the history of Merovingian *precaria*', in W. Davies and P. Fouracre (eds), *Property and Power in the Early Middle Ages* (Cambridge, 1995), pp. 31–52. See also Fouracre, *Charles Martel*, pp. 139–44.

# 3

# Light and power: the 'Carolingian moment'

Constantine, the first Christian emperor, had been astonishingly generous to the churches of Rome. As was seen in Chapter 1, this was recorded and celebrated in the *Liber Pontificalis* (the 'Book of the Popes').[1] It was noted there how the passages detailing Constantine's giving would go on to influence the text of the notorious 'Donation of Constantine', a later eighth-century forgery which purported to show how Constantine had not only massively enriched the Church, but also acknowledged the Pope, Sylvester, as the superior power in the world: Constantine ceded to Sylvester (i.e. to the Papacy) primacy over the Western half of the Roman Empire, no less. Though the narrative of how this happened is not drawn from the *Liber Pontificalis*, the details of Constantine's gifts clearly were. The motive for forging the 'Donation' seems to have been to persuade the Carolingian rulers of Francia of the Pope's supremacy in Italy at a time when those rulers were expanding their power south of the Alps. It was a moment at which they were, or were supposed to be, highly receptive to papal guidance. The 'Donation' gives Constantine a voice and what he says is that, having built the churches of Saint Peter and Saint Paul in Rome, he had given estates in East and West and on various islands to Pope Sylvester and his successors 'in order for lights to be provided' in the new churches.[2] That the forger should have given provision for lights as the reason for the handing over of the estates shows how the Frankish rulers had by the later eighth century firmly associated themselves with the burning of perpetual lights. It was their duty to ensure that churches had lights burning at all times, and making over resources to make this possible was something with which they could not disagree. This was one hook in the 'Donation'. Another, of course, was the unstated comparison with a great (and the first) Christian emperor. In this chapter I shall look at the Carolingian move into Italy and at how Italian oil began to provide for Frankish lights. I shall examine how the association between rulers and lights was built up, and look at examples of kings making grants for lighting to see how and why they did this. We will then turn to the legislation the Carolingian rulers put in place first to normalise the payment of rents to churches and second to maintain their buildings and equipment. This can be followed through to see how the cost of lights was spread throughout the Christian community, for it is now, from the mid-eighth century onwards, that there is finally some indication of how the injunction to burn lights at all times before the tabernacle was met at a general, rather than just elite, level. A combination of territorial expansion by the Franks, the incorporation of ecclesiastical needs into the political economy and the spreading of support for the Church into the wider population is what makes up the 'Carolingian moment'.[3]

In the last chapter it was shown how the Merovingian rulers of Francia helped their leading ecclesiastical institutions to acquire oil by granting them privileges of immunity which enabled them to raise cash to buy oil. Toll exemptions were also granted in order to facilitate travel to the Mediterranean ports where that oil might be purchased. The context for this, we saw, was the diminishing availability, and presumably the rising cost, of olive oil. Oil imports through Marseilles appear to have more or less ceased by the mid-eighth century, and it was noted that the production of oil in Provence came to an end with civil war and invasion. Spain, as was made clear in the last chapter, never seems to have produced oil for the Frankish market.[4] It did produce oil in great quantities in the Seville region, at least according to the tenth-century geographer Ahmad al-Rāzi. In his survey of Muslim Spain al-Rāzi said that so much top-grade oil was produced around Seville that it had to be exported by boat 'to the East', otherwise the price would have been too low for local sale.[5] It is striking that export to the Christian north does not seem to have been an option, something that reminds us that goods did not circulate in the early Middle Ages according to what we would identify as market forces. It also raises the question of whether the border zone between Muslim and Christian Spain was rather less permeable than recent studies have suggested.[6] What the oil was used for in 'the East' we cannot tell, although it is certain that eternal light played no part in Islam. Given that no oil came north from Spain, that left Italy as a possible source. Although the Italian evidence generally showed very local production of small amounts of oil, it was also seen that there was development of slightly larger-scale production in the Italian lakes area, especially around Lakes Garda and Como. A possible warming in the climate may be one explanation for a northward shift in the cultivation of olives, but another might be growing demand for oil from both the Lombard and the Frankish rulers. In 773 Charlemagne (ruled 768–814) invaded Italy, and in the late spring of 774 captured Desiderius and Ansa, king and queen of the Lombards. He took over as king there. For his decision to invade Italy numerous reasons have been given both by contemporaries and by modern historians: momentous events typically attract multiple explanations.[7]

Charlemagne is said to have felt obliged to protect the Papacy from the Lombards; he wished, according to evidence from the *Liber Pontificalis*, to protect his throne from two nephews who were being sheltered by Desiderius;[8] he wanted, it is reasoned, to step into the space created by the retreat of Byzantine influence in Italy, or, in a variant of this view, it was the Papacy that was set on using the Carolingians to free itself from Byzantium and to build up its own power.[9] Underlying all these possibilities is the certainty that Charlemagne simply wished to acquire more land and more resources to strengthen his position. It has also been emphasised that for him the invasion of Italy was a very big step and that he must have viewed the prospect of success with some trepidation.[10] From his actions shortly after the capture of Desiderius and Ansa, it is easily demonstrable that he did seize the opportunity to enrich himself in Italy. In June 774 Charlemagne made an extensive gift of land to Bobbio, an Italian monastery with strong Frankish connections. Bobbio's founder, Saint Columbanus, had inspired a wave of monastic foundations in mid- to late seventh-century Francia, and it was in the wake of this activity that the kings (and one queen, Balthild) had strengthened their ties with the leading monasteries by granting them immunities.[11] With this grant to Bobbio came a privilege of immunity. Documents of immunity continued to include the phrase that whatever was raised from the rights granted should go towards the lights of the church in question. Later this would be sometimes be replaced by a statement that the institution would remain under royal protection.[12] The Bobbio privilege, however, retains the lighting clause, and it can be seen from later documents that Bobbio indeed used its powers to collect and acquire oil. Before continuing with the transfer of Italian resources to Frankish monasteries, let us briefly look at what Bobbio was able to collect, for this gives us a rare, if rough, indication of the amounts of oil that might be obtained from northern Italy, and from the Garda region in particular. It should be noted, however, that Bobbio, situated as it was in the Trebbia valley in Piacenza, could, unlike the Frankish monasteries, collect its oil more or less locally. Olives could be grown in Liguria and in some of the valleys leading away from the coast, but Garda was the main source of its oil.[13]

The documents in question here are two ninth-century inventories drawn up for Bobbio in which the monastery made a list of properties that it held and stipulated what each of them owed. Other monasteries would do this but they were in Francia and oil cannot be seen to have been involved, although we shall examine these Frankish surveys in a later chapter because they have something to say about people who owed dues that were dedicated to lighting. Wala, who was Charlemagne's cousin, ended his life as abbot of Bobbio, a post he held from 834 to 836. He drew up the first of Bobbio's lists. A second survey of 862 added detail.[14] The dues included grain, chestnuts, wine and iron as well as oil. Out of 86 properties listed, seven owed amounts of oil. Garda, however, was designated by Wala solely to provide oil (*Garda deputavit ad oleum*). Apart from Garda, the amounts of oil owed, expressed in pounds, were meagre, being with one exception well under 100 lb.[15] One individual might owe as little as 5 lb. All told, Bobbio could expect to collect 2,885 lb of oil. The bulk of this, 2,430 lb, came 'in a good year' from just one place, next to Lake Garda. It can immediately be remarked that these amounts were in total small, a point which can be made even clearer if the pounds (that is, Roman pounds) are converted into litres.[16] One *libra* of oil equals 0.354 litres. Thus the person who owed 5 lb had to produce just 1.77 l of oil. Bobbio might collect in total 1,020 l per annum. It should also be noted that the amounts of other products were also small, 1,074 *amphorae* of wine, for instance. The 862 survey concludes with the phrase 'this is what the brothers were seen to have for their own use'. Bobbio, it seems clear, was not collecting a surplus either in oil or anything else that could be traded.[17] Oil, in other words, was not obviously being produced for the market. Hence the need to grant oil-producing properties to northern monasteries if they were to be provided with this kind of fuel for lighting purposes.

In July, a month after the gift to Bobbio, Charlemagne made over to the monastery of Saint Martin's at Tours lands stretching into the Alps, but also land around Lake Garda. Saint Martin was a patron saint of the Frankish kings and his support in military ventures was especially valued. We have already encountered Saint Martin's in the works of Gregory of Tours which furnished early evidence of the use of lights at the saint's shrine, and we have seen that Saint Martin's was a privileged institution which had in both the sixth and seventh centuries acquired oil from Marseilles. Janet Nelson has recently brought out the poignancy of the charter which recorded the 774 grant to Saint Martin's.[18] Using a Lombard style of charter-writing, Charlemagne showed how he and his wife Hildegard had replaced Desiderius and Ansa, who were at this point in captivity in Italy but facing what would be a lifetime of imprisonment in Francia. What had been theirs now belonged to Charlemagne and Hildegard, and this included the island of Sirmione in Lake Garda where Ansa had recently built a monastery.[19] The grant was ostensibly to enable Saint Martin's to acquire ecclesiastical vestments, but the island also had olive groves. New vestments and plentiful light were surely meant to demonstrate Charlemagne's triumph and his piety before his saintly patron. The next year (775) when Charlemagne was back in Francia, there would be a flurry of gifts, privileges and confirmations of privileges made over to the major Frankish monasteries: 27 in all for the years 774–5,[20] compared with just three for the year 776. Although Charlemagne presented himself as the most Christian of rulers, he was not in material terms actually very generous towards the Church.[21] It looks, therefore, as if in these years he was saying an enormous 'thank you' for his victory in Italy. Providing for the lights was a visible expression of gratitude. In the spring of 775, Saint Denis, another of the institutions which had received from the Merovingian kings a privilege of immunity, a toll exemption and cash grant enabling it to buy oil for lights, was granted extensive lands stretching towards the Alpine passes. This grant is revealed in what was actually a confirmation of the earlier immunity. Again, it was for the lights.[22] At the same time, Saint Denis had its earlier toll exemption confirmed, but now it was given exemption throughout Italy as well as Francia.[23] The grants secured passage to Italy for these powerful houses, and in this sense they fulfil the same purpose as those earlier privileges of immunity and toll exemptions which facilitated access to Marseilles. In 833 the Emperor Lothar, who ruled in Italy and the central part of Francia, donated to Saint Denis a property in Veltlin near Lake Como to set up a market at a place called Haenoheim. 'Veltlin' is the Valtellina, the valley of the River Adda which flows into the lake. At Haenoheim 12 free men under royal protection were designated to work for the monastery there.[24] Then In 843 Lothar confirmed Saint Denis's immunity, and also its possessions stretching out from Lake Como which were probably part of Charlemagne's original grant of 775.[25] That oil was involved is indicated both by the fact that this was land alongside the lake in an area that would later be the subject of a long-running dispute about the cultivation of olives, and by the assignment of the grant to lighting. This dispute will be examined in detail in the next chapter. By 840, however, Saint Denis had lost control of Veltlin, for in January 848 Lothar issued another charter restoring the property which was said to have been lost in the conflict between Lothar and his father Louis 'the Pious' who died in 840.[26]

Another powerful and influential monastery, but one founded too late to have received a Merovingian privilege, was Fulda in Hesse in Germany. Here the connection between grants in northern Italy and provision for the lights is made explicit. According to a fragment of a letter written by Hrabanus Maurus, one-time abbot of Fulda, Charlemagne's son and heir Louis promised Fulda an *olivetum* (olive plantation) in Italy.[27] This he had done when he saw that Fulda was reduced to burning pork tallow in its lamps. The *olivetum* was indeed given to Fulda by Louis and his wife Irmingard. This must have happened before Irmingard died in October 818. Then some time before 851 the monks wrote to Louis's son Lothar and his wife, also named Irmingard, to the palace arch-chancellor and to others 'about this matter'. It seems very likely that Fulda had lost control of the plantation and that the monks were trying to get it back because these Fulda letters, which are excerpted in fragments, are nearly all concerned with properties the monastery had lost, and with other injustices it had suffered. Again, the scarcity of oil is apparent here, and we have confirmation that a northern monastery was prepared to go to great lengths to acquire it. At such a distance this needed to be done with the support of the rulers. From the mid-ninth century onwards the Carolingian Empire was divided into separate kingdoms and these long-distance links were broken. The grants presented thus far were all made in the time of rulers who exercised power on both sides of the Alps. After Lothar died in 856 his kingdom was split into three. Apart from brief periods thereafter, Italy would be a separate kingdom and no more is heard of the northern monasteries being granted resources there. Nevertheless some oil did continue to get to Francia. In the mid-ninth century the cathedral of Le Mans burned 30 oil lamps and five candles each Sunday, and 90 lamps and ten candles were lit on feast days.[28] How the oil for the lamps got to Le Mans we cannot tell, nor even be sure that it came from Italy. As will be made clear in the next chapter, however, when in the later tenth century the Ottonian rulers of Germany in their turn brought northern Italy under a degree of control, the Lakes region and olives begin to appear in the sources again. This would be the context in which the dispute over the cultivation of olives by Lake Como, which was briefly mentioned above, would unfold.

Lothar's son, Lothar II, would continue to make grants to Saint Denis, and one of these was to be made solely in order to provide lights for the monastery. This, and the grants of other kings 'for the lights' would now be concerned with regions beyond Italy, that is, with places in what are modern France and Germany. The kings would generally donate farmed properties and it would be the income from these which would go to the lights. Sometimes it was stipulated that the people dwelling on the land should do the providing. An example of this, but one which shows that the links between providing for the lights and the projection of power continued as before, is the grant to Saint Denis from Lothar II, just mentioned. It was made in January 860. The charter says that Lothar had been asked by one of his followers (Werimundus) and the *archicustos* of Saint Denis (Deodatus) to give something towards its lights.[29] Accordingly he made over a single *mansus* (farmstead) taken from royal land in the area of Valenciennes. Along with the *mansus* came the *fiscalinus* (a kind of privileged royal serf) who held the *mansus*. He was called Valentinian and his wife and children were included in the gift. The farmstead, along with Valentinian and family (now termed *mancipia*, a standard word for serfs) would remain in Saint Denis's possession for ever 'for the lights'.[30] That means that Valentinian's descendants would have been tied to Saint Denis in this way. Whether they paid some kind of rent in money or kind to the monastery, or whether they collected wax, it is not possible to tell. I shall return to this issue of who paid what later in this chapter, but the point to be made here is that, although this seems to have been a rather small grant, it surely had a larger political significance. No grant from a king to Saint Denis could be insignificant, but the timing and placing of this one gave it special political meaning. It was made at the palace of Valenciennes which lay on the border between Lothar's kingdom (Lotharingia) and that of West Francia, which was ruled by Lothar's uncle, Charles the Bald. Saint Denis was at the heart of Charles's kingdom and it was a monastery with which Charles was particularly closely associated. Two years after Lothar's grant, Charles too would make grants to Saint Denis, to pay both for the lights and for meals to celebrate the various anniversaries of himself and his wife, with provision for an eternal light at the altar after his death.[31] The abbot of Saint Denis was Louis, son of Charlemagne's daughter Rotrude and thus, as Charlemagne's grandson, kin both to Charles (another grandson) and Lothar (great-grandson). It has been suggested that this charter was the result of a meeting between Charles and Lothar who were in 860 in the process of forming an alliance.[32] Lothar may have been invoking family ties in the 860 grant. A pressing reason for doing that was that in January 860 he was seeking (for a second time) to separate from his wife Theutberga in order to return to Waldrada, whom he had never formally married, but with whom he had a son, Hugh, as well as two daughters. The match with Waldrada may well have been one of love since he later referred to her as 'his most beloved'.[33] Abbot Louis, the son of an informal union himself (Charlemagne famously would not countenance the marriage of any of his daughters), might well have been sympathetic towards Waldrada and Hugh. Providing for the lights would have been a good cause around which all sides could rally, that is, a gesture of goodwill with which negotiations might open. The small size of the grant suggests that it had symbolic rather than material value. Providing for the lights of Saint Denis, moreover, was a statement of royalty.

In May 863 Lothar II made another grant for lights to be provided, the second of the four such grants he is recorded as having made.[34] This time the donation was very much larger: the *cella* (monastic dependency) of Saint Maxim's in the county of Maurienne, along with 35 *mansi* and the people on the farmsteads. These were granted to the convent of Saint Pierre (les Nonnais) in Lyons. It was made for lights to be provided there and also for the support of the nuns.[35] Again, the politics of family were involved, framed by the good deed of providing for a monastic community. In January 863 Lothar's younger brother Charles had died and Lothar divided Charles's kingdom of Provence with his elder brother Louis, ruler of Italy and also emperor. Lothar took the northern half of the kingdom and this included Lyons. Charles had been buried in the convent of Saint Pierre in the town. By endowing it Lothar was both honouring his family and asserting his power in the region. It was also a way of stating that Waldrada and Hugh were part of the family. The grant was made for the salvation of his parents, his brothers Charles and Louis, and for 'the salvation of my most beloved wife Waldrada and my son Hugh'.[36] It is in fact this charter that has persuaded some historians that Lothar's rejection of Theutberga and his move back to Waldrada was occasioned above all by his love for her.[37] At about this time Lothar sent envoys to Rome to ask for the pope's sanction for his divorce from Theutberga. So in May 863 it was an opportune moment to present himself as pious, and to inscribe Waldrada as his *coniunx* in association with that piety. This was also to say that Hugh was his legitimate son. As it turned out, Pope Nicholas I rather unexpectedly refused to agree to the divorce and Lothar was eventually forced to take Theutberga back. Nicholas was, in Janet Nelson's words, 'a man determined to extract the maximum authority from his official position', and in refusing to sanction the divorce he gained great influence with Lothar's uncles Charles the Bald and Louis the German.[38] They stood to gain if Lothar did not have a legitimate heir, and when Lothar died in 869 they divided his kingdom, Lotharingia, between them. Hugh could then do nothing but rebel against his uncles, without success.

There was a lot going on here. Might it be argued that providing for the lights of Saint Denis and for Saint Pierre's in Lyons was actually the least of Lothar's concerns? Was he just using a familiar form of grant as a vehicle for something else? And the same questions could be asked of Charlemagne's inclusion of lighting provision in his grants of Italian resources to Frankish monasteries. After all, as the evidence from Bobbio makes clear, the amount of material involved may have been meagre, and not only was the proportion of royal charters which mentioned lighting relatively small (not more than 8 per cent) but also these charters often confirmed earlier grants and privileges. They might, in other words, merely be repeating phrases that had become more or less formulaic and had little to do with actual provision for lights. On the other hand, the authors of the 'Donation of Constantine' thought that the provision of lighting was important enough to persuade the rulers of their duty to the Papacy. When Charlemagne made grants after his victory in Italy he was being thoughtful and deliberate in demonstrating his piety and giving due reward for prayers and support. One can go further in showing what providing lights meant to Charlemagne. On 30 April 783 his wife Hildegard died. She was only 25 years old but had borne him no fewer than six surviving children, three boys, all of whom would become kings, and three daughters.[39] The next day Charlemagne granted a *villa* (an estate) by the River Moselle to the church of Saint Arnulf's in Metz.[40] This was a church with which the Carolingian family had special ties, and at precisely this time it was claiming Saint Arnulf as an ancestor. The grant was to enable lights to be burned 'continuously day and night' before Hildegard's tomb, and the conditions of the grant were strongly worded: the abbots of Saint Arnulf's were forbidden ever to grant out the land as a 'benefice', that is, as a favour to a client or supporter, or to lease it out in *precaria* (a low-rent lease which was another kind of favour, a phenomenon to which I shall return later in this chapter).[41] Whatever was left over after paying for the lights was to go for masses and prayers to be said, and psalms to be sung, daily for Hildegard. There can be no doubt here: Charlemagne really did mean that lights should be burned 'incessantly' (*incessabiliter*) for his 'beloved wife'. At the same time this was also an overtly political act, for not only did the gift for the lights strengthen the putative ancestral connection with the saintly Arnulf but it also matched Charlemagne's most famous Merovingian predecessor, King Dagobert I, who had allegedly given 500 *solidi* a year to Saint Arnulf's for its lights.[42] This is in fact the first reference in Francia to commemorative lighting that we have since the one made way back in 615 in the Will of Bertramn of Le Mans, which was discussed in the last chapter. It seems unlikely that Charlemagne knew of this will, but he may have known of documents from the monastery of Farfa in Italy that recorded several grants for commemorative lighting that were made in the Lombard period, for he himself made grants to Farfa.[43] Perhaps this style of commemoration was something else that Charlemagne brought back from Italy. Whatever the case, it would now become increasingly common in Francia.

When Louis the Pious saw that the monks of Fulda had been reduced to burning tallow in their lamps, his response was anything but formulaic, and, when Lothar I restored the oil-producing lands round Lake Como to Saint Denis, he seems to have been genuinely concerned that the monks had lost these resources. Lothar II, as we have just seen, made grants for lighting at moments of great political and personal significance. The balance of the evidence therefore indicates that these rulers were not repeating empty phrases when they dedicated resources to lighting but that they were doing something they regarded as important in terms of religious duty and in securing the support of powerful allies. The historian Geoffrey Koziol has recently emphasised the performative element involved in the issuing of royal diplomas, seeing the charter as an artefact. It was, in his view, a prop in the public enactment of authority and legitimacy in which the ruler was associated with his predecessors. Koziol includes Lothar II's grant of 863 amongst his examples, noting that kings typically made such grants to prestigious religious institutions upon their accession to the throne or when they took over new territories.[44] Another example Koziol gives is a grant the Emperor Charles 'the Fat' made to the monastery of Saint Benigne de Dijon as he progressed northwards from Italy in 885.[45] Confirmations of earlier privileges were especially useful here as the present king listed his predecessors who had made and confirmed the grant, thus presenting himself as the latest in a long line of rulers. This was a statement of legitimacy. The diplomas were, Koziol argues, 'part of a political programme'. 'Both the language of the diploma', he continues, 'and the circumstances of its issuance were strongly, proactively and specifically crafted in order to further such programmes'.[46] On the other hand, however, he also thinks that the legal contents of these documents are more or less irrelevant, believing them often to be 'a verbatim transcription' of earlier charters, or, one might say, mindless copying.[47] On the basis of the argument just aired, namely that when kings made grants for lighting they were serious about providing it, I would beg to differ here. Koziol is following an older scholarly tradition which emphasised the formulaic nature of the royal diploma, a tradition most strongly emphasised in relation to grants of immunities, but one which as I argued in the last chapter has been challenged.[48] In concentrating on form and on the occasions when the documents were issued, it is arguable that he has not looked at their contents carefully enough. In discussing Lothar II's grant of 863, for instance, he correctly associates this with Lothar's move into northern Provence, but does not comment on the reference to Waldrada and Hugh, and he does not note that the grant was made for lighting. In fact Koziol scarcely mentions lighting: there are no entries for lights in the index of what is an impressive and otherwise comprehensive work. In the case of Charles the Fat's diploma of 885, which restored 12 *mansi* to Saint Benigne de Dijon, he does not comment on the fact that revenues from these farmsteads were meant to pay for the lights of the monastery. Far from being merely formulaic, the dedication of revenues to the lighting of prestigious institutions honoured by previous kings was another statement of royalty. This is seen most clearly in the charters issued by King Charles 'the Simple' (ruled 898–923), a Carolingian in competition with a non-Carolingian, and in particular need of identification with earlier kings of Francia, both Merovingian and Carolingian. Twenty out of the 122 charters that survive from his reign provided for the lights of the institution concerned, beginning at his accession in 898 with, unsurprisingly, a confirmation of Saint Denis's immunity.[49] At over 16 per cent this is by far the highest proportion of charters that dedicated resources to lights that were issued by any Carolingian king. The 'Carolingian moment' may have been fading at this point, but the kings presented themselves as just as pious and dutiful as their most illustrious ancestors. Nevertheless, after Charles, the number of all kinds of royal charters falls off sharply. For his son Louis IV ('d'Outremer') who ruled for 18 years (936–54), only 53 charters survive, and only one of these, the confirmation of an immunity couched in traditional terms, has a reference to lights.[50] In mid-tenth-century West Francia royal power was ebbing away, a phenomenon often understood by historians in starkly pejorative terms: something had 'gone wrong' with the Carolingian project. Yet one could argue that in at least one sense things had actually gone according to plan in that the Carolingians had long urged their counts, bishops and abbots to take on more of the responsibility for building a society worthy of salvation, and they had empowered them to do so. It was the power in these magnates' hands that now restricted the kings. Let us now turn to the legislation through which the Carolingian rulers sought to make their subjects accept their duty and to ensure that society was 'correctly' ordered, for this included maintaining the fabric of churches as well as making sure that each of them had lights burning in them. It is this impulse from the centre, or perhaps better from 'the establishment', that would help transform provision for the lights from the special to the ordinary, with important social consequences that we will go on to examine.

*Light and power*

In the first chapter of this book, I presented the evidence from the three sixth-century church councils from Visigothic Spain: two councils held in Braga (in present-day Portugal) and one in Toledo.[51] They were important for showing that provision and maintenance of lights were then regarded as essential for every church. Having lights, and the means to maintain them, was one of the minimum requirements for a church. According to the Second Council of Braga, churches should not be consecrated until bishops had written proof that they had the wherewithal to satisfy these requirements. The inference was that this concerned churches of lowly status, that is 'parochial churches', although parishes as we know them were not then in existence. It comes as something of a surprise to note that after the late sixth century there is very little reference to maintaining such churches either in church councils or in secular legislation. It is not until the mid-eighth century that they begin to appear again, now in Frankish sources.[52] One tiny, and rather curious, exception might be a later seventh-century Visigothic law which castigated those who quarrelled (presumably over the control of a church) and uncovered the altar and took away the lights.[53] Doing this would make the church defunct.[54] If we can assume that the numbers of such modest churches were growing throughout Western Europe in the sixth, seventh and early eighth centuries, and we have seen from Merovingian and Lombard charters that provision for the lights in churches was certainly a steady concern, and that to provide for the lights was seen as a good deed, then this silence is hard to explain.[55] What was carried on from the early councils through to the Carolingian period was the idea that the altar was central to the church, and there were careful instructions on how the altar should be consecrated.[56] The inspiration here was scriptural: Jacob's dream.[57] After waking from his dream (of a ladder that ascended to heaven) Jacob anointed with oil the stone on which he had rested his head, and declared that this was now the dwelling place of God. This is a good example of the Hebraic influence on the Church, and it was that influence, remember, that not only made the stone altar the centre of the church building but also placed an eternal light on that altar.

It can be remarked that both secular and ecclesiastical legislation tended to be focused on relations of power, that is, on who had authority over what. It dealt with faith, order and behaviour and was less concerned with the practicalities of maintaining buildings or running estates. As a recent study has demonstrated, neither secular nor ecclesiastical legislation had much to say on burial practices, something one might have thought would be essential in societies that stressed conformity in religious practice.[58] There are, in other words, silences in other areas one might expect to have been regarded as important. With regard to Francia, it is also the case that there is a hiatus in recorded secular legislation between the early seventh and the mid-eighth centuries, and, as Saint Boniface indignantly pointed out, there are no records of any church council being held there between 675 and 740. Both secular and ecclesiastical legislation in Spain ceased in 711 when the Visigothic kingdom fell to Arab invaders. So reasons for this legislative silence on the maintenance of churches can be adduced, but any explanations must ultimately remain speculative. As we shall see shortly, it is clear that in the mid-ninth century the canons of the Council of Braga of 572 were known, and were quoted in relation to the minimum requirements for a church. What cannot be shown is that they were in use in the intervening period.

The picture begins to change in Francia in the mid-eighth century when a series of councils was held with the aim of reforming the Church. The Council of Estinnes (in present-day Belgium), held in March 743, addressed the alienation of church property. It was argued that it was necessary for the rulers to make use of church property to defend the Christian community at a time of crisis ('because of the wars which threaten, and on account of the hostility of the rest of the peoples who surround us').[59] The land involved would be used to support soldiers. This is a key passage in what has been a long-running debate about the advent of 'feudalism', an arrangement in which, supposedly, land was systematically given out in return for military service, a form of reward for service which an earlier generation of modern historians often saw as the bedrock of Carolingian power.[60] That debate, which turns around the question of whether there ever was such a 'system',[61] cannot be entered into here, but what is of interest in the present study is the way in which Estinnes normalised a practice that had been developing over the previous half century. This was the letting out of land on easy terms, the so-called precarial grants (*precaria*) alluded to earlier in this chapter. The term *precaria* comes from the verb *precari*, 'to ask for'.[62] The grants were known as *beneficia* ('benefices'), a word that carries the meaning of 'favour', for letting out lands on such terms was a favour.[63] The request for *precaria/beneficia* came in three forms: someone might request a particular church to grant them some of its land in this way; someone might give land to a church and then ask to have continued use of that land ('usufruct') until they died; or rulers might request a church to lease out the land to one of their followers for the good of the community. In all three cases the lease, or grant, was understood to be in principle temporary and the church retained ultimate ownership of the property in question. Ecclesiastical ownership was signified in two ways: first, the lease had to be carefully recorded, and second, the tenant had to pay a nominal rent, known as *census*, to the church. The reform element in the Estinnes legislation lay in the insistence that these two conditions be observed, for this was meant to ensure that the land was not permanently alienated. A further condition, not always stipulated, but another one which signified that the land was church property, and thus to be used for the good of the Christian community (as should in theory be the case with all church property), was the convention that the rent should support liturgical activity. In many cases it was spelled out that the *census*, or at least part of the *census*, should go towards providing for the lights of the church. An example would be the Count Ratharius who in the year 734 was granted a massive *precarium* by his friend Teutsind, the wayward abbot of the abbey of Saint Wandrille. This was put forward in the history of the abbey as an example of how Saint Wandrille lost control of its lands, for Teutsind was regarded as a 'tyrant' and Ratharius as a usurper. Ratharius's *census* amounted to 60 *solidi* per annum to be paid *in luminaribus aecclisiae*. This sum, it was implied, was scant return on the 28 estates that had fallen into his hands.[64]

As Ian Wood has observed, Saint Wandrille actually let out great swathes of land in this way. Its complaint was about people rather than process. In the course of castigating Witlaic, another abbot who allegedly wasted resources, the history revealed that in 787 the abbey owned 3,964 *mansi*, of which 2,395 were let out as benefices (*in beneficiis relaxati*).[65] The point is that the great monasteries had acquired huge reserves of land over a relatively short period of time: Saint Wandrille, for instance, was less than a hundred years old when Teutsind took over. Much of this land, which presumably they could not control directly, was now flowing out as *precaria*. Churches also drew on precarial arrangements to facilitate the exchange of lands. One example will serve to illustrate how this was done. In 808 one Erbio gave lands to the monastery of Wissembourg in Alsace with which he seems to have been closely associated.[66] The grant included various farmsteads (here termed '*hoba*') and 10 *mancipia* (serfs). In return, Wissembourg gave Erbio and his two sons an equivalent amount of land and ten *mancipia* elsewhere, presumably both parties getting land in more convenient locations. What Wissembourg gave Erbio had been a *beneficium* of one of its clients, now, one assumes, deceased. So the land had at least once before been let out by the monastery. Now Erbio and his sons were to enjoy the usufruct of the land, on condition that they paid the *census* on it, and this amounted to 2 *solidi* per annum *ad luminaria sancti Petri in Uuizenburg*. The example shows us how institutions like Wissembourg were determined to have acknowledgement through the payment of the *census* that the land was ultimately theirs, at the same time as they were reorganising their holdings and entering into sometimes complex relations with clients. The effect was to reinforce *census* payment as a hallmark of land held from the church and in the process to strengthen the notion that their clients should contribute towards the provision of lighting. The tendency for *precaria/beneficia* to change hands would, as will be seen shortly, lead to legislation which aimed to ensure that the *census* did not get lost along the way.[67]

In the mid-ninth century, when the history of Saint Wandrille was being put together, churches began to try and regain control of much of this land, for by this time it had been in the hands of the 'tenants' for generations. The process of holding it had in the meantime done much to establish a landed clientele that might be termed a lesser nobility, and it did a great deal to create a *census*-paying peasantry, for it was the people on the *mansi* who ultimately paid the dues to the church. This was made clear at the Council of Estinnes at which it was stated that each *casata* ('homestead', a term that was equivalent in this context to *mansus*) was to pay one *solidus* as *census* on benefices held in *precaria*. This was a very high sum, to the extent that one wonders if there is some kind of error here. In 779 in the Capitulary of Herstal, Charlemagne's first major piece of reforming legislation, the sum appears as a fiftieth of the Estinnes render, i.e. one *solidus* per 50 homesteads. In addition, those who paid *census* should also pay 'ninths and tenths', a form of tithe which all Christians were supposed to pay.[68] The tithe was of scriptural origin and in early church councils (such as Braga) it was said that it should be divided into four parts: one each for the bishop, for the priest, for the poor and for the fabric of the church, and the latter part was often said to have included the maintenance of the lights. But it is also clear that the payment of tithe was at best fitful in this period.[69] The same legislation goes on to confirm 'long-standing arrangements' (unspecified) for ecclesiastical tributaries who pay their dues in wax.[70] Later, as we shall see, wax payers and *census* payers would be brought together in a single term: *cerocensuales*, 'payers of wax-census'. The use of such a term strengthens the impression that the payment of *census* and the provision of lights were closely associated. It was the more important ecclesiastical institutions, like Saint Wandrille, or, later, the church of Reims, that had most land and most precarial clients, and it was presumably important political players like these who were being reassured at Estinnes. Less visible, and much less vocal, are the innumerable churches and smaller monasteries which received gifts of land and then let it out again in usufruct to the donors. So common did this practice become that it has been described as an inheritance strategy adopted by the lesser nobility. In a society in which the custom was to divide inherited land amongst family members, it was likely, the argument goes, that subdivision over generations would leave individuals progressively poorer as the shares got smaller. As they became poorer, fewer would be able to afford the obligations required from those of noble status, and families would in effect drop out of the nobility. A solution for the individual was to give land to a church or monastery, and then to receive it back in usufruct as a precarial tenure. That tenure might then be passed on to a single individual and the disadvantages of subdivision might be by-passed. Noble status could thus be safeguarded, and, though other family members might miss out on a shared inheritance, they would gain by association with a noble relative. This way of doing things also brought spiritual benefits and an alliance with an ecclesiastical institution. Although one should be wary of labelling practices 'strategies' when contemporaries did not talk of aims and consequences (which they did not), there are indeed very many charters in which land was given and received back in this way. The argument was first put forward in relation to the evidence of Bavarian charters of the later eighth and ninth centuries, and one can see why the practice might have been particularly prevalent in Bavaria.[71] Bavaria was annexed by the Franks in 789, which no doubt encouraged indigenous nobles to intensify an existing practice in order to protect their lands from incomers by acquiring a degree of ecclesiastical protection and, importantly, getting the written evidence of rightful possession that was part of any precarial arrangement. It has also been shown that some Bavarians sold land in order to meet their public obligations, especially military obligations.[72] The Frankish conquest clearly put these people under great pressure. Ironically, however, conquest conditions in Bavaria saw Frankish-backed bishops asserting control over the churches and monasteries in the diocese: there are a series of court cases in which local families tried, and failed, to stop them doing this.[73] So in effect the bishops swept up control of these *precaria*. Alemannia may present a similar case, for in this region native landholding was similarly destabilised after the Franks had crushed the Alemmanic nobility at the battle of Canstatt in 746.[74] If we can generalise this to other parts of Germany in which bishops were instruments of territorial control, it could be one explanation for why *census* payers (*censuales* and *cerocensuales*) are so prevalent in Germany, and why there they are so often found under the control of bishops, much more so than in the West. The proliferation of the precariat in the East was a consequence of empire. This is an issue with great ramifications and I shall return to it in the next chapter. Everywhere in the Frankish lands north of the Alps, however, the development of precarial tenure of all kinds led to

*Eternal light and earthly concerns*

the spread of *census* payers. In this way large sections of the peasantry were bound into supporting churches, both large and small, and this happened somewhat before the regular payment of tithes became established.

Carolingian legislation, generally referred to as 'capitularies', addressed the upkeep of churches and the maintenance of lights on and off over roughly 140 years, that is, from the time of Charlemagne's father Pippin (ruled 751–68) to the death of his great-grandson Charles 'the Fat' who died in 888, and after whom there would be no more legislation. The maintenance of churches was a steady concern, but not a major one compared with, say, the performance of military service, the behaviour of officials or matters of faith or morality. Charlemagne's first piece of legislation, issued in 769, ordered parochial priests to obtain chrism from the bishops when they made a visitation.[75] Chrism, which was olive oil infused with balsam, was used in rituals of baptism and confirmation and had to be consecrated yearly by a bishop. Out-of-date chrism was not supposed to be used in baptism, and priests were instructed to burn it in the lamps. One imagines that tiny amounts of oil were involved here, so that burning it was not so much providing light as disposing of a substance that became religiously toxic once it had been superseded by a newly consecrated batch. It nevertheless shows us that oil for chrism was still available to bishops, even if it were to be measured in ampules rather than amphorae. The use of chrism was universal. As for the balsam, no study has ever explained where this came from, although in Scripture it was meant to come from Jericho in Palestine. The Capitulary of Frankfurt from 794 was the first to address the state of church buildings, complaining that some people robbed them of building materials which were used in their own houses. Then in legislation of 802 tithes were associated with the repair of church buildings. Some time between 801 and 810 in a capitulary issued by Charlemagne's son Pippin in Italy, bishops who received tithes 'from everyone' were told to make sure that the parochial churches under their care should be repaired and that they should be provided with lights. The bishops should also make sure that it was possible for priests to live in them.[76] Three more of Charlemagne's capitularies, issued between 802 and 813, insisted that to maintain churches meant, amongst other things, ensuring that the lights were in good order. As in the later sixth-century Visigothic legislation, it was the bishops who were to make sure each church had lights, and a roof.[77]

Two pieces of legislation issued by Louis 'the Pious' continued to put pressure on the bishops, and through them on the priests, to ensure that local churches were properly run and that their lights were maintained in good order. First, between 823 and 825, in a general complaint about the

*Light and power*

poor state of affairs, it was implied that where *mansi* had been donated to the church with the express purpose of providing for repairs and for the lights, some bishops and archdeacons had been drawing on the income for their own use. The resource was to be strictly reserved for the purpose for which it had been donated.[78] The inclusion of the archdeacons may suggest that income had been siphoned off from local churches for the use of the cathedral. Second, in 829 it was said that churches had been scandalously neglected, the first complaint being that priests had failed to repair them and had not taken care of the lights.[79] In wide-ranging legislation of 845–6, now in the reign of Charles the Bald, there was fresh complaint about the misuse of tithes. Lay people who had chapels and had given them a priest should use the tithes to repair the roofs and to provide 'decent' lights. Where they had given the tithe income over to 'others', these people should not use the tithe to feed dogs or to provide for women weavers (*canes aut geniciarias pascant*).[80] The priests should get the tithe and use it to repair their churches, maintain the lights and look after the poor. Quite apart from seeming to put women and dogs in the same category (the category of 'unclean'?), the complaint suggests that tithes were being appropriated for use on lordly estates, for that is where female weavers were to be found, and dogs are closely associated with the nobles' love of hunting. Finally, legislation of 853 suggests that instability had made things worse: after recent neglect and disturbance, churches were to be surveyed and the loss of lights and ornaments to be recorded.[81]

Church councils in this period shared the same concerns over the maintenance of local churches, as one would expect given the ecclesiastical focus of so much secular legislation, something which is characteristic of the 'Carolingian moment'. On the chrism, we learn from the Council of Chalons (813) that some priests were having to pay 2 or 4 *denarii* to buy the balsam from the bishops and also to pay for the lights. This should not happen: the bishops should provide the balsam and pay for the lights out of the income from church property.[82] Also in 813 it was stated at the Council of Tours that tithes were to be used to pay for the lights and for the support of the priests (*ordinati sunt ad luminaria et stipendia clericorum*).[83] At the Council of Rome in 826 it was declared that a church was defunct if it had neither liturgical vessels nor lights.[84] It was at the Council of Aachen of 836, or rather in a letter that the Council sent to Pippin, king of Aquitaine (814–38) and son of Louis 'the Pious', that we see the strongest statement to date about the duty of the priest to maintain a perpetual light in the church. In a passage that this work has already drawn attention to,[85] the council drew on the story of Nadab and and Abiu in Leviticus 10:1–2, 6 and

Numbers 3:4. These two, the sons of Aaron, progenitor of the priesthood, were charged with keeping a fire (*ignis perpetuus*) burning on the altar day and night. Through negligence they let the fire go out and then kindled it afresh. For this they were punished as God sent down a fire that burned them up.[86] The passage in the letter is so striking that it is worth quoting in full.

> The fire shall always burn on the altar and the priest shall tend it, laying on wood in the early morning each day and the burnt offerings placed upon it will be fragrant with the fat of peace offerings. That fire which shall never be lacking from the altar is perpetual. Those who should look after the perpetual fire, that is, the lights provided by the offerings of the faithful in the consecrated churches of the Lord, should give great weight to the words of the law and fear them greatly should they dare to take it [i.e. the fire] away. For that fire which was ordered to burn perpetually on the altar was extinguished due to the negligence of the sons of Aaron, Nadab and Abiu. And since on account of this they dared to offer a strange fire to the Lord [i.e. they relit it], fire came forth from the Lord and they were consumed by it, deservedly so. Because we cannot proceed without a great purity of the soul, those who rashly put out the fire of the Lord in the churches dedicated and consecrated to Him are to be devoured by a horrible death. And when we look at how it is put out, it is clear that when they take away that which should nurture the fire of the Lord, then they put it out. What is true is that the churches dedicated and consecrated to God should be sacred places and should also be the dwelling places of God. And they should be feared and venerated by all those who exist within the Christian religion.[87]

This is an admonition and should be read metaphorically rather than literally. It is Pippin who is failing to nurture the Church, and Pippin who will be horribly punished if he does not mend his ways and learn to venerate and fear the sanctuaries. According to the *Annals of Saint Bertin*, a key contemporary source for the political narrative of these times, the letter was sent to Pippin because his supporters had been taking church property. In the letter, said the *Annals*, the bishops 'warned him at some length about his own salvation'.[88] Our passage is part of that warning. Failure to nurture the perpetual fire of the altar will result in Pippin facing a very different kind of fire, the fire of damnation. It is nevertheless highly significant that the bishops chose this particular metaphor and translated the eternal fire of Leviticus into the lights (*luminaria*) on the altar. It is another indication that keeping a light burning at all times was regarded as essential. It was something that everyone would understand as important, and that is why letting the light go out could be used as a metaphor for failure to support the Christian religion itself. It was the same religious potency that we saw harnessed for political traction in the 'Donation of Constantine' and in some of the royal charters that have been discussed in this chapter.

The Council of Soissons, held in 853, returned to the issue of *beneficia* and the *census*: *missi* (agents of the church or of the king) were to look at church property that been given out as *beneficia* in order to see what *census* was being paid. They were to make sure that the church from which each *beneficium* had originated was being properly supported by the *census*, and this would be determined by how many priests and how many lights it had. If there was a shortfall in support, it had to be made up.[89] Finally, to bring us full circle, as it were, the Council of Worms of 868 repeated the injunction of the 572 Council of Braga that a church could not be consecrated unless there was written confirmation of its endowment, 'for it is seriously rash should it be without lights or without the resources to sustain those who serve there'.[90] From this raft of legislation it is clear that there was sustained pressure from above to ensure that churches were properly supported, and that this meant driving the burden of support deeper into the whole population. Carolingian society was relatively well organised to this end, or at least there was a coherence to its legislative efforts. On the ground, however, it was one thing to insist that people paid tithe and *census* to maintain local churches, but another to prevent these payments being appropriated for other purposes, to feed dogs and women weavers, as Charles the Bald's legislation put it. Quite what happened in other parts of Europe is not clear because there is not the quality nor the quantity of legislative complaint that would allow this to be seen. But everywhere, it is reasonable to assume, anybody with a degree of coercive power would have found it very tempting to siphon off at least something of what was effectively a tax on the peasantry: lords, in all periods of history, thought they were perennially short of money.[91] On the other hand, there was a degree of moral restraint, even if this came only from the threat of damnation, as the letter to Pippin of Aquitaine suggests. That lights should be provided for churches was an injunction that was now understood as a moral concern.

One last set of legislative texts from Carolingian Francia shows how individual bishops responded to the call from the court to 'correct' religious life by striving to improve the priesthood. This, as one historian, Carinne van Rhijn, has recently put it, would 'lead towards divine approval, salvation and the eternal rule of its [i.e. the Carolingian] kings'.[92] These documents are known as 'Episcopal Statutes' or *Capitula Episcoporum*. They are generally lengthy texts and there are 34 of them, issued between c. 800 and c. 970 with recent editions in the *Monumenta Germaniae Historica*.[93] Just under half of them (16) make some reference to the maintenance of lights.[94] They reinforce the notion that the priest should be responsible for the lights and that the lights should burn throughout the night. They confirm the demand that a quarter of the tithe should be spent on the roof, and go towards the lights. They also add fresh detail, such as dedication of burial fees to the lights,[95] and they reveal too that oil might still be burned as well as wax, although it is not possible to say where such oil might have come from.[96]

But these are minor points. What the statutes do rather more than the secular and conciliar legislation is to emphasise the special nature of the church as a building. It is the only place pure enough for the performance of the liturgy and nothing else should take place within it. It should contain only liturgical vessels (*ornamenta*, which included the lamps), vestments and books, but above all what distinguished a church from a house was the altar which had to be protected from defilement at all times.[97] An anonymous text from the ninth century (c. 840) known as 'The significance of the twelve candles' (*Quid significant duodecim candela*) gives instruction on how a church was to be consecrated.[98] 'It shows', according to van Rhijn, 'step by step how in its ritual of dedication a church is transformed from a building into something more'.[99] That 'more' was the way in which churches dedicated and consecrated to God became, in the words of the letter to Pippin, 'sacred places' and 'the dwelling places of God'.[100] The ritual itself has been compared with that of baptism.[101] Twelve candles were to be lit outside the building, the alphabet was to be written twice from corner to corner inside. The altar was to be wiped with oil and a cross drawn in oil from corner to corner. It would then be anointed with chrism, relics were to be placed within it, and a cloth placed upon it. Finally the *ornamenta* were put inside the building and then, as we might say, it was 'switched on' by the lighting of many lights (*accendunt luminaria multa*).[102] This ritual of consecration helps us to understand why the maintenance of the lights was of such concern in legislation, for a church could not properly be a church without them. It also gives us another angle on the repeated demands that church buildings, and especially their roofs, be kept in good repair. At stake was not just the weather-proofing of the building but also its very integrity as a sacred place. It had been spiritually sealed at the time of consecration and the ritual had encapsulated the host within it. Holes would puncture its integrity and let out the holy. If people imagined the holy spirit as heaven-bound, a hole in the roof would be particularly dangerous.

Because they were concerned with the ministry of the priesthood, the 'Episcopal Statutes' addressed the facilities available to the laity. It was the laity who stood to benefit from the encapsulation of the holy in the church building. If the laity were to pay tithes and the *census* they had to have proper access to the holy in return. As well as the top-down effort to 'correct' there may also be an element of demand from below here, something which must have added to the moral restraint against the appropriation of church income for other purposes. In one of his 'Statutes' Hincmar, who was archbishop of Reims from 845 to 882 and the leading churchman of the later Carolingian world, spoke of voluntary associations which supported churches. These 'guilds' or 'confraternities' might gather together for religious purposes such as to make offerings, for the lights, for mutual prayer, for ceremonies for the dead, for almsgiving and for other religious duties.[103] If this reflects demand, rather than wishful thinking on Hincmar's part, then it can be said that some element at least of the population had become engaged with the requirements of their religion over and beyond the payment of tithe and rent. This is another issue that will be followed through in the next chapter.

## Conclusion

In this chapter I began at the top with Charlemagne's move into Italy and his appropriation of Italian resources which were channelled towards the leading Frankish monasteries. Providing the wherewithal for these institutions to maintain perpetual light was seen as a good deed that might earn not only their political support but also prayers for the well-being of the king, his family and all the Christian community. To undertake that care was a projection of power, and it was shown how successive rulers made grants for lights as an expression of royalty at politically significant moments. At the same time they made efforts to improve or correct religious life across the whole community, again with well-being and success in mind. Such initiatives, which were carried forward in secular legislation, through church councils and in episcopal statutes, were not entirely new. Notably, there was some reiteration of injunctions first expressed in sixth-century councils. What was new was the consistency of effort and the conjunction of that effort with the spread of precarial landholding and a greater insistence on the payment of tithes. The result was to bind a larger section of the population into supporting the Church, or rather, supporting local churches. It was clear from legislative complaint that the dues paid by the peasantry were liable to be appropriated by the lords, and in the next chapter I will pursue this issue against the background of changing social and economic conditions. I shall also, as promised above when discussing

Hincmar's 'guilds', follow through on the subject of the initiatives that came from below. These, along with the growth of the class of *censuales* and other tributaries, are the key to understanding how providing for the lights had an impact on social organisation. Moving into the tenth century, I shall bring practices in Spain, Italy and England back into the picture, and this will require an explanation of regional differences, especially between practices in Germany and elsewhere.

Finally, the present chapter has thrown up what has become a perennial question in this study: was providing for the lights really that important? I have argued that the evidence is clear that it was important to rulers, that the duty to provide was taken up by the wider establishment and that there was some response from below which shows that the sacredness of the church as a temple was valued, and that the eternal light was an important part of that sacredness. But if the evidence is clear, why has not more been made of it in previous studies? The answer could be that it has simply been missed, and this is because historians have tended to look for other things in their sources, such as narrative, prosopographical or organisational information.[104] In Carolingian culture there was no sustained theology of light (though Hincmar did use a light or fire metaphor for the truth behind doctrine),[105] nor argument about the merits of burning lights. Concerns about behaviour loomed far larger than issues of lighting. Paradoxically, the low-level ubiquity of references to lights has made them all but invisible. What this chapter has shown is that, when those references are investigated, it turns out that the maintenance of lights was actually a subject of importance to the Carolingians, and so it should be important to the modern historian too.

## Notes

1 Above, p. 25.
2 'Donation of Constantine' (*Constitutum Constantini*), ed. H. Fuhrmann (Hanover, 1968), ch. 13: *Construximums itaque et ecclesias beatorum Petri et Pauli ... quibus pro concinnatione luminariorum possessionum praedia contulimus ... tam in oriente quam in occidente ... vel in diversis insulis*. See J. Nelson, *King and Emperor. A New Life of Charlemagne* (London, 2019), pp. 354–6.
3 The term 'the Carolingian moment' was coined by Pierre Toubert, in P. Toubert, 'The Carolingian moment (eighth century)' in A. Burguière (ed.), *L'histoire de la famille*, trans. S. Hanbury-Tenison, *The History of the Family* (Cambridge, 1996), pp. 379–406. The term in the broader sense used here is borrowed from Janet Nelson, to whom I am grateful for discussion of the issues raised in this chapter.

4 There are references to traders moving between Francia and Spain in the ninth century, but, with the exception of slaves, it is not clear what was being traded. See M. McCormick, *Origins of the European Economy. Communications and Commerce AD 300–900* (Cambridge, 2001), pp. 674–8. There are no extant toll exemptions for travel to Spain.
5 E. Lévi-Provençal, 'La "Description de l'Espagne" d'Ahmad al-Rāzi: essai de reconstitution de l'original arabe et traduction française', *Al-Aandalus* 18 (1953), 51–108, c. 58, pp. 93–4. I thank R. Portass for drawing my attention to this passage.
6 E. Manzano Moreno, *La frontera de al-Andalus en la época de los Omeyas* (Madrid, 1991), sets out the view of permeability.
7 For a compelling evocation of how things looked from Charlemagne's point of view in 773, J. Nelson, *King and Emperor*, pp. 123–4.
8 *Liber Pontificalis*, 'Life of Hadrian', trans. R. Davis, *Lives of the Eighth-Century Popes (Liber Pontificalis)* (Liverpool, 1992), pp. 107–72, c. 23, p. 133.
9 T. F. X. Noble, *The Republic of Saint Peter. The Birth of the Papal State, 680–825* (Philadelphia, 1984).
10 Nelson, *King and Emperor*, ch. 5.
11 See Chapter 2 above.
12 P. Fouracre, 'Eternal light and earthly needs: practical aspects of the development of Frankish immunities', in W. Davies and P. Fouracre (eds), *Property and Power in the Early Middle Ages* (Cambridge, 1995), p. 73.
13 R. Balzaretti, *Dark Age Liguria. Regional Identity and Local Power c. 400–1020* (London, 2013), pp. 13–34, for the ecology of the region.
14 *Codice Diplomatico del Monasterio di S. Columbano di Bobbio*, vol. 1, ed. C. Cipolla (Rome, 1918).
15 The directly controlled *olivetum* of Adra (*olivetum dominicum in Adra*) owed 150 lb.
16 Assuming a specific density of olive oil at 0.93 g, and given that the Roman pound was 328.9 g one *libra* was equivalent to 0.354 l.
17 In the light of the figures from Bobbio, P. Devroey's argument that the monasteries' ability to stimulate production by the better organisation of estates led to a recovery of the rural economy looks a trifle optimistic: P. Devroey, 'Réflexions sur l'économie des premiers temps carolingiens (768–877)', *Francia* 13 (1986), 475–88.
18 J. Nelson, 'The settings of the gift in the reign of Charlemagne', in W. Davies and P. Fouracre (eds), *The Languages of Gift in the Early Middle Ages* (Cambridge, 2010), pp. 116–48, at 120–5.
19 *MGH Diplomata Karolinorum* I, ed. E. Mühlbacher (Hanover, 1906), no. 81, pp. 115–17.
20 With one exception, *MGH Dip Karol* I, nos 82–110, drawn up between June 774 and December 775, all grants to monasteries and to one episcopal church. On the figures for the first half of the reign, J. Nelson, *King and Emperor*, p. 151.

21 Nelson, 'The settings of the gift', pp. 118–19.
22 *MGH Dip Karol* I, no. 94, pp. 135–6.
23 *MGH Dipl Karol* I, no. 93, p. 134.
24 *MGH Diplomata Karolinorum* III, ed. T. Schieffer (Berlin, 1966), no. 13, pp. 78–80.
25 *MGH Dipl Karol* III, no. 80, pp. 200–1.
26 *MGH Dip Karol* III, no. 100, pp. 238–40.
27 *Appendix ad Hrabanum, Epistolarum Fuldensium Fragmenta* c. 2, *MHG Epistolae* V, *Epistolae Karolini Aevi* 3, ed. E. Dümmler (Berlin, 1899), pp. 517–18. On this grant see M. Czock, *Gottes Haus. Untersuchungen zur Kirche als Heiligem Raum von der Spätantike bis ins Frühmittelalter* (Göttingen, 2012), p. 181.
28 Fouracre, 'Eternal light', p. 72.
29 'aliquantulum ex rebus nostrae proprietatis ad luminaria ipsius procuranda'. The request is slightly unusual because, strictly speaking, monasteries were not supposed to solicit gifts. I thank Rachel Stone for pointing this out to me.
30 *MGH Dip Karol* III, no. 13, pp. 402–4.
31 *Recueil des chartes de Charles II Le Chauve*, ed. G. Tessier, *Chartes et diplômes relatifs à l'histoire de France*, 3 vols (Paris 1941, 1952, 1955), vol. 1, no. 55, p. 55.
32 Schieffer, *MGH Dip Karol* III, p. 402.
33 The traditional view is that Theutberga was barren and that Lothar wanted to secure Hugh as his legitimate heir, but, as both Janet Nelson and Stuart Airlie have noted, Theutberga and Lothar had only been together for two years when he first rejected her, not long enough for her to be regarded as barren: J. Nelson, *Charles the Bald* (Harlow, 1992), pp. 198–9; S. Airlie, 'Private Bodies and the Body Politic in the Divorce Case of Lothar II', *Past and Present* 161 (1998), 3–38, at 11–12. Reprinted S. Airlie, *Power and Its Problems in Carolingian Europe* (Farnham, 2012), no. X. These works are invaluable guides to the so-called 'Lotharingian divorce'.
34 *MHG Dip Karol* III, no. 19, pp. 414–15. Out of the 50 charters published in the *MGH* edition for the reign of Lothar II, four were concerned with lighting, that is 8 per cent, a figure that compares with the 7 per cent issued over the three centuries covered in the Farfa cartulary. See Introduction, pp. 6–7.
35 *ad luminaria ibidi et concinnanda seu stipendia famulorum.*
36 For the *salvationem amantissimae coniugis nostra Waldradae et filii nostri Ugonis*. G. Koziol, *Politics of Memory and Identity in Carolingian Royal Diplomas. The West Frankish Kingdom (840–987)* (Turnhout, 2012), pp. 105–6, briefly discusses this charter as one in series in which rulers demonstrated their authority on taking over a region, but he does not mention Waldrada, Hugh or the lights.
37 Nelson, *Charles the Bald*, p. 199.
38 Nelson, *Charles the Bald*, p. 215.
39 Nelson, *King and Emperor*, pp. 203–5. Two more babies, one a twin, did not survive.
40 *MGH Dip Karol* I, no. 149, p. 203.

41 On benefices and favours, P. Fouracre, 'The use of the term *beneficium* in Frankish sources. A society based on favours?', in W. Davies and P. Fouracre (eds), *The Languages of Gift in the Early Middle Ages* (Cambridge, 2010), pp. 62–88.
42 On this grant and on Dagobert's generosity to Saint Arnulf's, P. Fouracre, 'Lights, Power and the Moral Economy in Early Medieval Europe', *Early Medieval Europe* 28–3 (2020), 1–21, here 7–9.
43 On the Farfa charters of the Lombard period, above p. 67.
44 See note 30 above.
45 Koziol, *Politics of Memory*, pp. 75–6. The document is no. 17 in *Die Urkunden Karls III*, ed. P. Kehr, *MGH Diplomata Regum Germaniae ex stirpe Karolinorum* II (Berlin, 1936).
46 Koziol, *Politics of Memory*, p. 39.
47 Koziol, *Politics of Memory*, p. 89.
48 Above, p. 53–5, and further, Fouracre, 'Eternal light', p. 68.
49 *Recueil des actes de Charles III le simple, vol. 1, text*, ed. F. Lot and Ph. Lauer (Paris, 1940), nos 10, 34, 45, 47, 48, 50, 53, 66, 71, 75, 77, 83, 86, 88, 93, 95, 96, 97, 104.
50 *Recueil des actes de Louis IV*, ed. M. Prou and Ph. Lauer (Paris, 1914), no. 16.
51 These strictures on the endowment and consecration of churches were regarded as important and would be repeated down the centuries. For Catalan examples of the twelfth century, see below, Chapter 4, pp. 138–9.
52 Merovingian Church Councils were concerned with new churches founded on lordly estates, but always in terms of the authority over the clergy who served them rather than with their fabric and equipment.
53 *MHG Lex Visigothorum* XII, 1.3, from the *Liber Iudicorum* recension under King Erwig, which dates it to 681.
54 See below p. 98.
55 Above, Chapter 2.
56 Czock, *Gottes Haus*, pp. 52–61.
57 Genesis 28:10–22.
58 C. Clark, 'Cultural Landscapes of Burial in Gaul 450–900', PhD thesis, Birkbeck College, London (2017).
59 *Concilium Liftinense*, ed. A. Werminghof, *MGH Concilia* Ii (Hanover and Leipzig, 1906), pp. 6–7, here c. 2, p. 7.
60 The literature on 'feudalism' is massive, but see F. L. Ganshof, *Feudalism*, trans. P. Grierson (London, 1964), for an account both of how the land/service relationship was formalised and of how it became the basis of Carolingian power. For a reading of Estinnes which does not support this argument, P. Fouracre, *The Age of Charles Martel* (Harlow, 2000), pp. 137–40. For a recent, and excellent, overview of how Carolingian power was constructed, M. Costambeys, M. Innes and S. MacLean, *The Carolingian World* (Cambridge, 2011), pp. 31–65.
61 The reaction against what might be termed the textbook notion of 'feudalism' begins with E. A. R. Brown, 'The Tyranny of a Construct: Feudalism and the

Historians of Medieval Europe', *American Historical Review* 79 (1974), 1063–88, and is developed at length in S. Reynolds, *Fiefs and Vassals. The Medieval Evidence Reconsidered* (Oxford, 1996).

62  The noun derived from the verb was, strictly speaking, *precarium*, second declension neuter singular, but the plural (*precaria*) beame a generic term and was soon treated as first declension feminine, with *precariae* sometimes used as the plural. Fouracre, *Age of Charles Martel*, pp. 137–8, on the development of the precarial grant.

63  Fouracre, 'The use of the term *beneficium*'.

64  *Gesta sanctorum patrum Fontanellensis coenobii*, ed. and French trans. P. Pradié, *Chronique des abbés de Fontanelle (Saint Wandrille)* (Paris, 1999), VI, c. 2, pp. 78–81. The passage is translated in I. Wood, 'Teutsind, Witlaic and the history of Merovingian *precaria*', in W. Davies and P. Fouracre (eds), *Property and Power in the Early Middle Ages* (Cambridge, 1995), pp. 31–52, at pp. 35–7.

65  *Gesta sanctorum partum Fontanellensis* XI, c. 3, pp. 132–3; Wood, 'Teutsind', pp. 38–9.

66  *Traditiones Wizenburgenses. Die Urkunden des Klosters Weissenburg 661–864*, ed. K. Glöckner and A. Doll (Darmstadt, 1979), no. 19, p. 200.

67  This was legislation from the Council of Soissons in 853. See below, p. 97.

68  On this form of tithe, G. Constable, 'Nona et Decima', *Speculum* 35 (1960), 224–50.

69  This is the impression that Charlemagne's adviser Alcuin gave in a letter of 794 in which he advised against demanding tithes from peoples recently conquered and forcibly converted: 'Why', he asked, 'should a yoke be placed on the necks recently converted which neither we nor our brothers have been able to sustain?', trans. P. King, *Charlemagne. Translated Sources* (Lambrigg, 1987), pp. 314–15. See J. Nelson, 'Alcuin's letter to Meginfrid', in A. Dierkens (ed.), *Penser la paysannerie medieval, un défi impossible? Recueil d'études offert à J.-P. Devroey* (Paris, 2017), pp. 105–19. On the growing acceptance of tithe in the ninth century, S. Wood, *The Proprietary Church in the Medieval West* (Oxford, 2006), pp. 459–78. On the tithe in Germany and its relation to episcopal power, J. Eldevik, *Episcopal Power and Ecclesiastical Reform in the German Empire. Tithes, Lordship and Community 950–1150* (Cambridge, 2012), pp. 2–95.

70  *MGH Capitularia regum Francorum* I, ed. A. Boretius (Hanover, 1883), no. 20, pp. 46–51, cc. 13, 15, p. 50, trans. King, *Charlemagne. Translated Sources*, pp. 203–5.

71  Two seminal papers are W. Hartung, 'Adel, Erbrecht, Schenkung: die strukturellen Ursachen der frühmittelalterlichen Besitzübertragungen an die Kirche', in F. Seibt (ed.), *Gesellschaftsgeschichte. Festschrift für Karl Bosl zum 80 Gerburtstag*, 2 vols (Munich, 1988), vol. 1, pp. 417–38, and J. Jahn, 'Tradere ad sanctum: politische und gesellschaftliche Aspekte der Traditionspraxis im agilolfingerische Bayern', in Seibt (ed.) *Gesellschaftsgeschichte*, vol. 1, pp. 400–16.

72  Carl I. Hammer, 'Land Sales in Eighth- and Ninth-century Bavaria: Legal, Economic and Social Aspects', *Early Medieval Europe* 6 (1997), 47–76, at 69–70.

## Light and power

73 P. Fouracre, 'Carolingian Justice: the Rhetoric of Improvement and Contexts of Abuse', *Settimane di Spoleto* 42 (1995), 771–803 [reprinted Fouracre, *Frankish History*, no. XI], at 784–6; W. Brown, *Unjust Siezure: Conflict, Interest and Authority in an Early Medieval Society* (Ithaca, 2001) is a book-length study of the situation in Carolingian Bavaria.
74 T. Reuter, *Germany in the Early Middle Ages 800–1056* (London, 1991), pp. 58, 60. In his perhaps overdramatic view, 'Canstatt did for Alemannic land-holding what Hastings did for Anglo-Saxon land-holding' (p. 60).
75 *MGH Capitularia* I, no. 19, c. 8, p. 45.
76 *MGH Capitularia* I, no. 102, c. 7, p. 210.
77 *MGH Capitularia* I, no. 43, c. 8, p. 121, no. 49, c. 4, p. 136, no. 83, c. 4, p. 182.
78 *MGH Capitularia* I, no. 150, c. 5, p. 304.
79 *MGH Capitularia* II, ed. V. Krause (Hanover, 1897), no. 196, c. 11, p. 33.
80 *MGH Capitularia* II, no. 293, c. 78, pp. 419–20, cf. *MHG Concilia* III, ed. W. Hartmann (Hanover, 1984), no. 11, c. 78, p. 125, for useful notes.
81 *MGH Capitularia* II, no. 267, c. 1, p. 267.
82 *MGH Concilia* I ii, ed. A. Werminghof (Hanover and Leipzig, 1908), no. 37, c. 16, p. 277.
83 *MGH Concilia* II ii, no. 38, c. 46, p. 292.
84 *MGH Concilia* II ii, no. 46, c. 6, p. 556.
85 Above, Chapter 1, p. 1.
86 *MGH Concilia* II I, no. 56, c. 28, p. 739.
87 This is the wording in the letter: *Ignis autem in altari semper ardebit, quem nutriet sacerdos subiciens ligna mane per singulos dies. et imposita holocausto desuper adolebit adipes pacificorum. ignis est iste perpetuus qui numquam deficit de altari. multum igitur haec verba praeponderanda et pertimescanda sunt his qui unde ignis perpetuus id est luminaria in basilicis Deo dicatis concinnari ex fidelium oblationibus debent, auferri praesumant. quoniam si filii Aaron, Nadab et Abiu, qui pro eo quod per suam negligentiam ignis qui iubetur in altari esse perpetuus extinctus est, et propterea ignem alienum coram Domino offerre paesumpserunt, ob id igne egress a Domino devorati sunt, merito. quod non sine magno animi merore prosequimur horribili morte devorandi sunt hi qui ignem Domini is basilicis sibi dicatis et consecratis audacter extinguunt. et si quaeriter qualiter illum extinguunt manifestum est quod quando ea auferrunt unde iste ignis Domino nutriti debet, tunc illum extinguunt. quod vero basilice Deo dictatae et consecratae loca sint divina, sint etiam Dei habitacula et omnibus in christiana religione consistentibus pavenda et veneranda.*
88 *The Annals of Saint-Bertin*, trans. J. Nelson (Manchester, 1991), s.a. 837, p. 36.
89 *MGH Concilia* III, ed. W. Hartmann (Hanover, 1984), no. 27, c. 3, 286.
90 *MGH Concilia* IV, ed. W. Hartmann (Hanover, 1998), no. 25, c. 38, p. 279.
91 On the way in which lords progressively appropriated the tithe to the point at which it was regarded as theirs to dispose of as they wished, S. Wood, *Proprietary Church*, pp. 486–512.

92 C. van Rhijn, *Shepherds of the Lord. Priests and Episcopal Statutes in the Carolingian Period* (Turnhout, 2007).
93 On the emergence of the Statutes, van Rhijn, *Shepherds*, pp. 47–8, and on the first texts, J. Gaudemet, 'Les status épiscopaux de la première decade du IX siècle', *Proceedings of the Fourth International Congress of Medieval Canon Law*, ed. S. Kuttner, *Monumenta Iuris Canonici*, series C, subsidia 5 (Vatican, 1976), pp. 303–49. They are edited by P. Brommer and R. Pokorny in three volumes: *MGH Capitula Episcoporum* (Hanover, 1985–95). A fourth volume by Pokorny (2005) adds a valuable commentary and index.
94 Van Rhijn, *Shepherds*, misses this observation. Note that her work as a published PhD thesis has no index, which makes it hard to find references to specific provisions in the statutes.
95 Atto of Vercelli (c. 970), c. 25, *MGH Capitula Episcoporum* III, p. 274.
96 Riculf of Soissons (after 889), c. 13, *MGH Capitula Episcorum* II, p. 106.
97 Van Rhijn, *Shepherds of the Lord*, pp. 124–38.
98 The text is in *Patrologia Latina* 131, cols 845a–866a.
99 Van Rhijn, *Shepherds of the Lord*, p. 135.
100 The wording here goes back to Genesis 28:10–22, Jacob's dream: when Jacob awoke he anointed with oil the stone on which he had been resting and declared that it was the dwelling place of God. See Gzock, *Gottes Haus*, p. 58.
101 D. Iogna-Prat, 'Lieu du culte et exégèse liturgique à l'époche carolingienne', in C. Chazelle and B. Van Nam Edwards (eds), *The Study of the Bible in the Carolingian Era*, Medieval Church Studies 3 (Turnout, 2003), pp. 215–44, at 231–4.
102 This ritual is similar to those prescribed in the Sacramentaries of Angoulême and Autun, roughly of the same date. 'The twelve candles', however is more exegetical in tone, drawing on Genesis. See Czock, *Gottes Haus*, pp. 258–65, and note 99, above.
103 Hincmar I (852), c. 16, *MGH Capitula Episcoporum* II, p. 43: *Ut de collectis, quas geldonias vel confratrias vulgo vocant, in omni obsequio religionis coniunguntur, videlicet in oblatione, in luminaribus, in orationibus mutuis, in exequiis defunctorum, in helemosinis, et in cetereis pietatis officiis.*
104 Czock, *Gottes Haus*, p. 181, does recognise the importance of lighting in Carolingian legislation, but makes no further comment on this.
105 D. Ganz, 'Theology and the organization of thought', ch. 28 in R. McKitterick (ed.), *New Cambridge Medieval History II* (Cambridge, 1995), pp. 758–85, at 761.

# 4

# Lighting, lords and peasants in post-Carolingian Europe

The last chapter examined the way in which the Carolingian rulers of Francia gave institutional backing to the scriptural injunction to keep lights burning before the tabernacle, that is, to have a perpetual light on every altar. This was revealed in normative sources (capitularies, the records of church councils, and the 'episcopal statutes'). At the same time, the evidence of royal charters showed that providing for the lights was regarded as politically and morally important. The spread of churches and the universalisation of obligations to the Church in the form of tithes also stimulated a push from below to become involved in the resourcing of local churches. The Carolingians, in other words, had been relatively successful in getting the message across that it was everybody's duty to support the Christian religion. References to guilds formed for this purpose were an early sign that at least some communities were responding to that message. In this chapter I will examine how the impetus from below developed and spread in a post-Carolingian era in which royal power weakened in West Francia, and in a context of increasing economic activity in the countryside and towns. It will be important to bring England, Italy and Spain back into the picture, for, although we have more information from Francia than from other areas, it is not the case that Francia can simply be equated with all of Europe, nor can the spread of support for the Church be simply put down to Carolingian initiative. But first I would like to return to the 'Carolingian moment' and to the evidence of charters both royal and private where we find the first hints of changing economic conditions and growing evidence for commemoration in the form of eternal lights, and through the instigation of anniversary feasts. I will then introduce the evidence of estate surveys (polyptychs), an early example of which was seen in the last chapter in the lists of dues owed to the monastery of Bobbio.

Polyptychs are important for showing the existence of tribute payers dedicated to the provision of light. For the first time they allow us to see a social layer between the nobility and the dependent peasantry. This layer, it will be argued, forms the constituency of those making small voluntary contributions towards the lights on a regular basis, and it was from this layer that guild members were drawn. With this constituency in mind, and having established the contours of the landscape in Francia, I will then make comparison with the situation in England, Italy and Spain. The chapter will end with thoughts about how the history of lighting provision fits with models for the development of Europe as a whole. This above all means seeing what part (if any) provision for lighting played in the so-called 'feudal transformation', a model based on West Francia, but one that historians have tried to apply to the wider area. That discussion leads to the theme for the next chapter (5) which is the apparent differences between what had been West and East Francia. The question there will be: why did a class of semi-free light providers (the so-called *Zensualität*) cohere in the East but not in the West?

West Francia was ruled for nearly forty years, from 838 to 877, by King Charles the Bald. Of his charters 468 survive, and of these 36, that is 7.7 per cent, make reference to the provision of lights.[1] There are a further ten charters that purport to have been issued by Charles and which have reference to lights, but these are judged by modern commentators to have been forgeries. Again, it is noteworthy that forgers (like the author(s) of the 'Donation of Constantine') seem to have believed that a gift looked more authentic if it was said to be for the purpose of lighting.[2] Charters from the monastery of Saint Bertin (in the present-day town of Saint Omer in the Pas de Calais, about 40 kilometres from the Channel coast) indicate how one such forgery was made in order to 'confirm' the monastery's takeover of a church and its resources. This case is worth considering at some length because it shows the relationship between the monastery and a local family over three generations, and reveals that the relationship was in part based on the provision of lighting. It is also important in relation to the polyptych compiled by officials at Saint Bertin at this time, that is, the mid-ninth century. The polyptych of Saint Bertin, which will be examined shortly, is unique in referring to a class of light providers, termed *luminarii*.

In 826 one Goibert and his mother Bertruda (or Trudlinda) donated the church of Saint Salvator in Stenetland (location unknown, but presumably in or near the Pas de Calais) to Saint Bertin as Goibert was about to go to Rome. A second grant followed in 828.[3] The church and its properties were given into the care of Goibert's son Gundebert. Further gifts followed in 831 and in 838, by which time Gundebert had become a monk at Saint Bertin.[4] In 857, at Gundebert's request, Adalard the abbot of Saint Bertin confirmed the gifts which now amounted to 18 places around Stenetland (some of which might well have come from other donors), income from these properties being designated to provide for the lights of Saint Salvator and for 'other necessities' as well.[5] The charter also confirmed Gundebert's right to manage the Stenetland properties and to choose his successor. Then in 866, Hilduin, Adalard's successor as abbot of Saint Bertin, took Saint Salvator and the Stenetland lands under his direct control, but in 867 Gundebert drew up a *brevis* or inventory of the properties in which he said that Hilduin had taken them *iniuste*.[6] Hilduin, formerly a cleric in the royal palace, had been appointed abbot only in 866. After drawing up this inventory, Gundebert left for Rome. It could be that Hilduin had more or less forced him out. Eighteen places were listed, and each was assessed according to land measured in *bunuaria*, a unit of about 3.3 acres.[7] Numbers of *mancipia* (here maybe not serfs, but dependants of the church) were listed and the income from each place was given.[8] The income was expressed in money (*solidi* or *denarii*). The money income was followed by the phrase 'this is what was yearly spent on light, wax, oil, fat and other necessaries for the church, and the feeding and clothing of eight clerics'.[9] Income in kind included flour, cheese, beer, fish, honey, wine and, very unusually, tiny amounts of pepper, cumin, cinnamon, cloves and ginger to be presented on Goibert's anniversary, for what might have been a rather spicy anniversary meal. The forged charter of Charles the Bald, which dated to itself to 866, was a confirmation of the history of grants to Stenetland which put them firmly under Saint Bertin's control.[10] It was drawn up by the monk Gombert at some time between 866 and 886, Hilduin having put Gombert in charge of Stenetland in 866. The forgery seems to have been based on the charter of 857, and it looks as if it had been prompted by a need to counter what was more than a hint of irregularity (carried in the term *iniuste*) in the 867 *brevis*. In the 866 charter the purpose of all the gifts of Bertruda, Goibert and Gundebert was said to be to provide for clothing and food for the clergy of Saint Salvator and for 'lights of wax and oil'. Control of resources to that end could, after all, hardly be 'unjust'.

The Stenetland sequence also reflects a shift in the nature of donations to churches, that is, from endowment to supply. Early charters had often recorded the gift of lands to establish or enrich churches, and, though large grants continue throughout the Middle Ages, documents from the ninth century onwards increasingly deal with the provisioning of churches that had already been established, and they are generally more specific about what was to be provided and for what purpose. This is the context in which more information about lights is revealed. Because Charles the Bald's reign was a long one, the run of genuine charters allows us to see these developments across the mid-ninth century. The royal charters that mention lights are of three kinds: confirmations of the donations of earlier kings, confirmations of transactions made by other (non-royal) parties, and gifts from Charles himself. Gifts from the king show a wider net of resources being dedicated to lights as well as to the support of monks and clergy. In a gift to Saint Denis of 861, made to help the monastery recover after Viking attacks, land (*mansi*), serfs, but also a mill and a fishery were given 'for lights to shine forth incessantly'.[11] In other charters, for the monasteries of Saint Bertin and Saint Philibert, the gift was the right to set up a market, the income from which was to go towards the lights.[12] In yet another gift to Saint Denis, made in 862, Charles coupled provision for the lights with commemorative meals: Charles's birth and accession, his marriage to Queen Ermintrude and her birthday were all to be celebrated. And after their deaths there were to be commemorative meals and masses. The amount of wine to be used is specified and, uniquely, a commemorative light was to be burned not on an altar but on the *gazofilacium*, the chest in which the offerings of the faithful were placed. Here, possibly for the first time, an explicit analogy was made between the burning of a perpetual light, and the eternal light enjoyed by the soul in heaven. Finally, nothing from the gift was ever to be given out as a *beneficium*, so that the income from the gift would remain for the purposes for which it was given, and to which it was to be devoted, beginning with the lights.[13] In a grant to Saint Riquier of 870 three oil lamps were to be set up to commemorate Charles, his wife Ermintrude and his son Carloman, and a fourth light was to burn night and day on the altar before the saint's shrine.[14] Then in 875, with Charles now emperor, seven lamps were to burn on the altar of the Trinity at Saint Denis to commemorate Charles's father, mother, Ermintrude, a second wife, Richildis, all his children and, unusually, two named followers.[15] What the charters reveal in general is an increasing cash element in donations, and this is in conjunction with references to markets, on which subject earlier sources are almost silent. Cash and markets together indicate greater economic activity in the countryside, with the production of a surplus that could be exchanged for a wider range of goods.[16] The Stenetland spices are an indication of this, and it is striking too that oil seems to have become more readily available again. Although the source of that oil is not evident, one might guess from earlier Carolingian tradition that it was Italy or Provence. The scriptural associations of the oil lamp

*Lighting, lords and peasants*

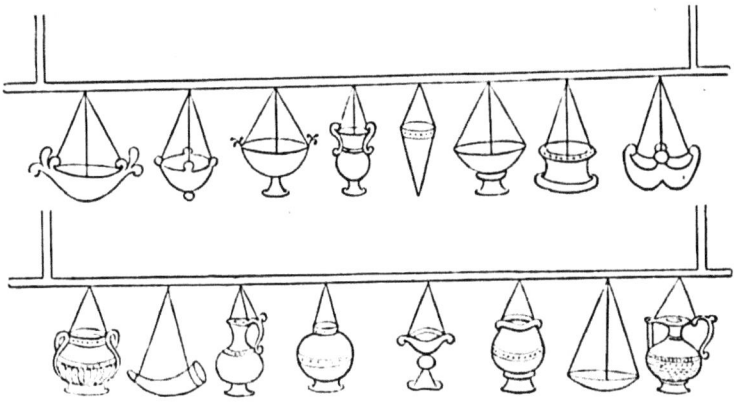

3 Depiction of hanging oil lamps taken from the 'Vivian Bible' of 845

remained strong, as can be seen from the illustrations of hanging lamps in the lavish bible presented to Charles at Christmas 845. The message in these illustrations was that a ruler who followed the Mosaic injunction to keep the flame alight would be favoured by God.

Charles the Bald's legislation reflects the economic diversification of this period with extensive measures put forward in 864 in the 'Edict of Pîtres' to control the minting of coins and the movement of what look like seasonal wage-labourers.[17] What this increased activity suggests is that a wider net of people could now afford the kind of commemoration that we see in the charters. At the same time, the documents show the continuing importance of the *census* from precarial tenancies, and the usual concern that those who held *beneficia* might divert the *census* from its proper destination, i.e. the church that was the ultimate owner of the land.

The written surveys of church resources known as polyptychs have their roots in later Roman surveys, but the drawing up of polyptychs was another strand in the Carolingian drive to bring order to the management of church resources. Not only was good stewardship of the land a religious duty, but it was also useful to bring order to a church's holdings after a period of land acquisition, land exchanges, and a turnover of tenancies, all these said by historians to have been taking place against the background of a growing population. Over the period 800–950 some thirty polyptychs were drawn up for institutions lying mostly in an area between the Rivers Rhine and Loire. Those of the monasteries of Saint Germain-des-Prés (Paris), Prüm (Eifel), Saint Remigius (Saint Rémi, Reims) and Lobbes (Hainault, Belgium) are the largest and most complete surveys.

*Eternal light and earthly concerns*

4 Location of the monasteries which produced the major polyptychs

These documents have become invaluable to historians for what they can tell us about the rural economy and the social structure of church estates.[18] The polyptych of Saint Bertin was put together sometime between 844 and 859. It is much smaller than the 'big three' because it was concerned only with those properties which supplied the monastery directly with its routine needs, rather as Gundebert's *brevis* concentrated on the income that supplied the church of Saint Salvator in Stenetland.[19] In fact the properties surveyed in the Stenetland *brevis* do not appear in the Saint Bertin survey because, although Saint Bertin was their ultimate owner, they formed part of the *ministerium* of Saint Salvator Stenetland, and income from them

112

went to that church. The polyptych of Saint Bertin thus details the abbey's holdings in just 15 places. As the Stenetland charters have shown, this was a time in which Saint Bertin was acquiring resources and reordering them, those of Saint Salvator included.[20]

In common with other surveys, the polyptych of Saint Bertin lists different types or categories of people on each *mansus*, telling us what they owed in terms of labour, money or kind. Some of these categories, *mancipia* for instance, are seen in all surveys, but some are unique to a given locality. In the case of Saint Bertin, three types of people are unique: *heriscarii*, *lunarii* and *luminarii*. *Heriscarii* sound as if they had some kind of military function, for the part *heri* means 'army' and *scara* means 'small troop'. *Lunarii* (from *luna*, 'moon') were presumably something to do with Mondays. Perhaps they were people who had to work on each Monday for the monastery, or maybe once a month. *Luminarii* owed dues that clearly went towards the monastery's lights. There are 621 of them[21] spread across nine different places which makes them the largest category of people in the survey.[22] *Luminarii* were, in the view of F. L Ganshof the survey's most recent editor, people, or the descendants of people, who were originally free, but had become dependants of the abbey by virtue of having sought its protection.[23] In return for that protection and in recognition of their ties to Saint Bertin, they paid a small sum to it each year. In the majority of cases that sum was 4 *denarii*. Four *denarii* (pennies) would later often be seen as the amount serfs ritually placed upon their heads to indicate that they 'belonged' to their lord. Four *denarii* was also often quoted as the price for a pound of wax. It is not possible to be sure of the social status or wealth of the Saint Bertin *luminarii* because they were not listed in relation to landholding, and they may not even have been living on the monastery's lands. They were clearly hereditary tribute payers, but the fact that their tribute was paid for the honourable purpose of providing lighting, and that the amount was meagre, or perhaps symbolic, suggests that they were of relatively high status amongst Saint Bertin's dependants. This puts them in roughly the same bracket as the census payers, the *censuales* and the *cerocensuales* found in Germany from the later ninth century onwards. But unlike the latter, *luminarii* were not widespread, for the term is not met outside of this one document.

Figures who look similar to the *luminarii* are also found in the polyptych of Saint Rémi (Reims). At Airoht, near Asfeld in the Ardennes, there were ten *cerarii* ('wax payers') who each paid 3 *denarii* or an equivalent amount of wax each year.[24] In the very different and better documented Paris region, 61 people were named in the polyptych of Saint-Germain-des-Prés as 'men who gave themselves for the lights of Saint Germain'.[25] In the same polyptych there are records of six donations of small *mansi* in which the donor, or the *mancipia* attached to the land, paid *ad luminaria*.[26] These look like precarial arrangements in which the payment was the *census*. The result was a class of people like the *luminarii* of Saint Bertin who were recognised dependants of the abbey but owed it nothing other than their contribution towards the lights. Another group that similarly owed little and performed only easy duties such as short-distance transport (services involving horses being seen as more honourable than, say, labour) were the *haistaldi* seen in the polyptychs of Prüm and Lobbes. The *haistaldi*, incidentally, look rather like the *geneats* mentioned in a later Anglo-Saxon account of conditions on estates, or the *radcnits* who were listed in the Domesday Survey.[27] The Lobbes *haistaldi* paid a head tax of 12 *denarii* for males and 2 *denarii* for females. Another feature common to these surveys is the relatively small size of many of the *mansi*. For example, with regard to the large estate of Poperinge (near Ypres in Belgium), the Saint Bertin polyptych said that there were 42 and a half *mansi*. Ten of these *mansi* consisted of 24 *bunuaria*, ten of 20 *bunuaria*, another ten of 15 *bunuaria*, the rest of 15, with the half *mansus* having eight *bunuaria*. Whole *mansi*, then, ranged in size from 81 to 51 acres. This is in contrast to the larger *mansi* held by two named *caballarii* (horsemen) on which there were many *mancipia*.[28] It has been observed that, across the survey as a whole, the size of the majority of Saint Bertin's *mansi* was in the region of 12 *bunuaria*.[29] That is around 40 acres, a holding that is in roughly the same order of size as the Anglo-Saxon *yardland* (30 acres) mentioned in the late seventh-century *Laws of Ine* and in one mid-eleventh century survey in which 12 pence was due in rent from each *yardland*.[30] The fact that fact that *yardlands* were not mentioned in the three centuries separating these references emphasises the fragmentary nature of the record from England. Holdings on the Prüm estates were even smaller, ranging from 12 to 37 acres, with the creation of numerous half or even quarter *mansi*. The smaller *mansus* and the subdivisions have been associated with a rising population and with the 'decomposition' of the estate structures that had characterised the early and mid-Carolingian periods. Alternatively, it has been argued that the smaller units showed that those estate structures were managing a creative response to changing conditions which maintained the dominance of monastic estate-management on a large scale.[31] Another possibility is that these smaller farming units had always been there, but do not become visible until the more detailed evidence of the polyptychs comes into view. It was the larger units of the *villa* and the undivided *mansi* as the *villa* appurtenances that appear in those earlier charters in which donations to the church were recorded. These were the resources of lords, whereas the smaller holdings were those of the peasants who worked them with their own hands.

Working out from the Prüm survey, Ludwig Kuchenbuch categorised the region between the Rivers Meuse, Scheldt and Lower Rhine (thus the area covered by the Saint Bertin, Lobbes, Saint Rémi and Prüm documents) as a *Rentenlandschaft*. By this he meant that typical of the region were 'free' *mansi* that did not owe labour services to their monastic lords, but paid a *census*, usually in cereals.[32] Kuchenbuch's model has been criticised for suggesting that this was a distinctively regional form of estate organisation as opposed to one arising from practical arrangements that responded to similar conditions.[33] He was, however, correct to emphasise the importance of rent payment and the fact that this element had been growing in proportion over the ninth century, and not just in this region, but also in mid-west and in south-west France. Services such as the *hostilicum*, for example, originally a military service, appear in the polyptychs as a money payment. Likewise personal payments such as the 4 *denarii* paid (usually by 'freedmen') to a church for protection, marriage tax and death tax were all dues appearing in different regions across the ninth and tenth centuries.[34] The evidence of the polyptychs thus points to a heterogeneous layer of rent- or tribute-paying peasants, holding units of land in the low tens of acres. This group included people of both free and un-free status, although the distinction between 'free' and 'un-free' is often hard to see. Free people could take part in public activity, owed military service, participated in assemblies, could dispose of property without interference and had some choice in marriage. Un-free people were unable to make contracts, were subject to distraint by lords and could be punished without recourse to public justice. Un-freedom was a hereditary condition, and un-free families were subject to division as the un-free could be directed by their lords to serve others.[35] Blurring the distinction between the two categories were people who had been servile but had been freed or 'manumitted', and who owed hereditary service to those (often a church) who protected them. A further complication is the way in which *mansi* were listed as either 'free' or 'servile', but servile tenants could occupy free *mansi*, and vice versa. On the estates surveyed in the Saint Rémi polyptych, 12.1 per cent of tenants listed were freedmen, 10.8 per cent were *servi*, and 71 per cent were free (*ingenui*).[36] These proportions are roughly similar across the West Frankish polyptychs, but east of the Rhine there is a far higher proportion of servile *mansi*.

The reason for going into some detail on the social landscape of the polyptychs is that it gives insight into the constituency from which light providers were drawn. That means provision that was in addition to the proportion of tithe that was earmarked for the lights. This pool of providers was set to grow. It has been seen that, apart from the *luminarii* in the Saint Bertin survey and the *cerarii* of Saint Rémi, there were the 61 named people in the Saint Germain polyptych who were said to 'have given themselves for the lights'. Giving oneself over to a church for the lights, and for other services, appears as an increasingly common act over the tenth and eleventh centuries. Such people, one imagines, would have had a relationship with the institution similar to that enjoyed by the *luminarii* of Saint Bertin. Their new condition was hereditary and carried with it some burdens, but also brought some protection, not least of social status. Furthermore, joining the *familia* of a church had spiritual benefits. Lords too might seek such benefits by freeing *mancipia* and then giving them over to a church as light providers. For instance in 945 the lady Irmina freed one male *servus* and five female *ancillae* and handed them over to the monastery of Gorze (in the Moselle region) 'on condition that the females each paid to the altar of Saint Gorgon one *denarius* on the saint's festival for lights to be kindled', whereas the one male would pay 2 *denarii*. All those born to these people in future generations would pay the same amounts.[37] The group would thus grow in size. Their dues were very easy, and it would therefore be reasonable to assume that these people were peasants of relatively high social status. At the same time, precarial grants continued to be made and new *censuales* to be created. On the other hand, *censuales* could be lost to the church as lords appropriated their dues. In a charter of 950, Otto the king of Germany (936–73) returned some *censuali homines* to the monastery of Wissembourg so that they could provide for the lights, and for food and clothing for the monks.[38] These people had once been Wissembourg *censuales* but had presumably been diverted to the king's service.

Although it is Francia that supplies the bulk of the evidence for these relatively well-off types whose obligations to those above them were easy, similarities of social structure, ecologies and agricultural practices would suggest that they were to be found across Western Europe. It may well be that it is often people of this sort (the 'middling sort'?) who are the named parties in many Spanish documents of the tenth century, or who appear as witnesses in manumission documents from later Anglo-Saxon England, or, maybe, as holders of fractions of a 'hide' in the Domesday survey in England. It was people of this standing, that is, those with the resources to make extra contributions to religious and social life, who participated in the activities of guilds and confraternities, again, across Europe.

Medieval guilds have often been studied as harbingers of the modern, that is, as early forms of economic association which by-passed lords and were organised around urban production. This may be true of some late medieval craft guilds, but guilds and confraternities have their origins in the early Middle Ages as associations formed for religious purposes: meeting the needs of churches and commemorating members. But whatever their origins the activities of the guilds and confraternities involved lights. In the last chapter we saw how Hincmar of Reims approved of guilds formed to support religion in this way, but in the same document (his 'episcopal statutes') he went on to say that they were prone to excessive drinking which provoked violence and even homicide.[39] Guilds were thus regarded with suspicion not only because members took oaths to each other but also because the memberships bonded through feasting and, especially, drinking.[40] In the ninth century guilds therefore tended to be regarded as subversive organisations that encouraged gluttony and dancing, said Hincmar.[41] Charlemagne famously declared against them in the 'Capitulary of Herstal' (779): 'Concerning oaths sworn through *gildonia*, sworn mutually and together, no-one is to presume to do this'.[42] Associations might be formed for almsgiving or against shipwreck or fire, but no oaths were to be taken. It is the mutuality of the oath (the *coniuratio*, 'swearing together') that bothered the king: Frankish rulers would have a long history of cracking down on *coniurationes* (sworn associations).[43] The word *gildonia* is of Germanic origin, and this has been taken to indicate that guilds were very old and somehow 'pagan' in origin, hence the excessive eating and drinking. Although some of the earliest guilds appeared in Anglo-Saxon England, Flanders and Frisia, areas particularly associated with pagan traditions, such origins cannot be demonstrated.[44] Alternatively, an old school of thought argued that the lay confraternities derived from the bestowal of monastic fraternity upon lay persons who supported the monastery, before becoming a separate lay organisation in the tenth century. More recent thinking is that these organisations then melded with the *gildonia*, the sworn associations of lay persons that feature in Carolingian legislation.[45] As O. G. Oexle has argued, there is a kind of third way in which they came into being: *coniurationes* first appear as associations of parish priests formed from the fifth century onwards for purposes of mutual self-help and the provision of charity, at a time when episcopal support for the rural priest was weak.[46] In the last chapter it was suggested that the rise of the lay guild was an indication that demands to support churches had met a response from the lay community. Three other elements can be identified in that response: first, as we have just seen, there was a layer of people able, as well as willing, to afford that support, and second, such people were perhaps following lords in their desire both to obtain spiritual benefits in return for their material support and to commemorate their own. Thirdly, solidarities for these purposes were easily formed, or perhaps grew out of pre-existing associations. Conviviality was certainly at the core of guild activity. The growth of guilds thus worked with the grain of social and religious development. That part of their organisation and activity should revolve around the provision of light was something that gave that provision a much wider and more powerful social dimension. Let us now review the situation across Western Europe, beginning with England.

## England in the late Saxon period

In the first chapter of this work it was shown that writers in England from the seventh and eighth centuries took very seriously the Mosaic injunction to keep lights of the purest olive oil burning before the tabernacle. In the early eighth century Bede conjured up the image of a church beaming out light in the middle of the night, as did the poet Æthelwulf a century later.[47] It was observed that there was an early commitment to pay for lights in Rome itself, and there is some archaeological evidence for the use of hanging lamps or bowls in both England and Rome. At the same time there were indications of a severe shortage of olive oil in England, and the hallowing of bees, and thus wax, in the works of Aldhelm at the end of the seventh century no doubt reflected that shortage. After this, the evidence for the maintenance of lights in England more or less disappears: only one document (a will from the year 995) refers to a gift for the provision of lighting. Nevertheless, as we shall see, there are a few normative statements that refer obliquely to lighting in that they are about the payment of dues which included wax or money for wax. In addition, there is a homiletic tradition which advocated giving alms for the lighting of churches.[48] The silence on the actual giving for the lights (as opposed to statements that they should be provided for) is puzzling, given that in other respects later Anglo-Saxon England had so much in common with those other European societies in which reference to the provision of lighting was maybe intermittent but never out of the record for long. On the other hand, there was something of an alternative diplomatic tradition in England. Anglo-Saxon charters tend not to use the formulae that provide stock phrases for charters across the continent, and many of the references to lights on the continent appear in such formulae. As suggested above, there is reason to think that the social structure of later Anglo-Saxon England included the kind of better-off peasants who would figure as light providers on the continent. In the discussion of the evidence of the continental polyptychs, it was noted that the late Saxon *geneat*, who paid rent and performed high-status services such as riding, appears similar to the *haistaldi* seen on the estates of the abbey of Lobbes. Likewise, Anglo-Saxon *yardlanders* who paid rent but owed no other service, look rather like the holders of small *mansi* in what Kuchenbuch termed the *Rentenlandschaft* of northern Francia.[49]

There is in England further evidence for an emergent class of socially active people between the nobility (the thegns) and the dependent peasantry. The witness list of a charter from Canterbury drawn up between 858 and 866 specifies four different groups of citizens, including *cnihtas*.[50] Such people were plainly 'law-worthy' but not obviously of noble status. More evidence of this kind of intermediate status comes in the next century. This, as suggested earlier, lies both in documents which recorded manumissions and in the regulations for guilds. Four sets of manumissions survive from the tenth, eleventh and early twelfth centuries, coming from Bath, Exeter and Bodmin, all in south-west England. About 120 manumissions survive in these documents.[51] Much thought has been given to the status of those being freed, and to conditions on which that freedom was granted, but the documents say virtually nothing on this.[52] Alice Rio has recently observed that they can tell us little about the state of slavery, or un-freedom in general, and she has argued that a key purpose of the documents was to showcase the institutions that produced them.[53] Our concern here, however, is with the witnesses to the manumissions. These included people with occupational elements to their names: shieldmaker, boatman, cook, for instance. There were descriptive elements too: Godric 'Buttock' stands out, or Ælfric 'Neck'. The Bodmin manumissions also have a significant proportion of Cornish names, which gives some indication of the relations between the Cornish and the English. Stuart Pracy has argued that the proportion of occupational names increases across the eleventh and into the twelfth century. His interim conclusion is that 'the corpus of late Anglo-Saxon and early Anglo-Norman manumissions provides evidence that tradesmen, merchants, village leaders and reeves were attesting and enacting legal performances. Importantly, these documents show these lower social classes were listed alongside thegns, thus illustrating that the thegnly classes were operating in conjunction with and sharing political space with peasants'.[54] Unlike manumissions in France, and especially unlike those in Germany, English manumissions did not produce a class of freedmen and freedwomen who were then committed to provide for the lights of the institutions which had freed them and no doubt protected them. It cannot be absolutely certain that manumissions in England did not lead to the freed becoming church tributaries, but the documents give no indication that they did.

There are ten references to guilds in later Anglo-Saxon England, and five sets of guild regulations. These complement the evidence of the manumissions in showing a peasant or townly elite working alongside the thegns. Unlike guilds on the continent, these organisations had a peacekeeping function as well as offering mutual aid, protection and commemoration. The peacekeeping perhaps came from the obligations to keep the peace supposedly placed on all free men in later Anglo-Saxon England, but, as on the continent, much eating and drinking was also involved.[55] Rare, however, is reference to any religious function. The statutes of the Abbotsbury Guild (1025–50) were an exception in stating that 'three days before Saint Peter's mass, from each guild brother one penny or one pennyworth of wax' to be paid to the local minster.[56] The statutes of the Exeter Guild (first half of the tenth century) began: 'This association was assembled at Exeter for the love of God and for our own souls' needs'.[57] The members would pay for masses for the dead, but there is no mention of any other commemorative or devotional activity. Laws and the records of church councils likewise said very little about lights, but they provide a little evidence that the cost of lighting was met by a general levy, sometimes referred to as *leohtgesceot* ('light-dues'). In the laws known as 'The Laws of Edward and Guthrum' from the early eleventh century, fines were to be paid 'if anyone does not pay light-dues'.[58] In the so-called 'Canons of Edgar' from the same period it was stated that there 'is always to be a light burning in the church when mass is sung'. Light-dues were to be paid three times a year.[59] This was repeated twice in the laws of King Æthelred. On the second occasion it was said that light-dues were to be rendered at Candlemas, but 'he who wishes may do so more often'.[60] This last is the only hint outside of the homiletic tradition that voluntary payments might be made. In conjunction with the Abbotsbury Guild statute calling for the brothers to pay wax to the local minster, it suggests that extra payments were indeed made. We have seen that there was a peasant or urban elite who might have been willing and able to pay, and we have seen that such people were sometimes organised in voluntary associations, the guilds. We are nevertheless left with the fact that the amount of evidence for the provision of lights is in England tiny by comparison with the continent.

Some modern historians of Anglo-Saxon England have held what is termed a 'maximalist' view of the Old English state. This is a view based largely on normative and narrative evidence which can be read as showing that late Saxon government was capable of widespread taxation, of raising armies on a national basis, of maintaining a single coinage and of rendering truly public justice.[61] The idea that provision for light, the *leohtgescot*, was raised nationally in a system analogous to taxation would fit well with the maximalist view. There would, in other words, be little need for any other measures. Hence the near-silence on lights in the sources. But such an arrangement would have been so unlike anything seen on the continent that, without a great deal more evidence of agency, one cannot be convinced that the collection of church dues was centralised in this way. In fact the same objection could be made the maximalist view in general, for it relies heavily on normative evidence which tells of what should be done but not of how it was done. What was different in England was the hold that so-called 'minster' or 'mother' churches had over the lesser churches. Only from the later tenth century were local churches allowed to raise their own revenues from burial fees and from tithes which previously went to the minster.[62] The dominance of the minsters may have something to do with the silence on the collection of lighting dues. In the words of John Blair, up to the later eighth century (and beyond) 'English minsters (at least in Wessex) had a form of systematic revenue from the laity, whereas Frankish churches [and one might add Spanish and Italian churches] did not', hence the lack of charters for lighting for England.[63] In eleventh-century Kent, oil for chrism was certainly distributed through the minsters. But we cannot see further than this, except to note that the later tenth and eleventh centuries were a time in which local lords founded many new local churches, especially in East Anglia.[64] These are the institutions which would attract the attention of parish guilds at a slightly later date.

Given the hints that extra payments for lights might be made, and since the normative evidence does point to the existence of 'light dues', and as guilds were well established in England, it seems certain that keeping a light burning in churches was normal practice in England, as it was elsewhere in Europe, but it is also true that the means by which those lights were provided are largely invisible to us, and that makes England look different. One could make the same point for Ireland and Wales, for which the sources are even more unyielding in this respect.[65] One reason why there is why there is so little insular material on providing for lights is that is that there were no precarial agreements in England, Ireland and Wales, and hence no *beneficia* and no *censuales*. There were leases, most notably from the West Midlands in the tenth century, but these never stipulate what the tenant will give as rent or tribute. Nor, with the one exception, is there any record in England of anyone simply giving to the church for lights. Such a difference may partly be understood in terms of the thinness and nature of the record in Anglo-Saxon England: if France and England are compared over the period up to 1000 CE, roughly ten times more charters survive from France than from England. Compared with charters from the continent, those from England are strong on locative indications, especially with regard to boundaries, but they are usually silent on who lived within those boundaries, and silent too on the conditions and obligations of the inhabitants. The charters, therefore, cannot tell us anything about lighting obligations. The final point to be made here is that, following the Norman Conquest, from the late eleventh century onwards the record from England came to resemble that from the continent, with gifts for lights and with guilds that had a more clearly devotional purpose. The change may suggest that new practices were imported from the continent after 1066, or, more likely in my view, it could be that a change in styles of documentation revealed more of existing practices. Or, of course, there could have been change both in practice and in styles of document.

## Italy between the Carolingians and the communes

It was shown in the last chapter how Italian oil was appropriated by the Frankish rulers after Charlemagne's takeover of the Lombard kingdom in 774, and how those rulers gifted olive plantations to northern monasteries for the purpose of lighting.[66] It was observed that, apart from these major donations, Italian charters made occasional references to gifts for lighting throughout the early Middle Ages. This is another case of that low but constant level of reference that was evident from Francia in the same period, and, like Francia, northern and central Italy, including Rome, saw capitulary and conciliar legislation that urged the payment of tithe and the reservation of revenue for lighting. In other respects the situation in Italy, or at least in some parts of Italy, bears some similarity to that in later Anglo-Saxon England in so far as the hold of the larger baptismal churches, the *plebes* (Italian, *pievi*), over baptism, burial and tithe was challenged by the foundation of smaller churches that served a more local population.[67] The similarity here is with the minster churches in England which from the tenth century onwards were giving ground to new parish churches. In both regions, and, it is logical to assume, everywhere that there was competition between old and new, there was fresh impetus and opportunity to support religious activity and to acquire the spiritual benefits that came from providing resources over and above payment of the tithe. It is surely no accident that the earliest evidence for associations founded for such purposes comes from England and Italy. In England, as we have just seen, this was, from the tenth century onwards, in the form of guild regulations, and in Italy there is evidence from the same period for the foundation of confraternities, sometimes termed *consortia*. These were usually linked through a patron saint to a particular church or monastery. The names of members, many of which are occupational, suggest a constituency of people, women and men, from a social layer beneath that of the nobility, perhaps more of the 'middling sort'. Both the Italian confraternities and the Anglo-Saxon guilds looked after the welfare of their members, and both were notorious for drinking sessions, but in Italy the confraternity rules or statutes gave the associations a more explicit religious framing. Typically, as in the case of statutes from Ivrea in the first half of the tenth century, or in Modena's statutes from 980, members of both sexes paid one *denarius* a year for lighting.[68] This was a kind of annual membership fee and the rule that it should be paid tended to come first in the statutes. As was suggested in the last chapter, providing for the lights was a statement of good intent, and thus a fitting opening to an association's account of its aims, objectives and regulations. These were the salvation of its members, their material welfare and the means to achieve its aims and objectives. As Susan Reynolds noted, by the thirteenth century 'the towns of Italy ... were positively riddled with fraternities'.[69] I shall return later to the urban contexts in which confraternities proliferated, but the point to be made here is that that, even if these members' fees were in each case quite small, collectively they amounted to a significant contribution to the costs of lighting.

The oil and wax that the confraternities supplied for lighting was produced locally. In Chapter 2 we saw this demonstrated in early charters from Italy.[70] Donations to the church were often of land that included small olive groves and it was suggested that this indicated that a small-scale local production of oil had replaced the large-scale imports and regional trade in oil of the later Roman and immediate post-Roman periods. An exception was the larger-scale production of oil in the northern lakes region. Later charters show this same pattern continuing. Donations for the explicit purpose of providing for the lights become rarer, but olive groves appear as a common feature in the descriptions of land in documents of donation, sale, lease and exchange. In the Italian documentary record from the ninth century onwards, leases in fact become increasingly common, or even predominant. For the present purpose of tracking gifts to the church, this presents difficulties, for whereas donations can indicate what the gift was meant for, i.e. on occasion to provide for the lights, leases do not say why there were made, just that they *were* made (usually to last for 29 years). Nevertheless, the terms of leases from churches to lay people indicate, that where olive groves featured, oil was produced and taken by the church in question as part of the rent for the land, or as the *exenium* owed by the peasants on the land. Sometimes the amount of oil was specified as in a grant from King Charles ('the Fat') to his follower (*fidelis*) Ansprand in 883. Ansprand received a small monastery, Saint Michele at Cerreto in Lombardy. This was to be Ansprand's as long as he lived. He was to restore it and pay 100 lb of oil in *census* each year to the bishop of Bergamo.[71] That such rent in oil was destined for the lights is indicated in three charters from Pistoia in Tuscany dated to the 970s. In a charter from 970–1 one Anselm was leased land that included an olive grove. In a second charter of 973, his rent was said to be of silver worth 6 *denarii*, plus the obligation to provide for lights to burn *diurno vel nocturne*, day and night. This is repeated in a third charter. One assumes that it was oil from Anselm's lands that filled the lamps.[72] Leases from the church of Ravenna take us a little further in showing how oil might be produced from the land. Typically, those who held land with olive groves were to deliver half the olives to the church, and it was the *coloni*, the peasants on the land, who were to collect and bring them in. Many of the Ravenna leases have a kind of pairing between between facility and product. Thus where cornfields (*sationales*) are specified in the description of the land, milled grain (*granum manoelictile*) is what is owed in rent or *exenium*.[73] Likewise where there are olives in the description, there is oil in the rent or *exenium*. The difference between rent and *exenium* was that rent was owed by the person who held the land, but *exenium*, originally an honourable gift of supplies from peasant to superior, was in theory owed by the cultivators directly to the person or institution from whom the land was leased, in most cases this being a church. In practice the *exenium* was little different from the rent in that it was collected from the peasants by the landlord, and by the tenth century it no longer had honourable connotations.[74] In a vestigial sense the peasants, the *coloni*, were ecclesiastical dependants, but not part of a wider group of light-providing *censuales*. The leases do show, however, that the church, here the church of Ravenna, did have some influence over the production and collection of a portion of the oil, even if the *coloni* were no longer in any practical sense tributaries of the church. In a lease of 907 the *coloni* were to press the olives and deliver the oil, and in another of 911 the tenant was instructed to look after and 'improve' the trees, which presumably means pruning them.[75] In a document of 952 one Count John was leased land with olives and had to deliver one-third of the oil they produced to the coastal town of Fano. It was John's *missus* (agent) who was to carry the oil to Fano.[76] In a lease of 1017, concerning a hilly property in the Ferrara region in which there were apparently no olives, 3 lb of wax was to be delivered to the church at Ravenna at Easter.[77] This last reference confirms the impression that Ravenna acquired at least some proportion of its lighting materials, amongst other products, from its tenants. Though leases were generally renewable, and rent to the church could be termed *census*, they were not *precaria* in the sense that their rents were more than token payments, and the leases were not generally drawn up on request as a special favour.[78] They did not create a new class of ecclesiastical tributaries. Where the leases concerned *plebes* (baptismal churches) the lordly tenants usually enjoyed the tithes from those churches so that their peasants may not have contributed towards the cost of lighting through the general levy.[79]

As the Ravenna charters suggest, it was no doubt the peasants (*coloni*) attached to the land who actually tended the trees, collected the olives and pressed them for the oil. A unique run of charters from Limonta by Lake Como have been seen as showing that such work was regarded as arduous and that the peasants resisted having to perform these tasks. This dispute between peasants and landlords is well known to historians since Rodney Hilton cited it as an early example of peasant resistance in a sequence that would culminate in the great 'English Rising' of 1381.[80] There is in fact rather more to the 'Limonta dispute' than peasant resistance, for two powerful monasteries fought over the property, and it may have been the competition between them that gave the peasants the opportunity to speak out, or the disputing parties may in effect have put words into their mouths. Limonta lies at the end of the Bellagio peninsula that divides the two arms of Lake Como in the south. That there are no fewer than 22 documents that concern Limonta, the first from 835, and the last, supposedly from 998, is indicative of its value to whichever monastery controlled it. Some of the documents are forgeries, but that fact serves to emphasise Limonta's importance. Half of the charters are originals. Though a small property, a favourable climate made Limonta exceptionally productive, and oil was the product the monasteries desired the most. I will briefly run through what the sequence of documents tell us before drawing out some of the wider implications of this extraordinary cache of evidence.[81]

In 835 the Carolingian King Lothar I donated the Limonta estate to the monastery of Sant' Ambrogio in Milan. This was at the request of his wife Irmingard whose brother Hugh was buried in the monastery. As Ross Balzaretti has suggested, the grant was very likely to have been made, in part at least, to provide oil for a memorial light to burn before Hugh's tomb. The land included olive groves, six *mansi* (farmsteads) and the *mancipia* who occupied them. Thus far the grant is like many of those discussed in

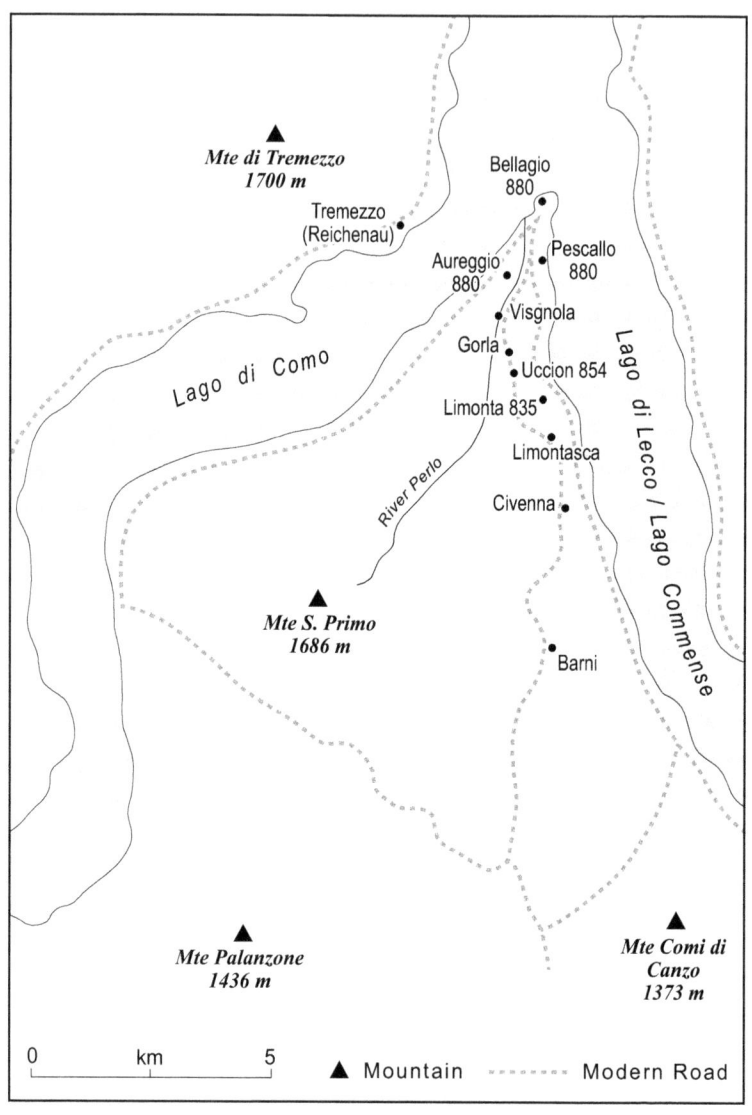

5 The Bellagio peninsula and the Limonta estate c. 880

the previous chapter: the donation by a Carolingian king of oil-producing lands in northern Italy to an important monastery, the gift having a political dimension. Lothar was seeking support in Italy after being driven out of Francia. Two years earlier, when he was still in with a chance of ruling north of the Alps, Lothar had made another grant by Lake Como, but that time it had been to the monastery of Saint Denis near Paris.[82] Now he concentrated on Italy, issuing 21 *diplomata* there between 834 and 840. In Limonta itself Sant' Ambrogio installed followers as clients, the transfer to tenants being witnessed by the locals. In 880 another Carolingian king, Charles 'the Fat', issued a confirmation of earlier grants which also gave the inhabitants of Limonta the right to hold an inquest (*inquisitum*) should there be a dispute over the property. It turns out, however, that all the witnesses in future inquests or inquiries would be clients of Sant' Ambrogio despite being local to the area. The 880 confirmation attracted the attention of the important monastery of Reichenau (at the southern tip of Germany), a monastery that was strongly supported by Charles the Fat. Reichenau claimed Limonta as its own. The locals testified that the six *mansi* did in fact belong to Sant' Ambrogio. Reichenau backed off, but it was by 896 in possession of the six *mansi* in Limonta, having, it seems, won the support of a king opposed to Sant' Ambrogio. This we know because in that year Sant' Ambrogio was said to have regained control. In 882 during the dispute with Reichenau, and, perhaps as Balzaretii suggests because that dispute opened up an opportunity, the *servi* (termed *mancipia* in the original grant) made their voices heard. Sant' Ambrogio claimed that the *servi* had to cultivate, collect and press the olives, and to transport the oil, like, as we have just seen, the *coloni* had to in some of the Ravenna leases. But the Limonta *servi* said 'it is not the case that we or our parents or our wives once had to collect, press and transport olives'. They were arguing that this was a new burden, for they were being treated as *servi* when they were not actually of that un-free status. They were, they said, descended from imperial *aldii*, peasants of a higher status.[83] Sant' Ambrogio used as witnesses clients who came from the region but were not inhabitants of Limonta itself, and, not surprisingly, the monastery won the day. In fact Sant' Ambrogio went further and claimed that all the inhabitants of Limonta were its *servi*, although earlier documents show that at least some of them had been free and independent of the monastery. A charter of 884, moreover, shows some of the so-called *servi* having property rights in and around the estate. Ross Balzaretti is surely right in arguing that here Sant' Ambrogio was seeking to increase its domination over all the inhabitants, hence the dispute.[84] The peasants, however, did not give up. At another court hearing in 905, they again lost and their burdens were actually increased. Between 906 and 910 the dispute moved to the royal court at Pavia where the peasants' claim to be *aldii* was again rejected. Finally, in 951 the German king, Otto I, issued a *diploma* which confirmed Sant' Ambrogio's possession of the six *mansi* and the olive groves in Limonta, but which did allow that the inhabitants included *aldii* as well as *servi*. No matter, for all of them were now under Sant' Ambrogio's control. Two further texts, purporting to be from 957 and 998 respectively, but which are regarded as later forgeries, 'recorded' Sant' Ambrogio's rights in Limonta, and in these the peasants' burdens with regard to the cultivation and processing of the olives were, unsurprisingly, even greater.[85]

What is immediately striking about the Limonta dossier is that such a small concern (six *mansi*) produced so many documents. The labour force in dispute numbered no more than 47 named people, unless these were just the heads of households, and even then fewer than three hundred souls could have been involved. The only figure for oil produced is from one part of the estate: an annual render of 60 lb of oil.[86] Even if that were but a fraction of overall production, given the size of the labour force, the whole must still have been tiny compared with, say, the 2,430 lb of oil the monastery of Bobbio hoped to collect from its properties around Lake Garda.[87] And since Limonta was far closer to Sant' Ambrogio in Milan than Garda was to Bobbio in the valley of the Trebbia, one wonders if Bobbio had just as much trouble in controlling its workforce in the olive groves. If so, we hear nothing about it. Ross Balzaretti has suggested that one reason for the outpouring of documents from Sant' Ambrogio was that it was aggressively expanding its interests in the Bellagio peninsula, and the pursuit of its seigneurial interests through the courts was a process that both required documentary evidence and resulted in production of yet more records.[88] Historians of a certain stripe (or perhaps one should say, 'of a certain age') might be inclined to side with Rodney Hilton in cheering on the peasants of Limonta. From another angle, however, it could be said that if Sant' Ambrogio was expanding its interests there, and thus in effect trying to increase production, it was making very slow progress. If it is possible to generalise from Sant' Ambrogio's experience, then it might be said that the difficulty in building up larger-scale production meant that oil would always be precious and scarce, even in climates and with soil which favoured the growing of olives. The difficulties in production meant that Limonta's oil was certainly worth fighting for, and worth fighting against.

That in Italy small amounts of oil could be obtained locally is another factor in the emergence of the confraternities that made small-scale donations of lighting materials to favoured ecclesiastical institutions throughout the peninsula. Episcopal churches such as Ravenna and large monasteries such as Sant' Ambrogio farmed or leased oil-producing land which met their lighting needs. Donations by individuals for the lights become rarer after the ninth century, and this may be because lighting needs were met by other means. The variety in the ways lights were provided for matches the complexity of conditions in Italy which comprehended regional differences in farming, and in political organization between the north, centre and south, and there were also differences in levels of urbanisation. As traditional powers waned in the north, towns developed levels of self-government which were moulded to their particular needs. To borrow the memorable title of Chris Wickham's book, they were 'sleepwalking into a new world', that is, into communal government.[89] Confraternities in the towns developed along similar lines as emerging interest groups consolidated their identities in organisations dedicated to the support of the towns' religious institutions, with lighting again at the forefront of their stated concerns. Around the year 1200 the scholar Boncampagno da Signa, who taught rhetoric at the University of Bologna, wrote in his work *Cedrus* of the proliferation of confraternities throughout 'much of Italy'.[90] Many were founded by young men and they had names like 'falcons', 'lions' and 'of the round table'. Boncampagno voiced the familiar concern that lots of people 'throughout the world' joined such confraternities, but only to fill their bellies.[91] In fact it was all getting out of hand: in the see of Florence there was a certain chapel built in honour of Saint Hilarius, where some rustics formed a fraternity to support the church, and they declared themselves to be 'parishoners of Saint Hilarius'. They were it seems, acting outside episcopal authority. Viewed from an urban lawyer's point of view, such confraternities needed rules, just as towns have officers and rules. Boncampagno's concern mirrors the growing complexity of Italian society. Towns were becoming larger and richer, and the constituency of those who supported the church was becoming more diverse. The ways in which lights were provided for in Italy in the central Middle Ages reflect that social and economic change.

## Spain

This study opened with the beginnings of the tradition that all churches should burn lights. It was seen that some of the earliest evidence for the practice came from Spain.[92] In Spain, being able to provide for the lights was a prerequisite for the founding and furnishing of a church. This was the instruction of the Councils of Braga and of Toledo which were held in the late sixth century. The second Council of Braga (572) had ruled that a church could not be consecrated unless there was written evidence of its endowment so that it was demonstrable that it could provide for the lights and for the upkeep of the building. There are at least 432 documents from Catalonia from the period from the ninth to the twelfth century which recorded the consecration of new or restored churches, and these indicate that the requirement to present evidence of endowment continued in at least one region south of the Pyrenees, although Catalonia looked north to Francia for much of this period.[93] There are 99 charters of consecration from the diocese of Urgell drawn up between 833 and 1219.[94] I shall draw on these, although what they say can be seen in charters across Catolonia. The Urgell charters list the possessions of the new churches and this served as the record of endowment. They also tell us what was owed by each church to the bishop in line with the stipulation of the earlier councils that church income was to be divided into three: one part for the bishop, another for the clergy serving the church and a third part for the maintenance of the building which included the lights. As late as 1080 we find a reference to one of the Visigothic councils, Toledo XI (675).[95] This was in the anathema clause of the document: whoever took from the endowment had to repay fourfold. In fact, after listing properties donated, the Urgell charters were mostly concerned with the bishop's third. Although this provides interesting information on what bishops hoped to get in terms of income from their parishes, it tells us less about lights. Sometimes, however, the *census* to the bishop included renders in wax, which might tell us how the cathedral lights were provided for.[96] There is also one reference to penance which asked for one *denarius* for the lights to pay for a minor infringement. For a larger sin the penitent was to provide to keep 40 lamps burning in the church throughout the 40 days before Easter.[97] All in all, 14 of the 99 Urgell documents can be associated with lighting.

It was shown in the last chapter how the instruction that a church had to have provision for lights as a condition of consecration was taken up by the Carolingian rulers in Francia, with the Council of Worms (868) repeating Braga more or less word for word. Though very few charters survive from Visigothic Spain, it was noted in an earlier discussion how what was in all probability a Visigothic formula (model document) for a charter of donation of land to a church for the provision of lights, for alms and for support of the clergy, was very similar in content and language to the actual donations recorded in charters from Francia from the eighth century onwards.[98] It was suggested then that this form of giving had its roots in late Roman law, hence its appearance in both Francia and Visigothic Spain. It might be assumed on the basis of this tradition and from the records of consecration that Francia and Spain would follow similar trajectories in the way in which the provision of lighting was addressed. But Spain and Francia did not in fact march in step here. For the first part, the destruction of the Visigothic polity in Spain by the forces of Islam meant that after the year 711 no more 'national' church councils were held and, with one exception, no more laws were issued by the kings. Visigothic law, however, continued to be cited. Whereas in Francia the rulers put themselves behind the effort to get lights into every church, in Spain this did not happen. Second, when charter evidence from Spain (from the north of the peninsula) does appear again in the later ninth century, there is no sign of anything like the Frankish *precaria*, hardly any leases of any other kind, very little commemoration through lights and no evidence of classes of light providers such as the *cerocensuales* or the *luminarii* that are to be found in Francia. Interestingly, though the Visigothic formula for donations is to be found in some tenth- and eleventh-century Spanish charters, one section that seems to have changed is the so-called 'dispositive', that is, where the donated land and its fixtures and fittings are described. In the original formula, *mancipia* (un-free people tied to the land) were to be named in family groups. This clause is missing in the later Spanish charters, in contrast to Frankish documents in which it often appears. It could be argued that such a difference between Frankish and Spanish documents reflected a social difference on the ground, with larger estates and more servile tenants (*mancipia*) in Francia than in Spain. The difference might alternatively be explained by divergency in scribal practice in the respective areas, but there are indications that it was more than this. Despite the early legislation ordering the resources of churches, Spain did not generally have organised parishes until the thirteenth century, although the process of parochialisation can be traced back into the eleventh century. From the Urgell and other Catalan documents there is some evidence for the levying of tithes and first fruits in Catalonia at least, but no evidence of revenue earmarked for the lights. Whether the bishops were able to bring in the revenues listed in the consecration documents is not clear, and there is no mention of tithes being allotted to third parties as they were in Francia. Churches in Spain seem often to have had several owners. Bishops had less influence over local churches. Local aristocrats were arguably less dominant. All of these factors had an impact on the way in which people gave to churches to maintain their lights.

The Arab conquest left only a few areas under Christian rule: the kingdom of Asturias to the north of the Cantabrian mountains, the

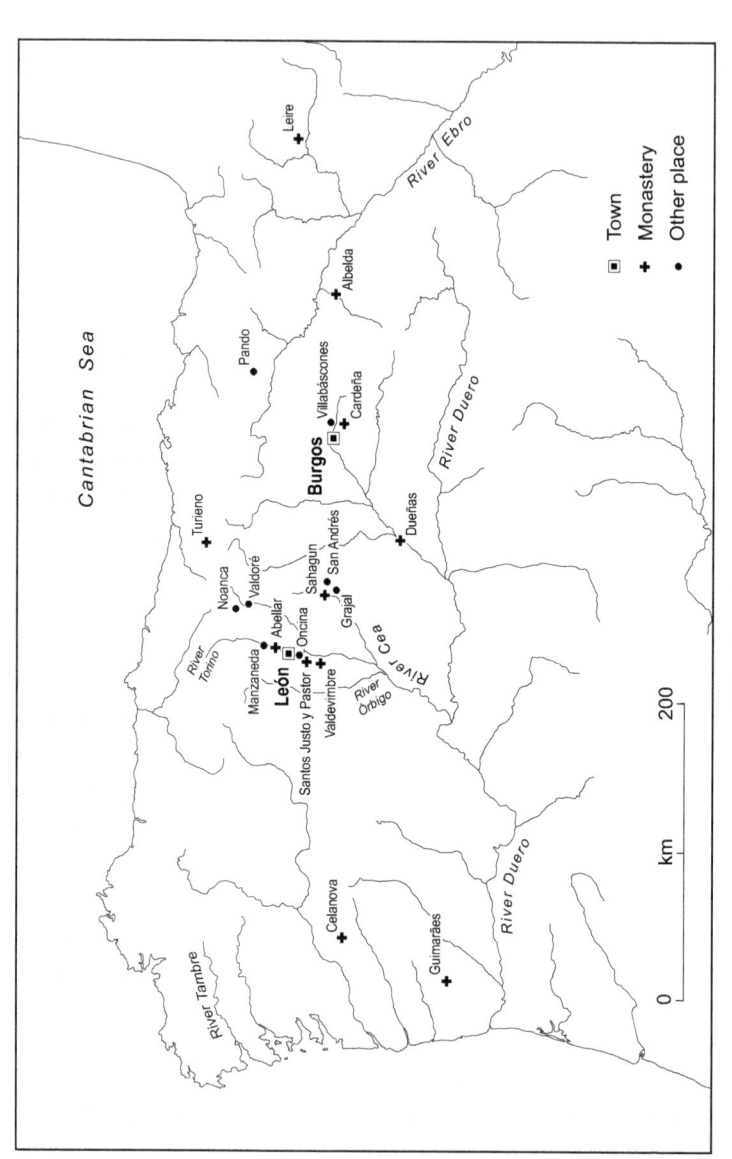

6 Northern Spain c. 950

kingdom of Pamplona and the several Catalan counties, some of which would be included in the later kingdom of Aragon. In the later ninth century the kingdom of Asturias would expand into the Duero valley in the northern *meseta* (table-land or plateau). What little evidence there is for the provision of lights often comes from the documents drawn up in the monasteries which were founded in this area. There are also documents from monasteries in the Asturias itself, from Galicia to the west, and from Pamplona/Navarre and Catalonia to the east. In all areas documents could also be drawn up by local priests or issued by royal and aristocratic households which had their own scribe. There are in addition some documents from the episcopal churches, the most important collection coming from Léon. An old nationalist school of Spanish history was dominated by the idea that Spain's development was driven by a determination to reconquer the territory lost to the Arabs after 711, a slow but at times dramatic process that lasted for over seven hundred years.[99] Part of this story was that the lands of the northern *meseta* were first depopulated by the Asturian kings and then repopulated with northerners as the Asturians advanced to the Duero. The implication was that the Duero territory was peopled by frontiersmen of a free and independent character, a people who had a subsequent impact on the very national character of the Spanish. Present thinking is that such a depopulation and repopulation are very unlikely to have taken place, for topographical and placename evidence suggests that there was a continuity of rural settlement in the area, and that this apparent frontier zone had in fact been very little affected by collapse of the Visigothic regime.[100] A supporting argument is that that regime had never been as centralised or as effective as its legislation gives one to believe.[101]

The essential problem here is that before the late ninth century there is very little written evidence from northern Spain. That dearth might itself be an indication of widespread disruption after 711, or it could suggest that bureaucratic organisation in the area had simply not developed before the later ninth century. On the other hand, the appearance of the Visigothic formula in charters of donation, plus the fact that a high proportion of charters were concerned with sales and exchanges of very small amounts of property between people who must have been peasants, argues for a relatively strong documentary habit.[102] The Catalan consecration documents, many of which purported to show small communities involved in the building of churches, likewise suggest great continuity in the bureaucratic tradition. When documents do appear, they give us an impression of a society in which political power was relatively weak and in which, for the tenth century at least, the aristocracy was still in the process of bringing peasant communities under their control, hence the lack of *mancipia*-types in the documents. The foundation and resourcing of monasteries were part of this process in which the nobles built up their landed resources and sought moral legitimation through pious donation. That is not to say that some monasteries had not been in existence before this time, and others were founded by influential clerics and committed religious who organised foundations.

Nearly all the references to lights in the Spanish charters of the tenth and eleventh centuries involve straightforward gifts of land to the church for the 'lights of the altar', for alms for the poor and for the support of the clergy. Remission of sins is generally what is hoped for in return for the gift. The proportion of charters that made provision for the lights is smallest in Catalonia which is surprising as this was the region most influenced by the Franks: it is the only region in which immunities were granted (at least 61 of them). Nevertheless there are very few Catalan charters that refer to lighting.[103] Privileges of immunity, the most royal of Frankish documents, had contained the clause that whatever income had formerly come from the 'fisc' should now go towards the lights. This clause is missing in all of the Catalan immunities, perhaps because in these documents the emphasis is on protection rather than income. From the cathedral of Léon 3.8 per cent of the 1,285 surviving charters up to the year 1230 mention lights.[104] The much smaller collection from the monastery of Valpuesta in Castile (78 documents in all) has a much higher proportion, 14 per cent, but the small size of the sample may distort the percentage here.[105] The large collection from the monastery of Sahagun near Léon runs at 7.7 per cent for the 727 charters produced up to the year 1073.[106] Sahagun does also have a large number of references to what look like oil lamps (*lucernae*) but this turns out to be part of a commonly used formula of 'anathema' (punishment clause): borrowing from Matthew 6:22 in which *lucerna* is used to mean 'eye' ('the eye is the lamp of the body'), the Sahagun formula is actually saying that whoever breaks the agreement or challenges the gift should have their eyes torn out of their living foreheads.[107] Fortunately there are no examples of this ever having happened. Each monastery or cathedral had variations on a few formulae. The Visigothic formula *ergo pro luminaribus ... donamus* is often shortened to *ut inde sit luminaria altariorum* which follows the gift, thus 'so that from this there may be lights for the altars'. Overall, these documents are businesslike and to the point. Their terseness may conceal the kind of detail to be found in Frankish and Italian charters, such as the spiritual setting of the gift, the precise arrangements for the lights, commemoration and, importantly, the link between the land and the lights. Despite the lack of detail, there is nevertheless sufficient material to make some basic observations about Spanish practice and to see that it had much in common with the other areas of Western Europe.

In northern Spain donations for the lights were made primarily by the powerful: kings, bishops, counts and other magnates. These were the patrons of the monasteries and the supporters of the episcopal churches. Not only could they afford to donate, in Spain as elsewhere in Europe, donation demonstrated social pre-eminence and showcased religious credentials. According to Wendy Davies, in the period up to 1000, 'Peasants were not much involved in making gifts in order to secure liturgical or some other form of commemoration or burial within the church'.[108] Perhaps they were 'not involved' because they could not afford to be. The fact that there were at least a few small gifts for lighting suggests that people were interested, if not involved, across the social spectrum.[109] Although there are no *mancipia* in the Spanish charters, there is evidence of landlord power over rural communities. The high number of peasant sales and exchanges might be linked to the growing pressure on those communities if peasants were mobilising wealth to meet new demands placed upon them. Davies cites one case of near starvation.[110] In a Valpuesta charter from 913 a couple sold land and 12 apple trees to another party for two pregnant sheep and 'a modius worth of wax'.[111] One wonders whether this couple were trying to meet a tribute payment in wax. In a charter from León dated to 936 one Ermenegild gave all his property to León.[112] This charter is very unusual in mentioning un-free people on the land. There were also *liberti*, formerly servile people whom Ermenegild had freed. They were to remain free on the sole condition that on the festivals of Saint James and Saint Eulalia they were to take candles and other offerings to the church. Ermenegild further gave one *villa* to León the income from which was to pay for his anniversary mass. Finally, Ermenegild's *pueri* (his servants or followers) 'from the least to the greatest' were to pay no form of *census*. Here we find all the elements that one might expect in a Frankish context, namely the un-free, the freed, commemoration and *census*. The difference between Francia and Spain is that these elements are common in Francia but rare in Spain. It is particularly interesting to see the protection for the freed in return for festival offerings including candles. The continuing obligations of the freed person to their former masters or mistresses was strongly emphasised in Visigothic law, so we are likely to be seeing a degree of social continuity here, but again the difference is one of scale. In Francia, especially in what would become Germany, the freed formed a substantial group in society. Each community was lined with *census* payers (the *Zensualität*) made up of the freed and of those on the lands of precarial lease holders. In Spain such groups cannot be identified, although a monastery such as Celanova did have large groups of dependants owing labour or dues (we shall meet some of its beekeepers shortly).[113] Payment for lights seems to have been ad hoc rather than systematic.

That actual payments for the lights came from the income from land is clear. In the Urgell consecrations the income can be seen to be made up of payments in kind, mostly in grain and animal products, especially ham, which were part of tithe or 'first fruits' (*primitiae*). Also frequently mentioned are *ebdomada*, weekly services provided by the inhabitants, but it is impossible to know what these amounted to, and what the status was of those who performed them. In tenth-century charters across the different regions it is notable that nearly all the lights were fuelled with wax, and from the Valpuesta charter we have just seen the possibility that there was some kind of tribute in wax. In the confirmation of a gift to the monastery of Celanova in Galicia dated to 986, people were included in the donation, but again their status cannot be known.[114] In addition there were 'men the bishop obtained' in various places. Possibly these were war captives. The donor, Vermudo III, also gave to Celanova 'for the lights of the church' the beekeepers (*mellarios*) dwelling in four named places.[115] These people produced the wax for the lights. What happened to the much greater quantities of honey they must also have produced is not mentioned. As in England two centuries earlier, wax was hallowed, or even venerated as a mysterious substance that was Christlike in the way in which it sacrificed itself to bring forth light. In an antiphonary (book of religious services, psalms, payers and responses) from León put together between 917and 970, there are instructions on how to conduct the ceremony of the Paschal candle and a prayer which venerates the wax.[116] In this dramatic Easter ritual, common throughout Europe, a special candle was lit to herald Christ's resurrection on the third day. Darkness was suddenly turned into light and a host of candles were lit from the original. In a dark church following a night of vigils this must have quite spectacular. The Christ analogy was literally marked by the bishop as he inscribed the letters 'alpha' and 'omega' (to symbolise the beginning and the end) on opposite sides of the candle separated by the sign of the cross. In the prayer to bless the candle, wax is eulogised for its purity. That was what made it the bringer of true light. Its origin in flowers meant that it came from a virginal source. It came from a parent which did not know the error of corruption. The candle wick was sheathed in a snow-white mystery and why should it not seek to enlarge itself under the cover of the flames?

None of this could happen without heavenly virtue through which the fire sought nourishment in the torrent.[117] Though this passage is a little hard to understand, it is clear that wax was a substance that was very special in the way in which it brought a spiritually nourishing light to the Christians. That it was so valued helps explain why people were keen to donate wax for the lights even where this was not demanded by way of tribute.

Despite the emphasis on lighting by wax, there are a few references to oil and oil lamps in the tenth century. For instance a Sahagun charter of 930 refers to a hanging lamp.[118] There are more references to oil in the eleventh and twelfth centuries when it seems to have become more available. There may have been an extension of olive farming in some micro-climates in the north-east. The Christian kingdoms were also a lot richer after the collapse of the Umayyad caliphate in 1031, for that resulted in the rise of numerous small Muslim kingdoms, the *ta'ifa*. The *ta'ifa* paid significant tribute or protection money to the Christian kingdoms. They may have supplied them with oil too. In a charter of 1071 from the monastery of Leire in Navarre, Leire was given a tithe of 70 silver *solidi* from four *villae* to buy oil, wax and incense.[119] The run of Leire charters in fact illustrates the changes taking place across the eleventh century and these included a measure of monastic reform as houses were encouraged to conform to the Benedictine rule, although whether they did conform in practice is questionable. In the 1071 charter a church transferred to Leire was given a monastic order said to have been according to the Rule of Saint Benedict. We also see more references to commemoration through lights as well as leases to followers which look rather like Frankish *beneficia*. A set of documents concerning the *villa* of Arascués to the north of Huesca makes the point about change.[120] First of all, in 1098 King Peter of Pamplona restored property unjustly taken from Leire. To this he added the *villa* Arascués 'to provide lights' for Leire. The grant included *census* and *tributum*, plus half the tolls from the town of Rosta, one-tenth of the market dues there and 1,000 '*solidi* of *denarii*' from the market dues of Huesca. In a second charter issued on the same day, the gifts were confirmed, with the interesting additional detail that the Rosta tolls were levied on the Jews. Peter also added part of an olive grove, which could explain Arascués's association with the lighting needs of Leire. Then in 1113 King Alfonso, Peter's brother, gave more of Arascués's resources, and this included the second half of the olive grove. This was to pay for eight lamps to burn every night for his soul and for the souls of his relatives. But in 1136 King Ramiro took the share Alfonso had donated to Leire and let it out to one Oto who swore that it would be returned to Leire on his death. This did not happen. In 1186 King Alfonso II recalled

Ramiro's charter which had been a chirograph. Oto's family produced their own charter saying that Arascués was theirs by hereditary right, but as their document it did not match Leire's half of the chirograph it was declared invalid and destroyed in court. Leire thus got back its olive grove. Apart from showing the changing fortunes of Aragon's rulers – sometime kings of Pamplona, then kings of Aragon and counts of Barcelona and *marchiones* of Provence – the Leire charters show rulers making lease agreements with followers, and also indicate that rulers were able to benefit from growing market activity. In the Urgell consecrations we see a similar change across the eleventh century. Endowments began to include income from, or interest in, mills and from rights held over people. *Castella*, *castra* and *turri* (fortified towers) appear more frequently. There are more olive groves and more olive oil in the gifts. Pierre Bonnassie read the Urgell sequence in the context of growing aristocratic power.[121] The early consecrations, he noted, were of churches built and endowed by local communities who then appointed the clergy and collected the tithe, distributing this themselves apart from the portion reserved, according to canon law, to the bishop. From the eleventh century an increasing proportion of church foundations came from the elite whose own lands and rights formed the endowments, and who then went on to control the new churches. Bonnassie discussed this in terms of the rise of 'feudalism', a subject in which he was supremely interested. He worked within a school of history that was keen to find the trigger for the decline of free communities and the rise of serfdom, calling this shift a veritable 'revolution'. The trigger was supposedly the collapse of central or 'public' authority. Present scholarship is less convinced that there was any sudden change here, and fears that relating social change to the fate of public authority is to exaggerate the speed of that authority's decline, and to overestimate the affective power it had supposedly once possessed. Another objection to the 'rise of feudalism' model is that its proponents read charters with the collapse of public authority too firmly in mind and missed other elements in the evidence. In the case of the Catalan consecration documents such as those from Urgell it has been convincingly argued that the community aspect is largely an episcopal fiction. There was a scribal tradition that churches had been newly founded by communities whereas in fact what was being recorded was bishops taking control of long-established churches.[122] Instead of a precipitate collapse of public authority, a gradual hardening of aristocratic rights is envisaged, a 'reification' of rights and privileges to borrow the term used by Charles West.[123] Despite strong regional differences, the charter evidence from northern Spain would support the picture of a gradual aristocratic encroachment on peasant communities, and the provision of lighting is as good a guide as any to this lengthy transformation, as well as to the variety in regional and local arrangements. But what the incidence of peasant transactions in that evidence also shows us is that a great deal of peasant and community affairs took place without the influence or interference of kings, nobles and the higher clergy.

Oil may have been becoming more available in the eleventh century, but as the dispute over Arascués's olive groves would indicate, it was still scarce and valuable. There is a strong contrast here with Muslim Spain, or at least with the far south of the peninsula. As was briefly noted in the last chapter, there was, according to the tenth-century geographer Ahmad al-Rāzi, such an abundance of oil in the Seville region that some of it had to be exported by boat to 'the East' to keep the price up in Spain. There is also a reference in one tenth-century Arabic formulary to the production and sale of oil, which, interestingly, distinguished between oil from the first pressing of the olive and oil produced by superheating the olives in water: the one being much more valuable than the other, just as we find in the modern supermarket.[124] The abundance of oil in the south raises the question of why more oil did not make it north from al-Andalus, especially during the *ta'ifa* period when the Christian kingdoms were raising large tributes from the southern city-territories. There is no obvious answer except to note that in the north the emphasis on the purity and spiritual efficacy of wax might mean that demand for oil remained low there. It could also be suggested that trade between north and south in Spain was in any case patchy, despite recent views on the permeability of the Christian–Muslim frontier. Arabic coins were indeed in use in the north and there was obvious trade in textiles and metalwork, which makes the absence of oil even more curious. It is true, however, that nowhere in Europe do we see the transfer of oil in any great amount from regions of abundance to areas of scarcity. Italy is another example: there too there is no evidence that oil travelled from the south, where it was produced in quantity, to the north which relied on small centres of production such as we saw in Limonta and the Lakes region.

There are no charters from al-Andalus which might indicate what the oil was used for, but something can be still said about the nature of pious donations in Muslim Spain. This comes from the *Mālikī* tradition of jurisprudence in which answers were given to questions about the nature and conditions of religious gifts. Spanning the period from the ninth to the sixteenth centuries these jurisprudential texts are said to respond to a certain social reality.[125] In the sense that norms were generated by genuine questions and cases, they have something in common with the Arabic formulary just mentioned, but also with the formularies from the Latin Christian world. The *hubs* (pl. *abbās*) was a pious endowment. The term more often used outside Spain is *waqf* (pl. *awqāf*). A donation could be made to equip a mosque with prayer mats, lighting oil and candles. There was a certain reverence for light as reflection of the truth, and following the Prophet's words in *sura* XXIV, 35 of the Qur'ān, a light was to be placed in the prayer niche (the *mihrāb*) of the mosque.[126] But as seen in the *Mālikī* texts, lighting in mosques was utilitarian. Evening prayers required illumination, and lights enabled the reading of the *hadith*, the collection of the Prophet's sayings.[127] The larger mosques had great numbers of lamps and candles. As in the Christian West rulers marked their status by the donation of lamps and candelabra. The mosque at Cordoba was said to have had 113 chandeliers, the largest of which held a thousand lamps, the smallest 12.[128] Just over 24 per cent of the jurisprudential texts deal with private or family endowments. These, known as *mu'aqqab*, had the same form as the pious endowment but were made to benefit the donor's descendants who were to enjoy the usufruct (*manfa'a*) of whatever was given. The element of piety comes only in the requirement that the donor name a *marja'* connected to the faith. The *marja'* was a beneficiary of last instance who would get the property when the donor's line of descent had become extinct. Given that that descent lines could be broadly defined, this was unlikely to happen. These family donations look similar to lease arrangements north of the Pyrenees where a strategy for preserving family inheritance was made possible through donation to a religious institution and the retention of usufruct. Usufruct arrangements in Europe had their origins in late Roman law. This is unlikely to be the case with the Islamic endowments which traced themselves back to precedent in the Qur'ān. It is thus striking to see how two separate traditions arrived at more or less the same point, that of 'keeping-while-giving', to borrow Annette Weiner's memorable formulation.[129] On the one hand the similarity in strategy suggests broadly comparable social conditions in which religious institutions backed family inheritance, albeit in their own long-term interests. But on the other hand, the similarity raises questions about difference, and the difference here lies in the very specific role of lights within Christian religious practice as opposed to the more utilitarian approach towards the lights in Islam.

Contrasting ecclesiastical and charter sources with the material from al-Andalus (and elsewhere in the Islamic world) points up the very precise way in which the Mosaic injunction to keep a light burning before the tabernacle had been incorporated by the medieval church. It was a universal demand, met everywhere, and it is very important to note that the proportion of references to lighting in the various kinds of written material is roughly similar (running at around 7 per cent) all across Europe, even though different regions had very different histories. What the Spanish evidence in particular shows is how that demand was met in the unique circumstances of northern Spain after the disappearance of the Visigothic regime. We have seen that there was strong continuity in documentary tradition and in religious norms there, but the growing prominence of the elite in providing material for the lights shows us how the influence of the nobility on communities was becoming more evident. One might be tempted to contrast Spain with England, Francia and Italy where we get the impression that a 'middling sort' of people was emerging as economic activity increased in town and country. This was a class that would form the guilds and confraternities that paid for so many of the lights in the central and late Middle Ages. The contrast may, however, be a false one, for the large proportion of transactions at peasant level in tenth- and eleventh-century Spain could suggest that the 'middling sort' did not so much emerge as had always been there, and would remain despite any growth in aristocratic power.

## Conclusion

People in each of the areas examined in this chapter made provision for perpetual lighting in ways that reflected their different histories. The salient point is that despite different local arrangements, say, the demand for apparently tax-like lighting dues in England as distinct from the raising of funds or material as part of lease agreements in Italy, provision *was* made everywhere, and this reveals the way in which providing for the lights had become a fixture in religious culture throughout Christian Europe. Some of the apparent difference relates to the nature and variety of the record. The Frankish polyptychs, for instance, give a picture of categories of people (like the *luminarii* or *haistaldi*) that are simply invisible in Spanish charters. The record from England is characteristically short of the kind of detail one finds in the Limonta dossier. But it is evident that throughout Western Europe people did voluntarily devote resources to the lights, and the impression is that the numbers of such people were growing in the tenth and eleventh centuries as guilds and confraternities proliferated. It may be tempting, but it is probably wrong, to try to align the evidence for lighting with a growth in the power of the nobility and the reification of rights and privileges that have been associated with the 'feudal revolution'. One feature that has been regarded as a consequence of that 'revolution' is the so-called 'Peace Movement', which was another form of religious solidarity. According to the mid-twentieth-century model in which the collapse of 'public authority' in the post-Carolingian world was said to have led to widespread oppression and the forcing of the peasantry into serfdom, the Church was believed to have stepped in to protect the powerless. They did this by calling a series of meetings or councils at which attempts were made to curtail the violence of the warrior class.[130] Such a way of thinking is no longer in vogue, just as the 'feudal revolution' itself is now also out of favour amongst historians,[131] and one reason for the change of mind about the aims of the 'Peace Movement' is that a discourse of peace can be found in regions in which there was apparently no 'feudal revolution'. England and Germany in the tenth and eleventh centuries are the prime examples here. The 'Peace Movement' now tends to be seen as another phase of that church reform once urged by the Carolingian rulers.[132] At the same time it is held to reflect a rise in piety and religious devotion in which monasteries were to be made fit for the purpose of salvation, and in which parishioners called for their priests to be more like monks, that is, celibate and disciplined. The next step, from the later eleventh century onwards, would be reform that not only aimed to bring discipline to the entire ecclesiastical hierarchy but also sought to disentangle the Church from secular involvement. This reform, known as 'Gregorian Reform', emanated from the Papacy, but fed off the dynamic of a rising piety amongst the laity. This is the context in which confraternities and guilds came to be established. A second element, strangely ignored in the debate about the 'feudal revolution', was a growth in economic activity that stimulated the development of towns. The result was not only that people wished (as some had always wished) to contribute material for worship, but also that an increasing range of people could now afford to do so, especially when they grouped themselves for this purpose. These are the kind of people I have characterised as the 'middling sort' and yet again it is notable that they appear right across Europe in the tenth and eleventh centuries. As their rules show, the fee for membership of the confraternities was generally low, often only 2 *denarii* a year. But collectively the members had considerable clout. A theme to be followed in the rest of this study is the way in which this influence was exercised, for lay associations came to play such an important part in funding the maintenance of lights that the withdrawal of their support meant that in large parts of Europe the practice of keeping a perpetual flame burning on the altar came to an abrupt end. This is what would happen in the early Protestant Reformation.

I began this chapter with a search for the kind of people who would later form fraternities and guilds. I end it at a point at which fraternities had become ubiquitous and with an illustrated charter that celebrates the formation of such a group in support of the monastery of Saint Martin's at Canigou in Roussillon in the eastern Pyrennees. This *communitatis confratria* was formed in 1195 and the charter was drawn up in about the year 1200.[133]

We see here in the top half of the illustration Christ in majesty surrounded by the four evangelists. Beneath Christ is the priest of the church of Saint Martin at Canigou celebrating mass, possibly signifying the saying of mass for a deceased member. To his right we see the members of the confraternity represented by three women and three men. One is kneeling and five are standing before two hanging lamps. These look like glass lamps of a kind that would be in fairly common use throughout the later Middle Ages, and underneath them is a device for catching drips.[134] The charter that follows the illustration says that the association has been formed for the remission of the sins of its members who will maintain a lamp burning before the altar 'day and night'. The members will each pay 2 *denarii* on the festival of Saint Martin. One day a week the priest in charge of this church will pray for deceased members and say mass at the altar for those still living. When a member dies a mass will be sung for them within thirty days and they will be buried in the monastery's cemetery. If there is anything left over after paying for the lights, it should be put to good use. The charter names 37 founding members before the manuscript breaks off. Despite the presence of the three women in the illustration, all the names on the charter are of males. The list includes monks and clergy. Some of the members have names such as 'of the tower' which would suggest that they were of the knightly class; most have a locative designation (for instance 'Petrus of Aspira'). There is a prior, a *capellanus* and a *camerarius* (treasurer). These are but faint indicators of social status, but given the low entry fee and the apparent mixture of lesser noble and non-noble it could be that the Canigou confraternity represented a social mix not unlike that seen in the eleventh- and twelfth-century manumissions from England. Finally, the Canigou list reminds us that, despite a Gregorian rhetoric of disentanglement from the secular, the rise of the confraternities in the twelfth century meant that churches of all kinds and monasteries were actually becoming more entangled with local communities.

Guilds, gifts and confraternities all relate to a strong voluntary element in the provision for lights. But it should be understood that there was also an involuntary element. The light providers in the polpytychs were hereditary payers who had no choice in the matter. The same is true of Italian

7 Illustration from the foundation charter of the confraternity of Saint Martin of Canigou

peasants made to collect olives and produce oil as part of their rent or in *exenia*. It would be hard to envisage the peasants of Limonta forming a confraternity in support of Sant' Ambrogio, an institution they were forced to work for. I shall return to this layer of providers in the next chapter. There the focus will be on the formation of the *Zensualität* in Germany and on the question of why a similar group did not form in France. Where payment was not voluntary, and where those who paid were under the control of others, there one might expect to see some effect of the hardening of rights and privileges that has been associated with the 'feudal revolution'. Did conditions deteriorate for such people? Or if they did not, might this suggest that the 'feudal revolution' is something of a historical red-herring?

**Notes**

1 *Recueil des chartes de Charles II Le Chauve*, ed. G. Tessier, 3 vols (Paris, 1941, 1952, 1955).
2 See above, Chapter 3.
3 *Diplomata Belgica ante Annum Millesimum Centesimum Scripta*, ed. M. Gysseling and A. Koch (Brussels, 1950), nos 26, 27, pp. 47, 48.
4 *Diplomatica Belgica*, nos 29, 31, pp. 51–2, 54.
5 *Diplomatica Belgica*, no. 33, pp. 56–7.
6 *Diplomatica Belgica*, no. 37, pp. 67–9. The document opens with the statement: *Brevis de substantia et censu et dispensa Domini Salvatore, quando Hilduinus abbas inuste kalendis septembris a manibus Gundeberti omnia abstulit.*
7 The dictionary definition of a *bunuarium* is one-quarter of an acre, as in the modern French *bonnier*: J.-F. Niermeyer, *Mediae Latinitatis Lexicon Minus* (Leiden, 1984), p. 107. *Bunuaria* calculated from amounts of land given in the polyptych of Saint Bertin and other documents of the ninth century are around the higher level of 1.28–1.38 hectares, which roughly equals 3.2–3.4 acres. Thus Ganshof in his commentary of the polyptych of Saint Bertin: *Le polyptyque de l'abbaye de Saint Bertin (844–859)*, ed. F. L. Ganshof (Paris, 1975), p. 10.
8 The reason for not equating *mancipia* with serfs here is that, in the polyptych of the abbey, *mancipia* are treated as a category separate from the *servi*. See below note 20.
9 *Item que annuatim ex his rebus expendebantur ad luminare, cera, oleum, pinguedo et universe necessitates in sanctuario Dei, clerici VIII pascebantur, vestiebantur.*
10 Tessier, *Recueil*, no. 489, vol. 2, pp. 624–5, included amongst the *actes faux* at the end of the edition. It was treated as genuine by Gysseling and Koch, *Diplomatica Belgica*, no. 36, pp. 65–6.
11 Tessier, *Recueil*, no. 230, vol. 2, p. 14.
12 Tessier, *Recueil*, nos 370, 378, pp. 324, 346.

13 Tessier, *Recueil*, no. 246, vol. 2, pp. 55–6.
14 Tessier, *Recueil*, no. 333, vol. 2, p. 237.
15 Tessier, *Recueil*, no. 379, p. 349.
16 For example a charter of 864 (Tessier, *Recueil*, no. 273, p. 114) has a reference to glassworkers (*vitrearii*) on lands given to the monastery of Saint Amand, this being a first reference to such specialists.
17 *Edictum Pistense, MGH Capitularia* II, ed. A. Boretius and V. Krause (Hanover, 1897), pp. 310–28. Cc. 8–24, pp. 314–20, dealt extensively with coinage, markets, weights and measures, c. 31, pp. 323–4, with the consequence of migration for seasonal labour.
18 The evidence of the poylptychs forms the backbone of studies of the Carolingian economy and rural society as for example in A. Verhulst, *The Carolingian Economy* (Cambridge, 2002), see especially pp. 37–52.
19 The Saint Bertin survey explicitly excluded lands let out as *beneficia* to warriors as these did not provide income for the monks, which implies that the monastery was not receiving *census* from them. The survey was of the lands that supplied the monks, but *absque his que in aliis ministeriis erant distribute* [e.g. like the *ministerium* of the Stenetland church] *vel qui militibus et cavallariis erant beneficiate. Polyptyque de Saint Bertin*, p. 13.
20 For a summary discussion of the document and the Saint Bertin social landscape, Y. Morimoto, 'Problèmes autour du polyptyque de Saint-Bertin (844–859)', in Y. Morimoto, *Études sur l'économie rurale du haut Moyen Âge. Historiographie, regime domanial, polyptyques carolingiennes* (Brussels, 2008), pp. 399–424, first published in A. Verhulst (ed.), *Le grand domaine aux époques mérovingienne et carolingienne / Die Grundherrschaft im frühen Mittelalter* (Ghent, 1985), pp. 125–52. See also Y. Morimoto, 'Aspects of the early medieval peasant economy as revealed in the polyptych of Prüm', in P. Linehan, J. Nelson and M. Costambeys (eds), *The Medieval World*, 2nd edn (London, 2017), pp. 705–19.
21 There were in addition seven *homines de lumine*, each of whom owed wax to the value of 2 *denarii*.
22 There were, by comparison, 262 *mancipia*, 101 *servi*, 65 *ancillae*, 217 *lunarii*, 141 *prebendarii* and 263 *herescarii*, plus 147 'men who did two days [work] a year' and 76 'men who did two days [work] a week'.
23 *Le polyptyque de Saint Bertin*, p. 29.
24 *Le polyptyque et le listes de cens de l'abbaye de Saint-Remi de Reims (IXe–XIe siècles)*, ed. J.-P. Devroey (Reims, 1984), p. 54.
25 *Das Polyptychon von Saint-Germain-des-Prés*, ed. D. Hägermann (Cologne, Weimar and Vienna, 1993), c. 24, pp. 209–10.
26 *Das Polyptychon von Saint-Germain*, pp. 83, 98, 99.
27 *Le polyptyque et les listes de biens de l'abbaye de Saint-Pierre de Lobbes (IXe–XIe siècles)*, ed J.-P. Devroey (Brussels, 1986), pp. cvii–cviii. On the *geneats* and their duties, *The Rights and Ranks of People*, trans. D. C. Douglas, *English Historical Documents* II (London, 1961), pp. 813–16.

28 *Le polyptyque de Saint Bertin*, pp. 18–19.
29 Morimoto, 'Polyptyque de Saint-Bertin', p. 416. He thought that the 12 *bunuaria mansi* were the result of the monastery reorganising peasant tenures in its vicinity.
30 *Laws of Ine*, trans. D. Whitelock, *English Historical Documents* I (London, 1968), pp. 364–72, c. 67, p. 271: yardlands held for fixed rents. No other services could be demanded unless a lord had furnished the yardlander with a dwelling; survey of Tidenham (c. 1060), trans. D. C. Douglas, *English Historical Documents* II, pp. 817–18.
31 For both sides of the argument, Y. Morimoto, 'Aspects of the early medieval peasant economy of Prüm', pp. 705–19.
32 L. Kuchenbuch, *Bäuerliche Gesellschaft und Klosterherrschaft im 9 Jahrhundert*, Vierteljahrschrift für social und Wirtschaftsgeschichte, Beiheft 61 (Wiesbaden, 1978), pp. 195–244.
33 Devroey, *Lobbes*, pp. cxxii–cxxiv.
34 Kuchenbuch, *Bäuerliche Gesellschaft*, pp. 157–68.
35 This useful listing of the conditions of 'freedom' and 'un-freedom' is drawn from J.-P. Devroey, *Puissants et misérables. Système social et monde paysan dans l'Europe des Francs (vi–ix siècles)* (Brussels, 2006), pp. 267–79. Alice Rio has more recently further undermined distinctions between free and un-free, arguing that conditions owed more to social negotiation than to legal category: A. Rio, *Slavery after Rome 500–1100* (Oxford, 2017), esp. pp. 98–112.
36 Devroey, *Puissants et misérables*, pp. 269–75.
37 *Cartulaire del'abbaye de Gorze*, ed. A. D'Herbomez (Paris, 1898), no. 100.
38 *MGH Diplomata Regum et Imperatorum Germaniae* I (Hanover, 1879–84), no. 121.
39 R. Kaiser, *Trunkenheit und Gewalt im Mittelalter* (Cologne, Weimar and Vienna, 2002), pp. 148–51.
40 Kaiser, *Trunkenheit*, pp. 144–65.
41 On the early associations, O. G. Oexle, '"Conjuratio" et "ghilde" dans l'Antiquité et dans le Haut Moyen Age. Remarques sur la continuité des forms de la vie sociale', *Francia* 19 (1982), 1–19.
42 *MGH Capitularia* I, no. 20, pp. 46–51, c. 16, p. 51: *De sacramentis per gildonia coniurantibus invicem, ut nemo facere praesumant*. See P. D. King, *Charlemagne. Tanslated Sources* (Lambrigg, 1987), no. 2, pp. 203–5, but note that King does not use the term 'guild' to translate *gildonia*.
43 The most notorious example of such a crackdown comes from the *Annals of Saint Bertin* for the year 859 when peasants on the Channel coast formed a *coniuratio* in order to resist Viking raids, but were massacred by Frankish lords who clearly regarded their *coniuratio* as a greater threat to order than the Vikings themselves: *Annals of Saint Bertin* s.a. 859, trans. J. Nelson (Manchester, 1991).
44 See above, Chapter 3, for Hincmar of Reims's reference to guild activities.
45 A.-J. Bijsterveld, 'Looking for common ground: from monastic *fraternitas* to lay confraternity in the southern Low Countries in the tenth to twelfth centuries',

in E. Jamroziak and J. Burton (eds), *Religious and Laity in Western Europe 1000–1400. Interaction, Negotiation and Power* (Turnhout, 2006), pp. 287–309.
46 Oexle, '"Conjuratio" et "ghilde"', 7–15.
47 Above, pp. 37–8.
48 *Vercelli Homily XVI*, ed. D. Scragg, *Old English Text Series* O.S. 300 (1992), p. 27.
49 See notes 27 and 30 above.
50 *Charters of Christ Church Canterbury*, ed. N. Brooks and S. Kelly (Oxford, 2013), no. 87.
51 I am indebted to Stuart Pracy for sharing with me his PhD research on this subject.
52 Thus D. Pelteret, *Slavery in Early Medieval England* (Woodbridge, 1995), pp. 131–62.
53 Rio, *Slavery after Rome*, pp. 114–26.
54 S. Pracy, 'Social Mobility and Manumissions in Early Medieval England', *Haskins Society Journal* 31 (forthcoming, 2020).
55 Kaiser, *Trunkenheit*, pp. 144–58; G. Rosser, 'The Anglo-Saxon gilds', in J. Blair (ed.), *Minsters and Parish Churches. The Local Church in Transition 950–1200* (Oxford, 1988), pp. 31–4. Note that Rosser assumed the 'pagan' origins of guilds. For the tendency towards association amongst peers, and further argument against 'pagan' and 'Germanic' influences, J. Nelson, 'Peers in the early Middle Ages', in P. Stafford, J.Nelson and J. Martindale (eds), *Law, Laity and Solidarities. Essays in Honour of Susan Reynolds* (Manchester, 2001), pp. 27–46, esp. pp. 33–46. See now also R. Naismith, 'Guilds, States and Societies in the Early Middle Ages', *Early Medieval Europe* (forthcoming), with emphasis on the guilds' social solidarity and their perceived social resistance.
56 *Councils and Synods with Other Documents Relating to the English Church*, part I, 871–1066, ed. D. Whitelock, M. Brett and C. N. L. Brooke (Oxford, 1981), no. 67, pp. 517–20.
57 *Councils and Synods* I, no. 16, pp. 58–9.
58 *Councils and Synods* I, no. 47, 6.2, p. 308.
59 *Councils and Synods* I, no. 48, c. 42, p. 328, c. 54, pp. 331–2.
60 *Councils and Synods* I, no 49, 11.1, p. 31. The Latin paraphrase of this injunction is *Lumina etiam cereorum ter in annis reddantur*; no. 52, 12.1, p. 393.
61 The clearest and strongest statement of the maximalist view is that of J. Campbell in 'Observations on English Government from the Tenth to the Twelfth Century', *Transactions of the Royal Historical Society* 5th series 25 (1975), 39–54, reprinted J. Campbell, *Essays in Anglo-Saxon History* (London, 1986), no. 10: 'The shires of the Midlands, the hundredal system, the burghal system, planned towns, Danegeld, and the currency reveal a capacity for change and for order hardly matched until the nineteenth century', at p. 159.
62 King Edgar's Code at Andover, cc. 1–3, trans. D. Whitelock, *English Historical Documents* I (London, 1955), p. 395.
63 J. Blair, *The Church in Anglo-Saxon Society* (Oxford, 2005), p. 436.

64 Blair, *The Church in Anglo-Saxon Society*, pp. 426–63.
65 Roy Flechner makes the point that from Irish material in this period it is scarcely possible even to describe the social structure on church estates: R. Flechner, 'Identifying Monks in Early Medieval Britain and Ireland: a Reflection on Legal and Economic Aspects', *Settimane di Spoleto* 64 (2017), 805–44.
66 Above, pp. 81–3.
67 This pertains above all to Lombardy and Tuscany. In the south of Italy there were fewer *plebes* and the payment of the tithe was hardly compulsory. See S. Wood, *The Proprietary Church in the Medieval West* (Oxford, 2006), pp. 86–91.
68 G. Meersseman, *Ordo Fraternitas. Confraternite e Pieta del Laici nel Medieovo*, 3 vols, *Italia Sacra. Studi e documenti di storia ecclesiastica* 24–6 (Rome, 1977), p. 95 on Ivrea, p. 97 on Modena. The latter's statutes open: 'those men and women named here give each year one *denarius* for the lights for the redemption of their souls, to light the church of God so that God might make their souls shine in paradise'.
69 S. Reynolds, *Kingdoms and Communities in Western Europe 900–1300* (Oxford, 1984), p. 74.
70 Above, pp. 63–6.
71 Wood, *Proprietary Church*, p. 396.
72 *Regesta Chartarum Pistorensium*, no editor given (Pistoia, 1973), nos 88, 91, 100, pp. 71–2, 74–5, 82–3.
73 This is a guess at the meaning of the word *manoelectile*, perhaps as grain milled by hand, for the term appears in no dictionary. The exception to the pairing is *salecta*, willows, which appear in most of the Ravenna leases. It is impossible to see what they were used for, unless they provided *pullum*, also frequently mentioned in the rents. *Pullum* means rope or net, and might just refer to the fish traps that are still common in the coastal region.
74 L. Kuchenbuch, 'Porcus donativus: language use and gifting in seigniorial records between the eighth and tenth centuries', in G. Algazi, V. Groebner and B. Jussen (eds), *Negotiating the Gift: Pre-modern Figuration of Exchange*, Veröffentlichungen des Max-Planck-Instituts für Geschichte 188 (Göttingen, 2003), pp. 193–246.
75 *Le carte del decimo secolo nell'archivio arcivescovile di Ravenna* I, ed. Ruggero Benericetti (Ravenna, 1999), nos 8, 18, pp. 21, 42–3.
76 *Le carte di Ravenna* I, no. 73, pp. 169–70.
77 *Le carte Ravennati del secolo undecismo* I (1001–1024), ed. Ruggero Benericetti (Bologna, 2003), no. 48, pp. 128–9.
78 On the significance of Frankish *precaria* and the creation of a class of *censuales* dedicated to the provision of lighting, see Chapter 3 above.
79 On *plebes*, tithes and leases, Wood, *Proprietary Church*, p. 505.
80 R. Hilton, *Bond Men Made Free. Medieval Peasant Movements and the English Rising of 1381* (London, 1973), pp. 66–8.

81 This analysis follows R. Balzaretti, *The Lands of Saint Ambrose. Monks and Society in Early Medieval Milan* (Turnhout, 2019), c. 9. 'Limonta and Inzago'. I am very grateful to Ross Balzaretti for sharing his thorough and compelling study of the Limonta documents prior to publication.
82 See above, Chapter 3.
83 Text in Balzaretti, *Lands of Saint Ambrose*, p. 435.
84 Balzaretti, *Lands of Saint Ambrose*, pp. 436–7. Sant' Ambrogio was also acquiring more land on the peninsula and then using incoming settlers as witnesses against the Limonta peasants.
85 Balzaretti, *Lands of Saint* Ambrose, pp. 442–6.
86 Balzaretti, *Lands of Saint* Ambrose, p. 442.
87 See above, Chapter 3, p. 81.
88 Balzaretti, *Lands of Saint Ambrose*, pp. 427–8.
89 C. Wickham, *Sleepwalking into a New World. The Emergence of Italian City Communes in the Twelfth Century (The Lawrence Stone Lectures)* (Oxford, 2015).
90 Meersseman, *Ordo Fraternitatis*, pp. 19–20. *Cedrus*, according to Meersseman, was a *manualetto per cancellieri*.
91 Text in Meerssema, *Ordo Fraternatis*, p. 19: *Multi populares per diversas mundi partes fraternitates et consortia secuntur, ut ventrem possint et stomachum adimplere*.
92 See above, Chapter 1.
93 The documents are most recently edited by Ramon Ordeig I. Mata, *Les Dotalies de les Esglésies de Catalunya (segles IX–XII)*, 7 vols (Vic, 1993–2000). On the early history of Catalonia, J. Jarrett, *Rulers and Ruled in Frontier Catalonia 800–1010* (Woodbridge, 2010).
94 These documents (which are also included in Ordeig's edition for Catalonia as a whole) have been published by C. Baraut first in C. Baraut, 'Les actes de consagracions d'esglésies del bisbat d'Urgell (segles IX–XII)', *Urgellia* 1 (1978), 11–182, and then C. Baraut, *Les actes de consagracions d'esglésies de l'antic bisbat d'Urgell (segles IX–XII)* (La Seu d'Urgell, 1986). In the later work Baraut added a further nine documents. Reference is to document number in the 1986 edition. In no. 2 from 839: 'it was shown by the aforesaid Sisebut the most illustrious bishop that no church should be dedicated unless beforehand the possession of all its property had been put down in writing' (*hostensum est a predicto Sisibuto illustrissimo aepiscopo quod nulla dedicacio ecclesiarum, nisi prius omnium rerum possessionibus per scripture tradite sint*). According to no. 1, the bishop was called to perform the consecration 'as was required in the books of the canons and the decrees of bishops'.
95 *Les actes*, no. 75.
96 For wax, *Les actes*, nos 3, 23, 28, 32.
97 *Les actes*, no. 46, from 1035.
98 See above, Chapter 2. It can be said only that the formula was 'in all probability' Visigothic because it survives only in a twelfth-century edition.

99  The classic exposition of this view is in the several works of C. Sánchez Albornoz, for example, his *Despoblación y Repoblación del Valle del Duero* (Buenos Aires, 1966).
100  J. Escalona, 'Mapping scale change: hierarchization and fission in Castilian rural communities in the tenth and eleventh centuries', in W. Davies, G. Halsall and A. Reynolds (eds), *People and Space in the Middle Ages 300–1300* (Turnhout, 2006), pp. 143–66.
101  S. Castellanos and I. Martin Viso, 'The Local Articulation of Central Power in the North of the Iberian Peninsula (500–1000)', *Early Medieval Europe* 13 (2005), 1–42.
102  W. Davies, *Acts of Giving. Individual, Community and Church in Tenth-century Christian Spain* (Oxford, 2007), notes that, of 1,960 charters produced in the tenth century, 950 recorded gifts and 850 sales and exchanges. The hundreds of examples of small-scale dealing were, says Davies, 'of a type that characterizes peasant-level rural society' (at pp. 17–18). In what follows I owe a great deal to Wendy Davies. In her later work, *Windows on Justice in Northern Iberia* (London, 2016), p. 12, she revises the number upwards to 2,700 charters, but with the same point about the proportions of gifts, sales and exchanges.
103  *Catalunya Carolingia II. Els diploms Carolingis a Catalunya*, ed. R. Abadal and I de Vinyals (Barcelona, 1926–50); *Catalunya Carolingia IV. Els comtats de Rosselló, Conflent, Vallespir I Fenollet*, ed. Ramon Ordeig Mata (Barcelona, 2006).
104  *Coleccion documental del archive de la Catedral de Léon (775–1230)*, ed. E. Saez (Léon, 1987). This collection has a very comprehensive index, vol. VII, *Apéndices e indices*, ed. José M. Fernández Catón and José Manuel Ruiz Ascensio (Léon, 2002).
105  *Cartulario de Valpuesta*, ed. M. Desamparados Perez Soles (Valcencia, 1970). The 78 documents are from the period 804–1073.
106  *Coleccion Diplomatica del Monasterio de Sahagun*, vol. 1 (*siglos IX y X*), ed. José María Minguez Fernández (Léon, 1976), vols 2 and 3, ed. M. Herrero de la Fuente (Léon, 1988), *Index verborum dela documentación Leonensa*, vols 2 and 3, *Monasterio de Sahagun*, ed. José María Fernández Catón (Léon, 1999).
107  *Sahagun*, no. 7 (904), for an example of the use of this anathema: *Quisquis vero quod absit ad disrupendum hoc testamentum ausu temerario su venire niterit, vivens suis a fronte careat lucernis postque picea non evadat baratri pena*. I have not seen *lucerna* used to mean 'eye' elsewhere.
108  Davies, *Acts of Giving*, p. 208.
109  Examples of small gifts, *Valpuesta*, nos 56, 58, 60, 61, which are dated from 1053 to 1057.
110  Davies, *Acts of Giving*, p. 152.
111  *Valpuesta*, no. 9.
112  *Léon*, no. 109. Davies, *Acts of Giving*, p. 19.
113  W. Davies, 'Free persons and landowners in the West', in J.-P. Devroey and A. Wilkin (eds), *Autour de Yoshiki Morimoto. Les structures agricoles en dehors du*

monde caroligien, forms et genes, *Revue Belge de philologie et d'histoire* 90 (2012), 381–90.
114 *O Tombo de Celanova*, vol. 1, ed. José. M. Adrade (Santiago de Compostello, 1995), no. 5, the gift included *homines hinc atque inde habitants*. See Davies, *Acts of Giving*, pp. 20–1. Against the assumption that these people were un-free are examples in charters in which people with allodial land were similarly 'given' away, although these came from Urgell, a different region.
115 *Damus etiam et pro luminaribus ecclesie mellarios qui sunt in* ... (four places are named).
116 *Antifonaria Visigotica Mozarabe de la Catedral de León*, ed. L. Brou and J. Vives (Barcelona and Madrid, 1959), pp. 280–3.
117 *Sed cera fammulantur ex lumine que non polluitur ex parente. Cuius natura de flore cuius orta est virgine. Cui ille dat genetrix nativitatis originem que corruptionis nescit errorem. Papirus quin etiam niveo adaperto sub tegimine flamarum exequitur incrementa. Neque hoc sine celestis agitur operatione virtutis quod fabet ignis res nutrita gurgitibus.*
118 *Sahagun*, no. 39. *Lucerna erea* is the term used.
119 *Documentación medieval de Leire (siglos IX a XII)*, ed. A. J. Martin Duque (Pamplona, 1983), no. 93.
120 *Leire*, nos 164, 165, 253, 308, 343. An interesting feature of no. 165 is that King Pedro signed his name in Arabic characters.
121 P. Bonnassie, 'Rural communities in Catalonia and Valencia (from the ninth to the mid-fourteenth centuries)', in P. Bonnassie, *From Slavery to Feudalism in South-western Europe*, trans. J. Birrell (Cambridge, 1991), pp. 243–87.
122 L. To Figueras, *Família i hereu a la Catalunya nord-oriental (segles X–XI)* (Montserrat, 1997).
123 C. West, *Reframing the Feudal Revolution. Political and Social Transformations between Marne and Moselle c. 800–1100* (Cambridge, 2013).
124 Ibn al-'Attār, *Formulario notarial y judicial andalusí del alfaquíy notario cordobés*, no. 12, 47, ed. and trans. with commentary P. Chalmeta and M. Marugán (Madrid, 2000), p. 137.
125 Alejandro Garcia Sanjuán, *Till God Inherits the Earth. Islamic Pious Endowment in al-Andalus (9th–15th Centuries)* (Leiden and Boston, 2007), pp. 24–54. I am grateful to Ann Christys for drawing my attention to this important work.
126 See above, Chapter 1.
127 Sanjuán, *Till God Inherits the Earth*, p. 515, for the eleventh-century text from which this is taken.
128 Sanjuán, *Till God Inherits the Earth*, p. 246.
129 A. Weiner, *Inalienable Possessions: the Paradox of Keeping-While-Giving* (Oxford, 1992).
130 For a conspectus of traditional scholarship on the 'Peace and Truce of God', see the papers in T. Head and R. Landes (eds), *The Peace of God: Social Violence and Religious Response in France around the Year 1000* (Ithaca, 1992).

131 Following a lively debate in several issues of the journal *Past and Present* from 1994 to 1997, the 'feudal revolution' has become a distinctly unfashionable subject.
132 K. Cushing, *Reform and the Papacy in the Eleventh Century. Spirituality and Social Change* (Manchester, 2005), ch. 3 'The Peace of God', pp. 39–54.
133 L. Blancard, 'Role de la confrérie de Saint-Martin de Canigou', *Bibliothèque de l'École des Chartes* 42 (1881), 5–7. See also Vincent, *Fiat lux*, p. 395.
134 This is the *canistra*, the appearance of which was noted in Chapter 1. On the glass lamps, see Chapter 6 below.

# 5

# Lights and social formation in the central Middle Ages

This study has been based upon the observation that throughout Western Europe it was regarded as not just spiritually useful but also a religious duty to burn eternal lights on the altar of each church, as well as lights by tombs, before the shrines of saints and during festivals. It can be said that by the year 1000 the lights were provided for in three basic ways, or to put it slightly differently, there were three kinds of providers who met what was presented as a universal obligation. There were gifts for the lights, and the givers were those with property to spare, ranging from kings to farmers and townspeople. There were tithes, a part of which went to the lights, plus other charges specifically for lights, often termed *census*, and these were laid upon people who had no choice in the matter. And thirdly there were groups of people who organised themselves into collectives, that is, guilds or confraternities, who paid a voluntary annual membership fee part of which went towards the lights. These latter solidarities had a dual social and religious purpose. In this chapter I will concentrate on the *census* payers, generally referred to as *censuales*, in what is conventionally termed the central Middle Ages, the period from about 950 to 1250. The focus here will be on France and Germany because that is where the bulk of the evidence for *census* payers comes from. An increasing amount of information from these areas allows one to investigate whether requirements to provide for the lights had the effect of calling social organisation into being, to ask, in other words, whether such requirements had by this time had any effect upon social structure.

This is a subject that goes to the very heart of the study in that it addresses the overall social and historical significance of the practice of burning eternal lights. But any attempt to explain and assess that significance by identifying the social consequences of putting belief into practice must be aware of the many other factors that shaped social development. For example, the *luminarii* discussed in the last chapter, who appeared in the polyptych of Saint Bertin as people whose status and social identity was tied to payments for the lights of the monastery, must be viewed in relation to other elements that could have contributed to their identity, such as where they lived, how they lived and what their relationship was with other clients or dependants of the monastery.[1] Across the various polyptychs there is evidence for people, such as the *haistaldi*, who look socially comparable to the *luminarii* in terms of their relatively privileged social status and minimal payments to monastic institutions, but these groups (if indeed they can strictly be called 'groups') were not apparently associated with lighting. It is more likely, for instance, that the *haistaldi* were bachelors. It can only be said, therefore, that whilst providing for the lights was a duty and obligation which did define the status and social identification of some people, it need not, and indeed does not, follow that it determined the social landscape at large. It could, however, have an effect on social structure locally where a church or monastery dominated the political and economic landscape, for what is also apparent is that there were more people designated as light payers in some regions than in others. In particular there were more people listed as payers of *census* for lighting in Germany than in France even though both France and Germany had been ruled by Carolingian kings and shared norms and traditions that emphasised the universal obligation to provide for the lights. It is the aim of the present chapter to worry away at this difference partly to see if it can tell us anything about the respective ways in which the western and eastern parts of Francia developed. It is important to consider separate development as one possible explanation for why there were noticeably more light payers in the east than in west. But at the same time it is necessary to consider whether differences of approach by modern French and German historians have had the effect of overemphasising separate development.

The identification of difference is essential to the assessment of historical significance. But complicating any comparison between France and Germany in the central Middle Ages is another difference, and that, as just suggested, is in historiography. To get to grips with this, and to set out the problem overall, a small excursus is required. This will take us some way away from the core subject of lights, for not only is it necessary to consider historiographical differences over the broader range but it is also important to examine the light providers in the wider context of social development. It is further the case that there may be problems in fitting words to practices. Words that were at one time associated with the providing of light may have changed their meaning. The term *censualis* designated a payer of rent for lights in the ninth century, but may not have done so in the thirteenth century. Lighting provision may have originally called some social organisation into being, but that does not necessarily mean that that organisation remained dedicated to provision. In addition, it is essential closely to interrogate the evidence in order to investigate whether the so-called *colliberti* in France were the equivalents of the German *censuales*, for both categories of persons seem to have evolved from formerly un-free people who were freed into the service of the Church. But this interrogation is of necessity quite lengthy as scholars cannot agree about the status and origins of the *colliberti*, and that makes comparison with the *censuales* quite complex. The comparison eventually draws a blank: it turns out that *colliberti* and *censuales* do not represent different regional forms of service to the Church and its lights. Yet forensic questioning of the evidence is in this case necessary to clear up questions of similarity and universality in the former Carolingian lands. The net result of taking these variables into consideration is much talk about peasants, about legal status and about the origins and obligations of *censuales* and *colliberti*, but less about the lights themselves. That is the consequence of attempting to place the subject in wider historical perspective. I begin with the historiography, but I shall end with the lights.

To put it rather baldly, French historians have tended to stick to France, and German historians to Germany, so that there is virtually no comparative discussion and very little communication between the two.[2] Few historians on either side tend to read widely in the language of the other. It was noted in the Introduction, for example, that, in her extensive history of lighting (*Fiat lux*), Catherine Vincent, who writes in French, listed only five secondary works in German, and this is in a bibliography consisting of around 350 items.[3] As a consequence, Vincent has almost nothing to say about Germany, although, as I shall argue, the provision of resources for the altar had a greater social effect in Germany than anywhere else in Europe. On the German side, in two classic papers on the *census* payers as a distinct social group, the so-called *Zensualität* ('Zum Problem der Zensualität' and 'Zensualität und Stadtentwicklung'), Knut Schulz referred to works in French in only four of his footnotes, and, where he did so, this included works on what is now Belgium, a partly francophone region which he treated (correctly) as part of the medieval German empire.[4] Although he included Flanders in his survey, rather surprisingly Schulz did not discuss the evidence from the monastery of Saint Peter's at Ghent possibly because Ghent was technically part of the French kingdom in the central Middle

Ages. This is unfortunate because the cartulary of Saint Peter's contains over a hundred charters concerned with *tributarii*, people who were directly equivalent to the *censuales*.[5] In fact the conditions of their service with regard to the yearly payment (*census*), the level of fee demanded for permission to marry and the death duties levied on the *tributarii* are basically the same as those found in documents dealing with *censuales* produced by institutions under German rule. A comparison would have suggested that it was not the political entity of a Franco-German border which determined the distribution of *censuales*, or *tributarii* as they were termed at Ghent. It would have been useful, to say the least, if Schulz had gone on to compare the situation in France in order to ask whether the importance of the *Zensualität* was a phenomenon unique to lands under German rule. If it was unique to Germany, as his work implies, this would require comment, but comparative comment is absent from that work.

There are also distinct national historical agendas, according to which issues of social and political development have been viewed within different frameworks. A French tradition of structural history has been concerned with the fate of public authority. Following a model famously set out by Georges Duby, mid-twentieth-century historians were convinced of the relatively sudden subjugation of the peasantry in the central Middle Ages, and this 'new' oppression was seen as a consequence of a 'privatisation' of power that was both the cause and the effect of a decline of royal authority.[6] An example of this line of thinking was discussed in the last chapter in relation to the consecrations of churches in the diocese of Urgell in the Pyrenees. Pierre Bonnassie used the charters of consecration to show how a landscape of free peasant communities allegedly gave way to a world dominated by an aristocratic elite. Such a transformation was, in Bonnassie's view, part of a 'feudal revolution'. This is an issue that impacts directly on our subject: did a structural change in the nature of power alter the ways in which lights were provided for? More recent thinking has challenged the notion of a 'feudal revolution', largely on a case-by-case basis. The Urgell consecrations, for example, are now seen to adhere to a conventional format in which episcopal direction was presented as community initiative.[7] The notion of a structural change in the nature of power in the central Middle Ages has more generally given way to a view that power relations were constructed through a process of social negotiation.[8] In line with a concentration on process there has also been more interest in the history of mentalities.[9] The nature of power nevertheless remains a focus of investigation, and such studies remain firmly located in France. The German tradition pays much more attention to the origins and history of institutions. A case in point is the term *Zensualität* itself which is the German-language collective noun for those who appear in documents as *censuales*, the payers of *census*. The German term has added an institutional flavour not necessarily conveyed by the Latin. For German historians legal status is as important an issue as the history of the state and the nature of power.[10] As Timothy Reuter pointed out over twenty years ago, the 'feudal revolution' is not a term of relevance for German medieval history.[11] Where *census* payers are concerned, the issues here are where they came from, what their status was and how that status changed as *censuales* were granted privileges. It was, in short, the *Recht* of the *census* payers that was the focus of investigation. What Schulz and others were looking forward to was the evolution of citizen-right (*Bürgerrecht*), and this was in some degree seen to grow out of the privileges of the *census* payers. Whereas for some French historians, and for perhaps even more Anglophone scholars, the relations of power and the vicissitudes of particular regimes have been central concerns, modern German historians of the central and later Middle Ages have arguably been more interested in the development of towns, in the interests vested in towns and in the relations between town and countryside. I will try to take these differences of approach and interest into account in order to try and think through the issue of why there should have been more *census* payers, the *censuales*, in Germany than in France. It will in fact be shown that the different historical agendas do roughly reflect the differences in nature and quantity of evidence from the two areas, but this question of difference is so important that an awareness of the differences in national historical traditions must play a part if a picture as accurate as possible is to be arrived at.

The term *census* was widely used in the Middle Ages for it could denote tax, tribute or rent. Any of these charges could be paid in cash, in kind, or in labour. *Censualis*, the term for one who paid *census*, could accordingly be applied to a broad range of persons. *Cerocensuales* referred to those who paid *census* in wax, so clearly for lighting, and there were so many who did so that the words *cerocensualis* and *censualis* were often used interchangeably. The terms *census* and *censualis* most often appear in relation to payments to the Church, if for no other reason than that most surviving documents are associated with the Church.[12] But it must also be noted that the Church as a landholder was a major force in the organisation of the countryside, and it would become a force in the development of towns too, especially in Germany. It has already been shown in this study that to pay *census* to a church was a recognition of that church's rights in land or over people. The sole justification for the church to mobilise resources via rent, labour or through the receipt of gifts or from the fruits of farming was to enable and support the practice of the Christian religion and to look after the poor. This is where the link between *census* and lights comes in. That link we saw in Chapter 3 in the spread of precarial grants in which the church in effect loaned out land to favoured clients in return for a (usually) nominal *census* which was in many cases designated for the provision of lights, for the upkeep of monks or clergy and for alms for the poor. It must be stressed again here how very widespread these *precariae* were in the early Middle Ages, and they were common both to West and East Francia, that is, the kingdoms that would become France and Germany. For example, out of the 24 charters listed in connection with the monastery of Stavelot-Malmedy in the Ardennes between 915 and 959, 11 recorded precarial agreements.[13] Although there was legislation safeguarding the exclusive ecclesiastical use of precarial *census*, there is almost nothing on how the rent was collected or on who actually paid it. Carolingian legislation from the later eighth century did, however, refer to *census* payment being reckoned according to homesteads (*casata*). If that is how it really was collected, then one can envisage a broad group of payers at peasant level, and the fact that the same legislation speaks of such people also having to pay tithes to the church could well support such an assumption. The legislation, which was issued by Charlemagne, referred to 'long-standing arrangements' for ecclesiastical tributaries who paid their dues in wax.[14] Nothing more was said, but such tributaries may well have been very like, or identical to, those *cerocensuales*, the wax-paying *censuales*, who appear in documents from the Central Middle Ages. A charter dated to 837 in which *ancillae* (un-free females) were given their freedom and their service transferred to the monastery of Wissembourg in Alsace, mentions other classes of dependants who were nominally free but bound for ever to the institution. The freed women were to pay a yearly *census* of 2 *denarii*, or of wax to the value of 2 *denarii*. They were to remain free 'like the other *tributarii*, *censarii* or *epistolarii*'.[15] The Wissembourg charter of 837 is one of the first recorded instances of people being manumitted and then given over to serve a church which would also act as their protector. Records of these kinds of manumission would increase steadily over the next two centuries. Alongside the evidence from the polyptychs, this charter indicates that there was a range of people paying *census* and other dues. It is the argument here that over the period 900–1200 the numbers of such people increased in German-ruled lands and that the local terms for them, and the arrangements that those terms represented, tended to be subsumed into the one generic description: *census* payer, or *censualis*. The question is whether these people continued to pay their *census* specifically for lighting.

Another example of people being given over to a church to become its *censuales* was presented in the previous chapter.[16] A charter of 945 from the monastery of Gorze in the Moselle region recorded how a lady, Irmina, freed one male *servus* and five female *ancillae* and handed them over to the monastery. These people then became Gorze *censuales*, their *census* being one *denarius* for the women, and 2 *denarii* for the man, and the money was to provide lights on the festival of the monastery's patron saint, Saint Gorgon. As was noted in the earlier discussion of this charter, it was made clear that the descendants of these people would continue serve Gorze as *censuales*.[17] It is therefore to be understood that the numbers of *censuales* would grow. When those who were manumitted were committed to giving wax for a light to be lit on the anniversary of the donor's death, increasing numbers and continuing service would serve as a memorial that in theory would grow rather than fade. This would have been encouraging to donors. Another way in which people became *censuales* was through self-gift, known to historians as 'auto-dedition'. Donors gave themselves into the service of a church or monastery. They received its protection but they, and their descendants, were bound to that service for ever. A ninth-century reference to auto-dedition was presented in the last chapter.[18] It comes from the polyptych of Saint Germain-des-Prés in which 61 people were named as 'men who gave themselves for the lights of Saint Germain'. Acts of auto-dedition increased throughout the tenth and eleventh centuries and then began to fall off in the later twelfth century, although the practice of self-giving continued to the end of Middle Ages, auto-dedition being valued for the legal protection it brought, as well as for its spiritual value.[19] Though the descendants of those who gave themselves in this way would remain dependants of the church and might be classed as 'un-free' in the sense that they faced restrictions on marriage and had to pay death duties, the conditions of service were generally better for these people than for the *mancipia* and *ancillae* who were given over to serve as *censuales*. The latter sometimes paid a higher *census* and faced heavier death and inheritance dues and had to pay substantial fines if they married outside the *familia* (group of dependants) of the church to which they were tied. Conditions and services were, however, subject to local arrangements. In a charter of 1035 the German king, Conrad II, made gifts to the monastery of Limburg, including *mancipia* who became Limburg's *censuales*. Their services varied according to age and marital status. The unmarried children of the former *mancipia* could be required to serve the abbot in the kitchens, in the bakery in the wash-house or as guards of the stud-farm. Married *censuales* could be asked to serve as cellarers, victuallers, toll-gatherers, foresters, as steward or cup-bearer, or as the abbot's soldiers.[20] Whether these last relatively high-status services were reserved for those who had formerly been free is not clear. Nevertheless, the effect of so many free people becoming *censuales* was to secure better conditions for all *censuales*. Behind these norms of giving, and self-giving, one can sometimes see the particular circumstances in which arrangements were made. Widows might give themselves to a church to protect themselves from male kindred. Or a parent might give over their children if a spouse had been un-free and they were in danger of a more severe servitude. In one unusual case from Regensburg in Bavaria, in about the year 1025 a young man gave his *ancilla* into the care of the bishop. It seems that the donor was physically very weak or even terminally ill. The *ancilla*, called Odalburg, was to care for the young man until he died, paying 2 *denarii*, or 2 *denarii* worth of wax, each year at the tomb of Wolfgang, an earlier bishop of Regensburg. When the young man died, Odalburg's *census* would be raised to 5 *denarii* or its equivalent in wax.[21] One wonders if the difference between the two payments, 3 *denarii*, bore some relation to the cost of nursing care for a year.

The large numbers of auto-deditions indicate that in becoming a *censualis* the advantages of protection might outweigh any restrictions on marriage, the payment of *census* and death duties. To protection should be added spiritual gain, and payment for lights signified a service that had a spiritual dimension. We have seen that there were several ways in which one could become a *censualis* or *cerocensualis*, but the only way out was down, back into a stricter servitude. Those who did not pay their *census* were in danger of reverting to their previous condition after three years' grace, although one presumes that this did not apply to those formerly free people who had become *censuales* through auto-dedition.[22] Given the variety of ways in which one could become a *censualis*, and the lack of opportunities to exit from the arrangement, numbers of *censuales* not surprisingly rose, although rates of manumission and auto-dedition started to decline towards the end of the twelfth century. In southern Germany in particular, from the end of the tenth century onwards, major churches and monasteries began to list separately those who became *censuales*. These so-called 'books of *censuales*' (*libri censualium*) contain thousands of notices of gift, manumission and auto-dedition.[23] Here is a typical short notice from the monastery of Saint Emmeram in Regensburg, dated to 1044–48: 'Diermot a free woman gave herself to Saint Emmeram so that she pays five denarii. Witnesses: Gutpold, Willipehrt and Werini'.[24] By the mid-twelfth century the *censuales* were to be counted in the tens of thousands, and they were numerous even at the end of the Middle Ages and beyond. In 1430 the monastery of Xanten in

Flanders recorded over four thousand *cerocensuales*. And in Münsterland there were traces of *censuales* into the eighteenth century.[25]

Although it was largely in German-ruled areas that high numbers of *censuales* were to be found in the central Middle Ages, the precarial arrangements, gifts, manumissions and auto-deditions that produced *census* payers were in origin common to all parts of Francia. In fact the earliest examples of people being freed and given over to churches and monasteries to maintain commemoration of their former lords come from the West. Two of these examples were discussed in Chapter 2 of this study but it will help to rehearse them here. First, from the year 616 there was the Will of Bertramn of Le Mans in which slaves were freed but on the condition that they maintain a perpetual light before Bertramn's tomb.[26] Second, there was a model for a will in the late seventh-century *Formulary of Marculf* in which slaves were freed with the stipulation that the freedmen and freedwomen would owe service to the children of those who had freed them. The former slaves had received documents of manumission which laid down that they, and their offspring, maintain lights at the tombs of those who freed them.[27] It could be that the *epistolarii* (people manumitted by charter) who appeared in the 837 Wissembourg charter were this kind of person who had received a document which stated the conditions upon which they had been freed.

The freeing of persons into the care of the Church can in theory be traced back to late Roman law in which the freed person remained in the debt of their former owners who also retained some claim over the wealth or the service of the one-time slaves.[28] Somehow (i.e. it is not clear how) the rights of the former owners were transferred to the Church when slaves were freed into its care. The early fourth-century Emperor Constantine gave the Church the right to conduct manumissions. Formerly this had been a civil right. According to the records of two of the Councils of Toledo (held in 633 and 638), former slaves who had been freed into the care of the Church were to remain under its protection, with the freed making a profession of obedience to the bishop.[29] This ruling would be quoted in the eleventh century when it was understood as saying that bishops had the right to conduct manumissions as long as the freed remained under the protection of a given church.[30] The actual Roman laws concerned with manumission were not quoted, and perhaps not known. In some eleventh-century documents from Poitiers there is a manumission formula which does purport to follow 'the old law of the Romans', but what it actually said was that, amongst the freed, those who were Roman citizens should be of higher status, and able to make wills in favour of descendants.[31] This might have been a way of indicating local identity, for the inhabitants of the Poitiers region often referred to themselves as 'Romans'. In one instance where the person involved was of low status, thus not a 'Roman citizen', this 'old Roman law' formula was not employed.[32] According to a manumission formula in the ninth-century *Formulary of Bourges*, Roman law stated that a freed person should have full liberty, even if they were freed in a church.[33] They were not necessarily under the protection and jurisdiction of the bishop. Were this generally to have been the case in Roman-law areas (like Poitiers, which is in the same region of northern Aquitaine as Bourges) it could help explain why a class of *censuales* did not form around the bishop, especially in the lands to the south of the River Loire. Nor did such a class form in Italy. In southern Germany, according to Carl Hammer, a higher proportion of dependent peasants were technically 'un-free' and, if he is right, this must have a bearing on the formation of the *censuales* as an intermediate group there.[34]

Since the Church was immortal as a patron, any protection and reciprocal obligation would remain permanent, passing to the descendants of the freed. The head tax, which was the essential charge that indicated the freed person's status, is said to have derived from the *capitatio*, the basic late Roman tax that was a mark of freedom, though again how this became the hallmark of the *censualis* is not clear. Stefan Esders suggests that it derived from the granting of fiscal rights to the Church by the later Merovingian and Carolingian rulers of Francia.[35] This is a reasonable suggestion given that royal immunities stated that whatever the *fisc* (public or royal treasury) had formerly been able to raise from the lands of those privileged by the grant of an immunity should now go to the church or monastery in question. As was shown in Chapter 2, in the early immunities it was spelled out that this income should go towards the maintenance of the lights, towards the upkeep of the clergy and for alms for the poor.[36] The dedication of income to the lights would in turn suggest that there was a well-established association between payment for the lights and the head tax (*Kopfzins*), and the link with the lights could be the main reason why the head tax of the freedman became the wax tribute (*Wachszins*) of the *cereocensualis*. It could also explain why such people lay outside of the jurisdiction of secular authorities for, as well as income from the *fisc*, the privilege of immunity granted rights of jurisdiction and legal protection to favoured institutions. As a result, the *censualis* was to appear before an ecclesiastical advocate or abbot rather than before the count, the key figure in secular government. The problem is that later documents never made these connections with the immunity or indeed refereed to prior immunities, and it must be said that by the eleventh century the immunity in its Carolingian form was long gone. It is clear, nevertheless, that by hypothecating the head tax (putting it to the use of worship) the Church was making the *censualis* a part of its *familia*, the circle that served its material and spiritual needs. Auto-deditions are rare at this point, that is before the mid-tenth century. Although early evidence for the freeing of slaves into the care of a church comes, as we have just seen, from the west of Francia (the Le Mans and Paris regions), the slightly later laws that deal with the subject are from the west and south of Germany, that is, in the laws of the Ripuarians, of the Alemans and of the Bavarians. Coupled with the probability that there was a larger proportion of un-free peasants in this southern region, it is unlikely to be pure coincidence that these are the areas in which the highest numbers of *censuales* appear in the central Middle Ages. Ripuarian law stated that a person freed into the care of a church, or freed by a church, lost the status of Roman citizenship and would remain under ecclesiastical patronage. Ripuarian law also dealt with the restrictions placed upon marriages between *tabularii* of the church and people outside of the *familia*: the effect was to keep these people and their descendants within the *familia*. Aleman law said that if a church freedman were to be killed, compensation (*wergild*) would be paid to the church in question. What these laws do in practice is to consolidate those under the protection and patronage of churches and monasteries as a separate group in society not subject to secular jurisdiction or to charges levied by secular rulers.

The question of why such a consolidation should have taken place in the East but not in the West remains difficult to answer, given that the two areas shared the same legal and canonical traditions. There were in the West, as in the East, lots of people who appear to have been freed or to be the descendants of freed people, but this appearance may often be misleading. From the late tenth century up into the mid-twelfth century western documents refer to *colliberti*. The term, rendered *culvert* in modern French, would seem to mean 'people freed together' or just 'freed'. Were such people similar to the freed who became *censuales* or *cerocensuales* in the East, that is, was the status called into being around provision for lighting? It seems not. In his seminal study of the *colliberti*, Marc Bloch saw them as a distinct class with their own place in law between the free and the serf. They were in this way like the German *censuales*.[37] The *colliberti* are, however, a category of people hard to pin down as an intermediary layer. The term does not become common until the early eleventh century and then it disappears in the course of the twelfth. *Colliberti* are well attested in western and northern France, but largely absent from Flanders, Picardy, Normandy, Brittany, eastern France and from the far south-west. Bloch was convinced that the *colliberti* were in some ways socially and economically superior to the *servi* and *mancipia*, but he was unable to say exactly how. They were indeed referred to as 'different' from the *servi*. In a list of fines for La Chapelle in Aude from 1065, offenders were said to have owed fines according to what law they lived under, 'be they free, be they *servus*, or be they *colibertus*'.[38] Occasionally a person protested that he was a *collibertus* rather than a *servus*. One such case comes from the monastery of Marmoutier near Tours and can be dated to between 1032 and 1084. At the end of the eleventh century Marmoutier compiled a cartulary known as 'The Book of Serfs' (*Liber de Servis Majoris Monasterii*) that was solely concerned with relations between the monastery and its serfs.[39] 'The Book of Serfs' is an invaluable source for evidence of attempts to keep serfs within the *familia*.[40] It is very striking that it never refers to *censuales*, to lights, or to the spiritual benefits of becoming part of the *familia*. In this case of contested status, Engelric, a recalcitrant serf, had claimed to be a *collibertus*, but the person who had given Engelric's father to Marmoutier said that he had been given *lege servi* ('by the laws of a serf'), and this made his son a serf too.[41] Engelric's party then argued that his mother had been a *colliberta* rather than an *ancilla*, but this was refuted by one of the monastery's men. Engelric's case thus collapsed. Quite what he would have gained had he been successful in claiming *collibertus* status cannot be known. In the late nineteenth century, Ch. Grandmaison, the second editor of the 'Book of Serfs', noted that in these documents *colliberti* were generally identified by place, that is, by the estate they came from. *Servi*, however, were identified by parentage, as Engelric was here. In fact, to name his parents as serfs in this way was to reinforce the denial to him of a higher status. Grandmaison went on to reason that, in having strong links with the land on which they were born, the *colliberti* were analogous to the late Roman *coloni* who were tied to the soil but who had a degree of freedom.[42] But similarity does not prove origins. If the *colliberti* emerged from the ranks of the *coloni*, then it is hard to see why they do not appear until the end of the tenth century. On the other hand, that the *colliberti* should have been a type of peasant whose status and conditions were in steady decline seems quite possible. That would fit with what Chris Wickham has called 'the caging of the peasantry' across the early medieval period. In other words, peasants lost privileges and rights and faced heavier burdens as lords attempted to increase income from land. This should be seen, however, as a process of encroachment rather than as the result of any sudden 'feudal revolution'.[43] That scenario would give the *colliberti* the vestiges of a higher status and better conditions, something to be remembered and honoured, but that had very little meaning in practical terms, hence the difficulty of distinguishing between the *collibertus* and the *servus*. If this line of thinking is correct, it follows that the emergence of the *colliberti* has nothing to do with lighting, or even with manumission. They were not like *censuales*. But there is one strong similarity between peasants east and west and that is the payment of 4 *denarii*, placed on the head or the altar, which signified dependent status. In several of the Marmoutier cases in which the serf contested his or her status the dispute ended with the ritual placing of the coins on the head. Four *denarii* was the amount of *census* paid by the *luminarii* of Saint Bertin. It was very often the amount paid in head tax by the *censuales* and *cerocensuales* in German-ruled areas in the central Middle Ages, and 4 *denarii* was conventionally the price of a pound of wax. It is not possible to say that this ritual acknowledgement of dependence and even de facto servility was derived from a universal obligation to provide material and money for the lights. But the fact that the 4-*denarii* charge did mark out those who *were* obliged to contribute towards the costs of maintaining the lights could well have influenced the social acceptability of imposing the charge on a much wider section of the dependent or servile population.

Dominique Barthélemy remarked apropos the Engelric case that the people involved may have known what was at stake in claiming *collibertus* status, but the texts simply do not reveal what it was. Barthélemy was convinced that there was in fact no practical difference between the *servus* and the *collibertus* and no general deterioration in peasant conditions over the period.[44] But here there is another example of the 'feudal revolution' debate muddying the waters: Barthélemy was reacting, or arguably over-reacting, to Bloch's position that there was in the central Middle Ages a deterioration of the conditions in which the peasantry lived, as various early medieval types of free, semi-free, freed and tributary peasant were squashed into a single category of the servile, all now being termed *servi*.[45] But according to Barthélemy, and also to Alice Rio, servitude was always multifaceted as a result of the different negotiating strengths of particular peasants or groups of peasants.[46] As proof of this, says Barthélemy, is the phenomenon of auto-dedition: people would not voluntarily have entered serfdom were it equally oppressive, everywhere. So, what Barthélemy argued in relation to the *colliberti* was that they were not created by manumission, nor did they have special privileges, nor did they perform lighter services, nor did they face fewer restrictions than the *servi*. They were, he added, far more likely to be mentioned in documents concerned with lay lords than in documents that related to the church. They were thus unlike the *censuales* in a further sense: they were not essentially people of the Church.

There was more similarity between the *censuales* in Germany and those in France who entered the *familia* of a church or monastery through an act of auto-dedition. This self-giving was common to both East and West. Just over half of the documents copied into the 'Book of Serfs', that is 65 out of the 125 charters, were concerned with auto-dedition. In terms of the proportion of all charters in the cartulary, this compares with the thousands of gifts-of-self which are evident in the *libri censualium* drawn up by German institutions. Another institution that recorded large numbers of auto-deditions was the monastery of Saint Peter's at Ghent. These, in which people gave themselves to become *tributarii* rather than *censuales*, are like the German acts in that they involve large numbers of women seeking the protection of the monastery.[47] They also stipulated what the new member of the *familia* would pay as a yearly *tributum* or *census* (2 *denarii*), as a marriage fee (6 *denarii*), and as death duties (12 *denarii*). Though Barthélemy quoted the Ghent auto-deditions to show that the phenomenon was not limited to Marmoutier, he did not note that the two sets of auto-deditions are quite different in that at Marmoutier protection was not spelled out, nor were any charges or services specified.[48] In the Ghent documents conditions were consistently set down, both for those *mancipia* who were manumitted into the care of the monastery and for the free, even sometimes noble, people who submitted themselves. For the three hundred years from the mid-tenth to the mid-thirteenth centuries, the Ghent cartulary contains just over five hundred charters.[49] Of these about 114 (thus 23 per cent) were concerned with *tributarii*, people who entered the *familia* of the monastery. These people look indistinguishable from the *censuales*, although what was done with the charges laid upon them was never mentioned. That is, there was no reference to lights or to wax. The conditions of entry into the Ghent *familia*, both for the manumitted and for those who gave themselves into it, were standard over the three-hundred-year period: a charter of 950 is word-for-word almost identical to a charter of 1250, though this may reflect continuity in recording tradition instead of, or as well as, social and religious practice. Each member of the *familia* would pay the charges just detailed, but they would also enjoy the legal protection (*defensio*) of the monastery via its advocate under whose *mundeburdium* (legal guardianship) they were, and occasionally this was linked to the 2 *denarii* payment. A few favoured people would enjoy the personal protection of the abbot.[50] A preponderance of women amongst the self-givers could relate to the emphasis on protection. But in all cases, the conditions were to be permanent, and later in the run of charters there are several lists of *tributarii* from various estates owned by the monastery, which suggests that Ghent kept a close eye on its growing *familia*. Likewise, several of the later charters were renewals of earlier gifts, going back generations.[51] Ghent was in Flanders, and Flanders was nominally part of the French kingdom. It was this fact that seems to have led Barthélemy to refer to the monastery's dossier to make the point that Marmoutier's auto-deditions were paralleled elsewhere. But in this case difference outweighs similarity, and, as just mentioned, the Ghent charters are much more like the German notices. The similarity lies in the way in which at Ghent charges were detailed and entry into the *familia* conferred protection to the point of privilege.[52] At Marmoutier, by contrast, even in the auto-deditions the emphasis was on complete submission and servitude. In the words of Alice Rio, at Marmoutier the adoption of un-free status was 'symbolized in a uniquely powerful way'.[53] The oblate presented himself before the Marmoutier chapter with a rope around his neck. He (and it is always a man who commits his wife and children) then placed the 4 *denarii* on the altar. In this way the person was becoming a serf, and committing himself, his family and his descendants to eternal servitude. He was not becoming a *censualis* but a serf. After about the year 1050 the rope around the neck no longer featured in the Marmoutier documents, but this change does not seem to indicate any improvement in conditions.[54]

Grandmaison, struck by the finality and harshness of the enserfment in the Marmoutier documents, believed that whoever gave themselves into servitude in this way must have been in desperate straits. Famine and plague were probably the main causes of destitution.[55] Here Grandmaison was no doubt influenced by another much earlier document from the Tours area. This was from the early eighth-century *Formulary of Tours* in which there is a model for entry into servitude: people enter the service of a lord when compelled by necessity. They give up their freedom, and the freedom of their descendants, in return for clothing and housing; the lord pledges that these needs will always be met. The Tours formula has been regarded as essential in explaining how the peasantry started to move towards serfdom. For F. L. Ganshof it kick-started the narrative of 'feudalisation'.[56] Reacting against that narrative, Barthélemy did not accept that the Marmoutier auto-deditions were brought about by desperation. His argument was that to enter the *familia* of the monastery was to gain security. If the conditions of serfdom were negotiable rather than cast in stone, as it were, then becoming a serf of Marmoutier could actually have been a good career move. As in Conrad II's grant to Limburg in 1035, the dependants of the monastery could serve in a variety of honourable or even prestigious positions, such as stewards or grooms or cellarers.[57] Yet, as Rio observed, in the ritual of submission the monastery was making a strong statement about the complete power it had over these new members of its *familia*. A rope around the neck symbolised the powerlessness of the serf. The 'Book of Serfs' contains numerous cases like that of Engelric in which the monastery's serfs contested their status. Families could be split up if there was marriage between serfs belonging to different masters. Inheritance was another issue of contention.[58] Relations between the monastery and its serfs could even turn to violence, and serfdom could be imposed as a punishment. The documents from Marmoutier concerned with auto-dedition have remarkably little to say about any religious duties, or about spiritual benefits apart from very occasionally assuring a serf that they could be buried in the monastery's cemetery. It is therefore hard to see what advantages there could have been in becoming a Marmoutier serf. The 'Book of Serfs' was not, however, concerned with duties or charges or benefits. Marmoutier's overwhelming concern was its human assets and it tried very hard to prevent people leaving the *familia* either by forming a family with the people of another lord, or by refusing to acknowledge their serf status.[59] Lights, wax and even alms for the poor and the maintenance of the monks do not feature at all. Barthélemy was surely right to think that for *some* people in the monastery's *familia*, and not just for those who entered it via gift of self, there could have been advantages and privileges, but there is a strong contrast with the German *censuales* or the Flemish *tributarii* whose conditions, charges and privileges were made clear. It is the fact of the latter definition that makes it possible to speak of the *censuales* as a distinct category or group of people. With regard to the West, however, the argument from the silence on advantages and privileges is a strong one given that self-gift is relatively well documented. I will now turn to the German *censuales/cerocensuales* themselves to see what can be gleaned from their conditions and privileges.

In a charter of 1025 King Conrad II of Germany confirmed the manumission of 11 *mancipia* of the church of Speyer.[60] The bishop of Speyer 'had with the consent of the clergy and people turned them from servile people into *censuales*'.[61] This was no arbitrary act on behalf of the bishop, Walter. Rather, it was done according to the authority of the canons of the Church and the capitularies of Conrad's predecessors Charles, Louis and Lothar. The canons were those of the fifth Council of Toledo which gave bishops the right to manumit *mancipia*. Although the wrong council was quoted here (it was actually Toledo IV at which this right was set down),[62] and although it is not possible to pin down which of the capitularies of Charles, Louis and Lothar were being referred to, or even which Charles, Louis and Lothar were regarded as Conrad's *antecessores*, it is clear that the *censuales* were seen as having rights and obligations that were long established, and were recognised and protected by rulers and the Church. The new *censuales* would live for ever *infra legem censualem* ('under the law of the *censuales*'). This was a *lex* (law) that came from the canons and the capitularies, and it stated that the *censuales* should pay 2 *denarii*, or the equivalent amount of wax, on the festival of the nativity of the Virgin Mary. Thereafter they should live like free people and like the other *censuales*.[63] This charter is similar to the document discussed above as one of the earliest examples in which *mancipia* were freed and made *censuales*. In that charter, from the monastery of Wissembourg and drawn up in the year 837, the conditions for the *censuales* were the same as in 1025: 2 *denarii* or 2 *denarii* worth of wax to be paid annually, and the *censuales* to remain free, like the other tribute payers. But what was referred to in 837 as the 'way' or 'condition' (*ratio* or *conditio*) in which they would exist henceforth has in the 1025 charter become the *lex* under which they would live. The change in terminology, from *conditio* to *lex*, may reflect the way in which the *censuales* had become consolidated and recognised as a distinct category or group of persons, and reading out from the 1025 charter, it was a consolidation underwritten by the rulers and the Church drawing upon ancient capitularies and canons. An obvious thought is that in West Francia, which shared the same capitularies and canons, the rulers and the Church had not been able to, or perhaps had chosen not to, support the *censuales*, *tributarii* or *epistolarii* to anything like the same extent.

The *censuales* or *cerocensuales* in the East thus look to have been relatively privileged by comparison with the *servi* tied to the Church in the West. Later documents make it clear that in the East they were indeed protected, and that their privileges were gradually extended.[64] The obligations of the *censuales* might vary according to local arrangements. In the Rhineland and Flanders the *census* tended to be 2 *denarii* for wax and 2 for protection, whereas in Bavaria it was more often 5 *denarii* without distinction between lighting dues and protection.[65] It is nevertheless clear that the association with lighting remained an essential element of their condition. In 1118, for instance, the monastery of Stavelot-Malmedy reckoned up the income of its *familia* from one estate. Each member of the *familia* paid one *denarius* in *census*, amounting to 8 *solidi* in total. The sum was paid for 'for lights every day'.[66] Another Stavelot-Malmedy document, this time from the year 1153, connects protection, privilege and the provision of lights even more explicitly.[67] *Censuales* living between the forest of Fagnes and the River Vesdre had been wrongly appropriated by one Count Eberhard as part of his *beneficium*. Whereas they should only be liable for the head tax (*census*),

Eberhard was vexing them with 'dire exactions' (the bundle of dues and fines commonly paid by peasants). 'About 200' of these *censuales* proceeded to Aachen to complain before the emperor, Frederick I (Barbarossa), who upheld the complaint against Eberhard. It was stated that income from the *censuales* could go only towards the lights and the roofs of the church.[68] *Census* could never be granted out to lay people as part of a benefice. Further, the Stavelot-Malmedy *censuales* were given the right to choose a *censuarius*, that is, their own administrator and a figure similar to the *villicus*.[69] The *censuarius* was to collect the *census* and administer justice in minor matters. In cases of 'high justice' the *censuales* would appear before the abbey's advocate, but they would also have access to justice in the royal court. In terms of privilege the *censuales*, and especially the *censuarius*, here look to be close to the level of the *ministeriales* (nominally 'un-free' dependants who by virtue of military leadership and administrative role could have quasi-noble status), although the *censuales* had no other administrative duties or any military function. It is again notable that it was the ruler working with a senior churchman who guaranteed these privileges, and together they had the clout to bring the local count into line. One suspects that in much of what had become France the count might well have prevailed in such a case, meaning that the *censuales* would have been reduced to the status of *mancipia* or *servi*. Incidentally, it is of note that the most recent scholarship on this case, in a fine book by Nicholas Schroeder on the social and economic history of Stavelot-Malmedy (published in 2015), has the kind of blind-spot with regard to lights that was highlighted in the Introduction to the present work. Despite discussing the Eberhard case, and despite quoting a charter of 1082 in which *mancipia* were given in order to pay for the commemoration of the donor in lights,[70] and despite quoting a survey of 1131 which begins with a list of churches which owed lighting dues to the monastery,[71] Schroeder does not mention lighting as a factor in the economic and social structure of Stavelot-Malmedy's 'seigneurie', as it surely was. But if the 1118 charter is anything to go by, the *censuales* who paid for the 'lights every day' could have been a source of considerable income. Or to put it another way, the cost of lighting was obviously a considerable charge upon the monastery.

It was in the towns, especially the new towns, of the Rhineland and Flanders that the *censuales* most rapidly won concessions, as we have just seen with the case of Speyer in Conrad II's charter of 1025 in which the *cenusales* were referred to as having their own *lex*. In towns the pressure points were on death duties and fines for marriage outside the *familia*.[72] Death duties were traditionally levied in the form of the best beast for males or best item of clothing for women, but in monetary terms they were often as high as 12 *denarii* per person, and were seen to hamper the ability to inherit and to build up wealth. Outmarriage for those who had formerly been *mancipia* could be fined at two-thirds of a person's inheritance, but marrying outside the *familia* became harder to avoid as several churches might have dependants in a single town.[73] *Censuales* benefited from privileges that were given more widely to towns in order to stimulate growth and trade, but there was also a political dimension to these concessions as various Salian and Staufer rulers sought the support of towns and their bishops, beginning with Conrad II. In the late eleventh century the Emperor Henry IV was in particular need of support in his protracted struggle with the Papacy and the pro-reform Church. His son, Henry V, granted privileges to Speyer, both to support the commemoration of his father (whose power he had effectively usurped) and to shore up support in his own dispute with Rome.[74] The terms of these privileges were famously inscribed in golden letters around the porch of the cathedral of Speyer. In 1114 a document was produced in the town of Worms which imitated the Speyer privileges that had become something of a template for town freedoms. In 1182 the Emperor Frederick Barbarossa confirmed the Speyer and Worms privileges and extended them to end the death duty of best beast or best item of clothing, as well as ending head tax for all the citizens.[75] In imitation of the Speyer inscription, the Worms privileges were inscribed on a tablet in the porch of the Cathedral. This was part of a text in praise of the town which celebrated its citizens. Their privilege was to be 'free from the head tax' (*a censu capitum sis libera*) by the gift of the emperor.[76] According to Knut Schulz, these two imperial privileges marked the beginning of a gathering change in the status of the *censuales*, and the disappearance of the last restrictions was the result of the rapid growth of towns.[77] The *censuales* were becoming indistinguishable from the other citizens, and their once distinct legal status disappeared as they became subject to the law that applied to all citizens (*Bürgerrecht*).

The fading away of the *censuales* as a distinct category of people was in fact a gradual process that took place at different times in different places: as was noted at the outset of this discussion there were still thousands of *cerocensuales* attached to the monastery of Xanten in the fifteenth century. The convent of Kappenberg gave its *cerocensuales* in the town of Lünen privileges in 1279: they were freed from 'the common law of all our *cerocensuales*' (*a iure communi cerocensualium nostrorum*). That meant that their death duties were reduced, marriage outside the *familia* was no longer penalised and they joined the ranks of the citizens (*recipient in ipsorum civile consortium*).[78]

*Lights and social formation*

Over the thirteenth century in south-east Germany the class of *censuales* diminished as people either became independent farmers or slipped under the control of secular lords who subjected them to heavier burdens.[79] Interestingly, the head tax, the *census*, was usually the last element of the charges to be abandoned, and as a consequence the association with lighting provision lasted well into the thirteenth century. In some towns this meant that there was but a short interval, or even a temporal overlap, between the payment of *census* for lighting and the provision for lighting by the *Zechen*, and other street, parish or trade organisations dedicated to supporting the needs of the church. The *familiae* of the churches cannot actually be seen to morph into parish organisations such as the *Zechen*, but it is possible that townspeople were generally influenced by the long history of wax payments (*Wachszins*). The *Zechen* will be discussed in the next chapter, as will the way in which lights were paid for outside Germany.

## Conclusion

At the root of this chapter has been the question of whether the requirement to provide for the lights had a significant effect upon social formation in the central Middle Ages. The answer has been a tentative 'yes' for Germany but a qualified 'no' with regard to France. Why the two halves of the former Carolingian Empire north of the Alps should have been different in this respect has been a secondary question, and the extent to which differences between the two have been exaggerated by different historical approaches has been a third issue of concern. The evidence of charters makes it clear that there were large numbers, that is, tens of thousands, of *censuales* (*census* payers) or *cerocensuales* (payers of *census* in wax) attached to monasteries and churches in German-ruled areas. This was not simply a matter of language and culture, for some of these areas, such as the Ardennes, were Francophone regions. Nor was it strictly a matter of political boundaries: the monastery of Saint Peter's at Ghent which was nominally in the French kingdom organised its *census* payers in exactly the same way as any German monastery. The association of these people with lighting is well evidenced. Shared features gave the *censuales* a clear identity in that they had common obligations in the payment of a head tax, marriage fees and death duties, and these charges were roughly of the same order, everywhere. It was above all the head tax, the *census*, often paid in wax or for wax, which linked them to provision for the lights. The sources are very clear on how people became *censuales* or *cerocensuales*. According to the privilege of 1114, in the town of Worms, for instance, 'they handed themselves over voluntarily or they came by being made free and handed over by others'.[80] It is equally clear that, for the *censuales*, status overrode origins in relation to the conditions under which they lived. That status, or privilege, was, according to Conrad II's charter of 1025, derived from Carolingian tradition. Their *lex* was drawn from earlier capitularies and church canons, and, as was made clear in Chapter 3 of this work, Carolingian legislation had been crafted with the explicit aim of supporting the Church. Support involved more than provision for the lights, but providing for the lights was a visible organising principle in keeping the *familia* of each church together, hence the continuing emphasis on the link between *census*, lights, and sanctions against *censuales* marrying outside the circle of people attached to a particular church.

It is important to state again that East and West Francia, that is, the kingdoms that had by the central Middle Ages become Germany and France, shared the same legislative tradition. Manumission into ecclesiastical care, auto-dedition and measures to conserve the *familia* of each church were common to both areas of Western Europe. Serfs in the West also paid a head tax, marriage fee and death duties (*chevage*, *formariage* and *mainmorte*). Yet whereas in the East these traditions gave rise to formation of the *censuales* as a distinct category of people, in the West they did not. The question of whether the people designated as *colliberti* in western charters were similar to the eastern *censuales* has been examined in some detail, but despite the term itself suggesting that the *colliberti* were freed people[81] and were in terms of origins thus similar to many of the *censuales*, there was apparently no evidence that they were indeed people who had been freed, or that they were specifically linked with the church, and there was certainly no sign that they were associated with the provision of lighting. They were thus unlike the *censuales*, and in fact they were in practice indistinguishable from *servi*, the mass of un-free in the West. Scholarly opinion is divided over the origins and status of the *colliberti* because whatever had once distinguished them from the *servi* is now not visible, although, given the fact that *colliberti* did very occasionally protest a superior status, it is plausible to suggest that there was some vestigial memory of difference. That observation may provide a clue as to the difference between East and West, if it can be said that in the West a once privileged category of people like the *colliberti* had lost ground to lords, whereas in the East the *censuales* had not. To the contrary, their position was steadily improving. The crux would thus lie in the relative power of lords over dependent peasants in West and East. This is, however, a highly complex issue and one fraught with the danger of overgeneralisation, made worse by the lack of comparative discussion and differences in national historical traditions.

## Lights and social formation

What preserved privilege in the East and eroded it in the West could have been the differing degree of attention paid to Carolingian legislation. As Conrad II's charter indicates, it was apparently strong in the East, but that legislation seems effectively to have dropped off the radar in the West. One could contrast the way in which Stavelot-Malmedy's *censuales* were able to defend themselves against the depredations of Count Eberhard, with the powerlessness of Engelric when contesting his status against Marmoutier. In the Eberhard case the winning principle, backed by abbot and king, was that ecclesiastical resources could not be wound into the *beneficium* of a lay person. This was a principle stated in numerous Carolingian capitularies. In Engelric's case, as in other Marmoutier cases, and in cases of a secular nature too, there was no defence against witnesses. It was declared status (that is, a declaration of strict dependency) and coercion that kept the Marmoutier *familia* together. In contrast it was the supposedly written norms that preserved Stavelot-Malmedy's *familia*, and writing as a means of preservation also entailed a recognition of right and privilege. Such reasoning may seem to come close to a narrative of separate development in East and West, with the East hanging on to norms of Carolingian authority as opposed to the disintegration of central authority, if not a 'feudal revolution' in the West. But the objection to these two characterisations, quite apart from the fact that they make comparative thinking nigh-on impossible, is not that they are wholly wide of the mark but that they concern only certain aspects of the whole picture, and that this leads to a degree of determinism. In other respects, say in gender relations, or economic structures, building techniques or military technology, West and East were of course virtually indistinguishable. In the case of the formation of the *censuales* as a category of people, Stefan Esders points to historical difference. In the East, he argues, in areas newly absorbed into the Frankish realm, kings had a particular need to build up clienteles around newly founded churches.[82] Those clienteles were the basis of the *Zensualität*. One could add that, as was explained in Chapter 3, the Carolingians made use of bishops in the East to consolidate territories and to bring local churches under control. This meant that a large proportion of the *precariae* came into episcopal hands, and the *precariae* were a significant source of *census* payers. This situation may explain the concentration of *censuales* in episcopal *familiae*, and also why bishops were likely to defend *censuales* against depredations from outside. It is an axiom of post-Carolingian German history that the Carolingian comital structure never really took hold in the East. Advocates (the legal representatives of churches and monasteries) were more prominent than counts, and advocates were charged with defending the *censuales*.

One of the latter's privileges was to be heard in the advocate's court, or, better, in the court of the abbot or bishop. Again, over-generalisation is a danger here, and this picture ignores significant regional differences east of the Rhine. Nevertheless, *censuales* were present, even if in different numbers, in all areas. Did the association with the provision of lighting play a part in the formation of these groups? The answer must be in the affirmative. Were they a socially significant category of persons? Their relatively privileged position and the increasing freedoms conferred on them in towns again indicates an affirmative answer.

## Notes

1. Above, pp. 113–14.
2. These remarks apply less to historians of the early Middle Ages, that is, of the period before the formation of France and Germany, and an exception for all periods must be made for the truly international scholarship that has emerged from Vienna and the Österreichische Akademie der Wissenschaften. An English-language work which does show the value of a comparative approach is C. West, *Reframing the Feudal Revolution. Political and Social Transformation between Marne and Moselle c. 800 – c. 1100* (Cambridge, 2013).
3. C. Vincent, *Fiat Lux. Lumière et luminaires dans la vie religieuse du XIIIe au XVIe siècle* (Paris, 2004), pp. 639–59.
4. K. Schulz, 'Zum Problem der Zensualität im Hochmittelalter', in K. Schulz, *Die Freiheit des Bürgers. Städtische Gesellschaft in Hoch- und Spätmittelalter* (Darmstadt, 2008), pp. 69–105, notes 5 and 25; K. Schulz, 'Zensualität und Stadtentwicklung im 11/12 Jahrhundert', in Schulz, *Die Freiheit*, pp. 106–30, notes 5 and 15.
5. *Chartes et documents de l'abbaye de Saint-Pierre au Mont-Blandin à Gand*, ed. A. van Lockeren, 2 vols (Ghent, 1868, 1871).
6. The seminal work is G. Duby, *La société aux XIe et XIIe siècles dans la region mâconaise* (Paris, 1953).
7. Above, pp. 130, 133.
8. For a trenchant critique of the French 'feudal revolution' model and for a processual alternative, S. White, 'Tenth-century courts at Mâcon and the perils of structuralist history: re-reading Burgundian judicial institutions', in W. Brown and P. Górecki (eds), *Conflict in Medieval Europe: Changing Perspectives on Society and Culture* (Aldershot, 2003), pp. 37–68. The first note of this work contains an excellent bibliography on the whole subject.
9. As Paul Freedman wistfully remarked, peasant studies were eclipsed by the history of mentalities from the 1970s onwards: P. Freedman, 'Peasants, the seigneurial regime and serfdom', in T. F. X. Noble and J. van Engen (eds), *European Transformations. The Long Twelfth Century* (Notre Dame, Ind., 2012), pp. 259–78, at 260.

## Lights and social formation

10 This approach is encapsulated in the title of Stefan Esders's recent monograph on the *censuales*: S. Esders, *Die Formierung der Zensualität, Vorträge und Forschungen*, Sonderband 54 (Ostfilde, 2010).

11 T. Reuter, 'Debate. The "Feudal Revolution" III', *Past and Present* 155 (1997), 177–95.

12 For this reason M. Matheus thinks that the importance of the *Zensualität* has been overestimated. He also notes that an attempt by K. Bosl to identify three social groups below the level of nobility has led to the *Zensualität* being declared a general social phenomenon, whereas in actuality it emerged from different local arrangements: M. Matheus, 'Forms of social mobility: the example of the *Zensualität*', in A. Haverkampf and H. Vollrath (eds), *England and Germany in the High Middle Ages* (Oxford, 1996), pp. 357–69, at 368–9.

13 *Recueil des chartes de l'abbaye de Stavelot-Malmedy*, ed. J. Halkin and C. Roland (Brussels, 1910–30), nos 53, 54, 55, 56, 57, 58, 64, 65, 68, 69, 77.

14 See above, Chapter 3.

15 *Chartes de Stavelot-Malmedy*, no. 165, p. 367. J.-F. Niermeyer, *Mediae Latinitatis Lexicon Minus* (Leiden, 1984), p. 377, gives the meaning of *epistolarius* in this charter as 'former serf who has been manumitted by charter'.

16 Above, p. 116.

17 Above, p. 116.

18 Above, p. 116.

19 C. de Miramon, *Les 'données' au Moyen Age. Une forme de vie religieuse laïque v. 1180 – v. 1500* (Paris, 1999).

20 *Monumenta Germaniae Historica, Diplomata Regum IV (die Urkunden der deutschen Könige und Kaiser IV)*, ed. H. Bresslau (Hanover and Leipzig, 1909), no. 216, pp. 295–6.

21 *Die Traditionen des Hochstifts Regensburg und des Klosters S. Emmeram*, ed. J. Widemann (Munich, 1943, repr. Aalen, 1969), no. 353, p. 254.

22 Schulz, 'Zum Problem', pp. 87–8.

23 J. Wild, 'Libri censualium', in G. Hetzer and B. Uhl (eds), *Festschrift Hermann Rumschöttel zum 65. Geburtstag*, 2 vols (Cologne, Weimar and Vienna, 2006), pp. 1105–21.

24 *Die Traditionen des Hochstifts Regensburg und des Klosters S. Emmeram*, no. 500, p. 284: *Diermot libera tradidit se ipsam ad S. Emmerammum ut v den[arii] sol[vat]. Testes Gutpolt, Willipehrt, Werini.*

25 Schulz, 'Zum Problem', pp. 74–5.

26 Above, Chapter 2, pp. 51–2.

27 Marculf II, 17, see above, Chapter 2, p. 52.

28 For a clear account of the conditions upon which people were freed in later Roman law as seen from Visigothic versions of the law, D. Claude, 'Freedmen in the Visigothic Kingdom', in E. James (ed.), *Visigothic Spain. New Approaches* (Oxford, 1980), pp. 159–88.

29 Esders, *Die Formierung*, pp. 33, 37–8.

30 Quoted in a charter of Conrad II from the year 1025 in which the king confirmed the freeing and granting of *censualis* status of 11 *mancipia* of the church of Speyer. The Toledo reference is slightly wrong, being to Toledo V, c. 65, whereas the quote comes from Toledo IV, c. 68: *MGH Diplomata Regum* IV, no. 41, p. 47. Manumission into the care of a church does not mean that this was the only form of manumission, but it is this particular form that has a bearing on the provision for lights, especially on commemoration by keeping a light burning.
31 *Chartes et documents pour server à l'histoire de l'abbaye de Saint-Maxient de Poitiers*, ed A. Richard (Poitiers, 1886), nos 92, 104, 111, pp. 112, 130, 139–40.
32 *Chartes et documents*, no. 115, p. 144.
33 *Formula Bituricensis*, ed. K. Zeumer, *Formulae Merowingici et Karolini* Aevi (Hanover, 1886), no. 9, pp. 173–3; Esders, *Die Formierung*, p. 49.
34 C. Hammer, *A Large-scale Slave Society of the Early Middle Ages: Slaves and Their Families in Early Medieval Bavaria* (Aldershot, 2002).
35 Esders, *Die Formierung*, pp. 37–8, 65–9.
36 See above, pp. 53–4.
37 M. Bloch, 'Les *colliberti*. Étude de la formation de la classe servile', *Revue Historique* 157 (1928), 1–48 and 225–63 [repr. Bloch, *Mélanges historiques I*, pp. 385–451].
38 Bloch, 'Les *colliberti*', 389: they were fined according to *talem legem qua vixerit, sive sit liber, sive servus, sive colibertus*.
39 *Liber de Servis Majoris Monasterii*, ed. Ch. L. Grandmaison (Tours, 1864).
40 On Marmoutier, its serfs and its *familia*, P. Fouracre, 'Marmoutier and Its Serfs in the Eleventh Century', *Transactions of the Royal Historical Society* 6th series 15 (2005), 29–49 [repr. Fouracre, *Frankish History*, no. XV]; P. Fouracre, 'Marmoutier: *Familia* versus family. The relations between monastery and serfs in eleventh-century north-west France', in W. Davies, G. Halsall and A. Reynolds (eds), *People and Space in the Middle Ages 300–1300* (Turnhout, 2006), pp. 255–73; P. Fouracre, 'The "Book of Serfs" of Marmoutier (eleventh century): reflections on the development of servitude', in B. Hudson (ed.), *'Familia' and Household in the Medieval Atlantic World*, Penn State Medieval Studies 3 (Tempe, Az., 2011), pp. 123–39.
41 *Liber de Servis*, no. 101, pp. 94–5.
42 Grandmaison, *Liber de Servis*, pp. X–XII.
43 C. Wickham, *The Inheritance of Rome* (London, 2009), ch. 22, and C. Wickham, *Framing the Early Middle Ages. Europe and the Mediterranean, 400–800* (Oxford, 2005), pp. 570–88. On the process of subjugation, in which the *eulogia*, or voluntary and honourable gifts from peasant to lord, became another involuntary charge, see L. Kuchenbuch, '*Porcus donativus*: language use and gifting in seigniorial records between the eighth and tenth centuries', in G. Algazi, V. Groebner and B. Jussen (eds), *Negotiating the Gift: Pre-modern Figurations of Exchange*, Veröffentlichungen des Max-Planck-Instituts für Geschichte 188 (Göttingen, 2003),

pp. 193–246. On the *eulogiae* as part of peasant renders in Italy, see above Chapter 4, p. 124.
44 D. Barthélemy, *La société dans la comté de Vendôme de l'an mil au XIVe siècle* (Paris, 1991), pp. 481–90.
45 This reaction runs throughout Barthélemy's work, but see in particular D. Barthélemy, *The Serf, the Knight and the Historian*, trans. G. Edwards (Ithaca and London, 2009), and D. Barthélemy, *La société dans la comté de Vendôme*, esp. pp. 474–90. The frequent use of exclamation marks in these works is an indication of the strength of feeling with which Barthélemy challenges the Bloch-Duby-Bonnassie 'feudal revolution' tradition.
46 Rio, *Slavery after Rome*, pp. 108–11, extends this argument to manumission, thinking that Barthélemy was too categorical in judging that there was no difference between the manumitted and the serfs, whereas, according to Rio, p. 109: manumission was 'an intensely customizable practice, capable of taking on as many different functions as there were different kinds of dependants'.
47 Rio, *Slavery after Rome*, p. 55.
48 Barthélemy, *The Serf, the Knight and the Historian*, p. 37.
49 *Chartes et documents de l'abbaye de Saint-Pierre au Mont-Blandin à Gand*, ed. A. van Lockeren, 2 vols (Ghent, 1868, 1871).
50 See for instance *Chartes et documents de Saint-Pierre*, no. 191, p. 120 (from the year 1108) in which a woman, her niece and three daughters gave themselves into the *familia*, paid the usual charges but would have no legal representative other than the abbot.
51 Lists of tributaries: *Chartes et documents de Saint-Pierre*, nos 412, 455, 508. Renewal of documents nos 423, 431, 451, 452. These are all from the period 1200–32.
52 German historians do not seem to have followed up this comparison, possibly because Ghent was seen as part of the French kingdom, although note that Ghent was not in a Francophone region.
53 Rio, *Slavery after Rome*, p. 56.
54 Barthélemy, *The Serf, the Knight and the Historian*, pp. 44–50.
55 Grandmaison, *Liber de Servis*, pp. X–XIII.
56 F. L. Ganshof, *Feudalism*, trans. P. Grierson (3rd edn, London, 1964), pp. 6–9.
57 See above, p. 160, Barthélemy, *La société dans le comté de Vendôme*, pp. 474–5; Barthélemy, *The Serf, the Knight and the Historian*, pp. 51–4.
58 For disputes over status, inheritance and marriage, Fouracre, 'Marmoutier and its serfs'; Fouracre, 'Marmoutier: *familia* versus family'; Fouracre, '"The Book of Serfs" of Marmoutier'.
59 Fouracre, 'Reflections on the development of servitude', pp. 138–9.
60 *MGH Diplomata Regum* III, no. 41, pp. 46–7.
61 *Ex servilibus personis censuales fecisset, consentiente clero et populo*.
62 Toledo IV, c. 68, pp. 30–1.
63 *... postea sic ingenui sicut ceteri censuales persistant*.

64 For a typical example, in 1191–92 the monastery of Saint Emmeram pledged to protect its *censuales* from the depredations of a neighbouring count who was the advocate of another church: *Die Traditionen des Hochstifts Regensburg und des Klosters S. Emmeram*, no. 997.

65 Schulz, 'Zum Problem', pp. 69–71. The total of 4 *denarii*, in the Rhineland and Flanders (2 for wax and 2 for protection) is reminiscent of the 4 *denarii* paid by the *luminarii* of Saint Bertin in the ninth century and may suggest that *luminarii* were in effect *cerocensuales*.

66 *Stavelot-Malmedy*, no. 140, it was to be paid *ad cotidianum luminare*. If the conventional ratio of 12 *denarii* to the *solidus* holds here, this would indicate that there were 96 *census* payers.

67 *Stavelot-Malmedy*, no. 244, pp. 467–9. The document is discussed in E. Link, *Sozialer Wandel in Klösterlichen Grundherrschaft der 11 bis 13 Jahrhunderts. Studien zu den familiae von Gembloux, Stablo-Malmedy und Saint Trond* (Göttingen, 1979), pp. 85–7, and N. Schroeder, *Les hommes et la terre de Saint Remacle. Histoire sociale et économique de l'abbaye de Stavelot-Malmedy, VIIe–XIVe siècles* (Brussels, 2015), pp. 162–8.

68 On the importance of maintaining roofs, see above, Chapter 3.

69 Niermeyer, *Lexicon*, p. 167, defined this use of *censuarius* as 'rent collector'.

70 Schroeder, *Les hommes et la terre*, p. 151, n. 23.

71 Schroeder, *Les hommes et la terre*, p. 222, n. 17.

72 Schulz, 'Zensualität und Stadtentwicklung', pp. 116–20.

73 For the 'bittere Klage' that these restrictions engendered, Schulz, 'Zensualität und Stadtentwicklung', p. 117.

74 K. Andermann, 'Bürgerrecht. Die Speyer Priviligien von 1111 und die Anfänge persönlicher Freiheitsrechte in deutschen Städten des hohen Mittelalters', *Historische Zeitschrift* 296 (2012), 593–624.

75 *MGH Diplomata Regum et Imperatorum Germaniae X*, Friderici I, 4 (Hanover, 1990), nos 827, 828, pp. 34–6.

76 For the full inscription, Schulz, 'Zensualität und Stadtentwiccklung', p. 121.

77 K. Schulz, 'Stadtrecht und Zensualität am Niederrhein (12–14 Jahrhundert)', in E. Ennen and K. Flink (eds), *Soziale und wirtschaftliche Bindungen in Mittelalter der Niederrhein*, Klever Archiv 3 (Cleves, 1981), pp. 13–36.

78 Schulz, 'Stadtrecht und Zensualität', pp. 16–17.

79 Schulz, 'Zensualität und Stadtentwicklung', p. 112.

80 *Sponte ex libertate se tradiderunt vel servitude liberati aliorum traditione venerunt*, quoted in Schulz, 'Zum Problem', p. 69.

81 This was the opinion, perhaps based on folk etymology, of an eleventh-century Regensburg author who believed that *co-llibertus* meant 'co-freed' and that the *colliberti* paid *census*, but there are no examples of this in the East. Text quoted in Esders, *Die Formierung*, p. 95.

82 Esders, *Die Formierung*, p. 97.

# 6

## Lights in the later Middle Ages: from devotion to destruction

It was in the later medieval period that the use of lights in worship reached a high point, before being challenged and brought to a sudden end in some regions of Europe in the movement known as the 'Reformation'. The argument over the course of this study has been that pressure from the top over several centuries helped to generate support from below with the effect that more and more people became involved in meeting the costs of religious practice. By the time of the later Middle Ages most areas in Western Europe were wealthier than they had ever been, and an increasing number of people, who now came from a wider social range, could afford the wax and oil needed to keep lights burning in churches.[1] In consequence there were now more lights than ever. These included, of course, the eternal lights that burned on the altar and before shrines, but there was more generally a significant increase in the numbers of candles used in religious services, especially during festivals. The celebration of the purification of the Virgin Mary which takes place on the second day of February became known as Candlemas. This was when candles were distributed and as a festival it grew in importance. The number of lights kept burning to honour the dead rose sharply not only because people increasingly often organised into collectives to support the commemoration of their members but also because ever more individual bequests were made to pay for them. It became evident that belonging to organisations supporting churches and monasteries had become socially normal: this is clear from the spread down to parish level of confraternities and guilds that commemorated members with lights, maintained lights before saints' shrines, and which otherwise funded a growing range of religious practices.

The later eleventh and the twelfth centuries was a time of ecclesiastical reform. Religious excitement was generated by the Crusades, and, as has been made clear, confraternities and guilds began to proliferate. Higher standards were demanded of the clergy, the authority of the popes was strengthened and new, stricter, monastic orders were founded. A new departure in the early thirteenth century was 'the coming of the friars', that is, the invention of the mendicant orders which sent wandering preachers and ministers into the towns and across the countryside. Although support for what might be termed 'traditional monasteries' continued, lay persons across Europe began to express religious devotion from within their own communities. The friars provided a strong example of good works performed outside of the cloister, but still within strict religious discipline. The Fourth Lateran Council of 1215 exalted apostolic action, and the contemplative life of the monastery became less attractive. Confraternities and guilds, by contrast, became major social forces as they threw their weight behind charitable works, and as crafts and trade guilds, which had begun as religious confraternities, became economically and socially more powerful. Yet, as Robert Swanson has remarked, 'the amount these organizations spent on candles invariably exceeded the sum paid in formal charity'.[2]

In this, my final chapter, I shall look at the way in which a hardening of the concept of Purgatory affected giving for the lights, and, at the same time, I will show how demand for wax increased in the later Middle Ages and led to imports. These discussions are closely tied into the development and spread of confraternities and guilds. In André Vauchez's words (in translation), in the fourteenth and fifteenth centuries, 'the golden age of the laity', people were heavily concerned with 'book-keeping for the beyond'.[3] Giving for the lights was one way people hoped to shorten their time in Purgatory. Not surprisingly, this was a moment when records (the 'book-keeping') proliferated. Thus far, my approach has been to squeeze the relatively little evidence available for all it can tell us about the lights. In this chapter, though, I am dealing with a comparative superabundance of records, and I can do no more than pick examples from them to illustrate general trends. Although I shall look at the different regions of Europe in order to show how earlier ways of giving for the lights changed in rather different historical contexts, the emphasis will be on the phenomenon as a whole rather than upon the specific developments in each area. It will, however, be necessary to look in more detail at those areas which were most receptive to early reform teaching, for these, Germany and England, are where the very practice of burning eternal lights came to a sudden, and sometimes violent, end. Another reason for a more general approach is that, for the later period, the historical setting and the social and material consequences of providing for the lights have already been well treated by modern historians, not least by Vauchez himself and by Catherine Vincent. Ending with the Reformation will also bring us back to something like the starting point of the study: a moment at which belief in the efficacy of burning lights was challenged. Thinking again about how and to what effect that belief was accepted and came to be integral to the social practice of Catholic Christianity for over a millennium will form the final conclusion to this work.

I begin with Purgatory. In short, when people came to believe that a time of cleansing, but also of suffering (purgatory), preceded entry into heaven, they sought to shorten that period for themselves and for their loved ones by giving to the Church. This was in effect to buy out the suffering, and the process of doing so became systematised to the extent that the amount of time by which Purgatory might be shortened was calculated and costed. In fact every aspect of religious life and the life of Christ was subject to numerical calculation in a kind of holy arithmetic.[4] In mid-thirteenth-century England, episcopal statutes encouraged giving for the lights by promising ten days' indulgence (time off Purgatory) for those who did so.[5] There were, not surprisingly, confraternities dedicated to the relief of Purgatory. In the mid-fifteenth century the Confraternity of Purgatory of Lavaur in the Midi of France sought to shorten Purgatory for its members by burning an eternal lamp before 'the holy crucifix of Purgatory'. They paid for 3 to 4 l of oil which would be sufficient to keep the lamp burning for 15 days. That means they purchased over 85 l per year.[6] The cheapest letter of indulgence that might shorten the pains of purgatory cost 4 pence in early sixteenth-century England. The cost of a single mass which might have the same effect was also 4 pence.[7] This would seem to indicate a kind of 'entry-level' piety which a substantial element of the population could afford, and it is interesting to note that the annual render of those earlier tributaries had often been 4 pence, and 4 pence placed on the head had symbolised the recognition of serf status in the Marmoutier documents discussed in the last chapter. Were this amount to have been related to the price of a pound of wax, as I suggested earlier, it could be an indication of the extent to which the purchase of spiritual favours had become integral to the wider economy. Not unlike those merchants who gave cattle to provide lighting fuel for Hindu temples in Andhra Pradesh, people in Europe gave or lent out sheep and cattle the income from which paid for lighting.[8] In Germany the cattle were known as *ewige Rindern*, 'eternal cattle', for they paid for *ewiges Licht*, 'eternal light'. The rent for one cow for one year was one pound of wax.[9] In England sheep and cattle were bequeathed in wills, with the income from them going towards the lights.[10] In Kent, for instance, in 1358 Sir Otho de Grandison the lord of the manor of Chelsfield left to the church there 'four good cows and 20 good mother sheep' to provide two candles each of 18 lb weight 'to be lighted every day at the elevation of the sacrament'. He also left two cows for another light in Chelsfield church and another 40 sheep to provide for a 10 lb candle for yet another light to be burned on festival days. Only after these bequests did the will turn to people, with one shilling going to each of 40 tenants.[11] Sir Otho was clearly wealthy. To give cash on this scale was a mark of social as well as pious distinction. A social commodification of the means of salvation had taken place. I now turn to the confraternities themselves, to the growing demand for wax, and the imports that were needed to meet the demand.

Chapter 4 closed with a typical example of a confraternity being founded. It came into being at the very end of the twelfth century to support the monastery of Saint Martin at Canigou in the French Pyrenees, and the illustration accompanying the founding charter shows very clearly that providing for the lights of the monastery was an organising principle of the new foundation.[12] The confraternity of Saint Martin's Canigou stands, as it were, at the beginning of a flood in the numbers of such foundations. Another example of a confraternity founded around this time shows the veneration accorded to wax and also how confraternities could invent new festivals and traditions. This was the Confraternity of Notre Dame des Ardents, the 'Dame' being the Virgin Mary and the 'Ardents' being those who suffered from the affliction of ergotism, also known as 'Saint Anthony's Fire'. Following an outbreak of this distressing disease in the Arras area, allegedly in 1105, the Virgin appeared before two jugglers who were told to prepare the cathedral of Arras for her. She visited, carrying a large candle. Drips of wax from the candle fell into a vessel containing water, and then that water cured those suffering from ergotism. A confraternity that honoured the miracle of 'the holy candle' formed in 1175, and its members were made up of musicians and jugglers as well as other townspeople. In 1215 a chapel was built in the cathedral to honour the holy candle, and the latter, encased in silver, was housed in a tall pyramidical tower built for that purpose. The confraternity made an annual gift of wax to the monastery of Saint Vaast. Vaast, or Vedast, had been an early Merovingian bishop of Arras. His cult was firmly established by the ninth century. The wax the confraternity gave was moulded into the shape of a bear, Vedast being associated with bears.[13] The history of the Confraternity of Notre Dame des Ardents at Arras reflects the local traditions that might give identity to an organisation. It also shows the rising importance of the cult of the Virgin, and it reveals the widening social range of those involved in confraternities.

Here jugglers and musicians could demonstrate their social importance by contributing to the resourcing of the cathedral and monastery and by honouring Saint Vaast, for this anchored them into a distant past, represented by the wax bear. That more and more people were able and willing to pay for the lights was evident too in a massive increase in the amount of wax consumed by European religious institutions, especially in the fifteenth century. According to Catherine Vincent, there was in this century a 30 per cent increase in the amount of money spent on wax in the diocese of Cambrai.[14] The use of wax grew to the point that West European bees could no longer supply enough material for all this activity. Wax eventually had to be imported from the Baltic regions, and even from North Africa, the very place that had once supplied the oil which fuelled lights back in the late Roman period when burning lights at all times first began.[15] Alexandra Sapoznik's careful reading of late medieval English churchwarden and parish records shows that in the early sixteenth century the purchase of wax was typically the largest single expense of the parish church. At a minimum, 159,000 lb of wax was consumed annually to fulfil 'the most rudimentary Christian observance', not to mention the huge amounts of wax consumed in the lighting of shrines and at tombs. Hence the need for imports, and these amounted to about a fifth of all the wax consumed in England.[16] The imported wax was mostly said to be 'from Poland', which means the Baltic hinterland roughly from Novgorod to Warsaw. The trade was generally handled by Hanseatic merchants who guaranteed its quality. Wax from North Africa was imported through Lisbon. It came in much smaller quantities and was of poorer quality. Oil, which probably came from Provence and Italy, was also used, especially where an eternal light was required. This was above all in the major churches and cathedrals where chandeliers were made up of numerous lamps. Oil burned much more slowly than wax: one estimation has been that a litre of oil could fuel a lamp for 134 hours. For longer services and vigils in larger buildings, the oil-fed chandelier was a more reliable and longer-lasting source of light than the candle, even though it was trickier to operate, having to be lowered on a pulley system in order for the lamps to be filled.[17] Given that oil was now more available and at price comparable to that of wax, it is striking that it was not used more in the later Middle Ages. The apparent preference for wax might relate to the hallowing of wax over the earlier period: qualities of Christ-like purity and sacrifice were attributed to wax, as was made clear in prayers for the blessing of the paschal candle.[18] This, as well as its universal availability, may have given wax the edge over the purest olive oil that the original Mosaic injunction said should be burned before the tabernacle.[19]

In the last chapter it was shown that the categories of people who were *obliged*, often on a hereditary basis, to pay a charge for the lights and for other forms of support for the churches and monasteries were in decline in the central Middle Ages, although tithes, of which a part was assigned to payment for the lights, continued as a supposedly universal obligation. The hereditary tribute payers, and in particular the *censuales* or *cerocesuales* in Germany, lost their identity as privileged but dependent or 'semi-free' persons. This happened either as lords, lay or ecclesiastical, forced them into a less privileged position, i.e. stricter dependence, or, better evidenced, as their exclusive association with a particular religious institution was weakened in towns that were growing rapidly. In the face of increasing social complexity in the towns, and especially given the growing numbers of urban parishes, institutions in towns could no longer hold back marriage between members of different church *familiae*. The *censuales*, freed from marriage restrictions and the punitive inheritance dues that were likely to be imposed if those restrictions were ignored, steadily gained rights and improved their status until they became indistinguishable from the rest of the citizens. These developments took place for the most part over the course of the twelfth century. But as I have just suggested, confraternities, guilds and other parish organisations such as the *Zechen*, more than filled any gaps in lighting provision left by the fading away of tributary groups.

Alongside the guilds and confraternities, and sometimes in rivalry with them, were the lay adherents of monasteries and hospitals. These are revealed in acts of self-giving which are descended from the acts of auto-dedition that are so prominent in the early and central Middle Ages. But differences between the later acts, usually termed 'auto-traditions', and the earlier practices are, nevertheless, significant. These latter-day donors gave themselves and their possessions (the formula is *se et sua*) and became like monastic oblates, but remained in the outside world, their new status being marked by clothing or badges. They nevertheless intended to enter their chosen institution at the end of their lives. Until then they did not have to remain sexually abstinent. As a community they were different from a confraternity that supported a monastery in that they were now in a semi-monastic state and could hope to earn an indulgence by virtue of being more intensely religious.[20] Having a particular emotional connection to the mass, those who donated *se et sua* were criticised by some clergy for an extreme devotion which allegedly led them to interfere in the liturgy.[21] As with the earlier donations of self, women were prominent givers, and these donors like their predecessors enjoyed the protection of the church in taking on the fiscal immunity of their host institution. This was resented, especially in the Italian communes. What is clear is that these self-givers did not enter the servant *familia* of the monastery, they were not tied to tributes to be paid to an institution and they had the right to enter the monastery when close to death.[22] This speaks of a world rather different from that in which to give one's self was to enter a kind of religious servitude. Again, in terms of providing for the lights the shift was from a tributary mode towards devotion organised and funded by lay people. The idea that a religious life was possible while remaining a lay person would give rise to new communities of lay religious such as the penitents, beguines and beghards, and tertiaries. From the end of the fourteenth century in the Low Countries and parts of Germany there was a particularly strong lay movement, the *Devotio Moderna*, that sought spiritual excellence.[23] There is a paradox in that these movements may have been formed in the heat of religious devotion, but they had the effect of eating away at the comparative virtue of the priestly order. Concomitant with the rise of the lay religious was a decline in the power and prestige of bishops, though not everywhere in Europe: in the Auvergne in France, for instance, bishops enjoyed near princely power over the diocese. But in many areas bishops came under pressure from citizens, from rulers or princes. They lost control over their advocates and thus over their lands. They were forced to mortgage ancient rights such as the right to mint coins or to control markets. In short, despite reservoirs of prestige and power over cathedral, monasteries and saints' cults, bishops lost out to new forces in and around towns.[24]

The later Middle Ages was thus a time in which traditional forms of religious life that went back to the very establishment of the Catholic Church were under pressure from newly mobilised lay patrons. It was certainly not a time of waning religious enthusiasm or of a kind of cultural exhaustion as Johan Huizinger thought.[25] The growth of the *Devotio Moderna* alone serves to puncture that impression.[26] If giving for the lights is a sure indicator, then support for the Church was at a height, and this is something that can be roughly quantified according to the figures for the purchases of wax which were recorded across a range of documents: parish accounts, wills, cathedral records, guild records and the records of central government.[27] The expenditure on wax by King Henry III of England (1216–72) provides a good example of the level of detail in government records, and these show the king providing for eternal lights at chosen shrines, sometimes on a six-monthly basis. These payments appear relatively small (as low as half a mark) considering that they often included the stipend of the clerk who was to tend the light. It is notable that this ruler was concerned with the provision of single lights at named shrines, which is suggestive of a personal devotion that is mirrored in the thousands of small donations across society. In other contexts the royal court paid for and transported 'in strong carts' very large amounts of wax, that is, into the thousands of pounds in weight.[28] King Henry stored his wax in depots and took from them as it was needed. One suspects that this wax was imported: it was of high quality and some of the depots were on or near the coast. On the one hand devotion was personal and even intimate, but on the other hand rulers might demonstrate their power and standing by the public consumption of very large amounts of wax. The light it produced reflected a glory that was as earthly as it was ethereal. It was no doubt the personal element, particularly in relation to salvation, that drew in the mass of donors, but it was an association between light and power that kept the elite interested in providing for the lights. The attraction of doing so across the social spectrum is an important element in the whole history of the use of light in worship. It explains why practices originally the preserve of the elite spread so widely, and, further, why the elite continued to give even when the Church's needs seem to have been met.

Although there was diversification in forms of religious organisation in the later Middle Ages, there was also great continuity in worship and commemoration. The belief that a church could not be consecrated unless the founder could demonstrate that it had an endowment sufficient to maintain a light had been established in the sixth century. This was a condition stipulated at the councils of Braga in later sixth-century Spain and it would be repeated by the Carolingian rulers of Francia in the ninth century.[29] It was seen again in eleventh-century Germany, and appears in the mid-twelfth century in the *Decretum* of Gratian where the stipulation is expressed in wording close to that of Braga.[30] Gratian's canon law collection would be highly influential for the rest of the Middle Ages. This element of continuity is a good illustration of how beliefs and practices promoted in the early Middle Ages had by the later Middle Ages become a cornerstone of religious life, and how the common nature of practices helped to mediate between different social classes. Salvation was the aim across the social spectrum, and providing for the lights was something a richer peasant could do as well as a noble in order to earn it. At the same time, providing for the lights and other needs actually had the effect of reinforcing the social hierarchy where the ability to provide was associated with power, and where the very process of collecting lighting and other dues strengthened the hands of the lords. I will come back to these continuities and common themes in a final review of the subject, but I will now briefly look at the situation in the different parts of Europe before turning to the way in which the veneration of light began to be challenged. I shall have relatively little to say about Italy, Spain and France where traditional practices continued to flourish; confraternities still involved a broad social spectrum; and gifts for the lights remained important. But in all these regions too, the provision for the lights became less prominent in the record as the cost of providing them declined in relation to rising incomes and increasing wealth generally. It is also the case that in the larger churches there was from the seventeenth century onward more natural light as developments in building techniques allowed bigger spaces that were undivided by the supporting walls of aisles, and sometimes domes let light in from the centre. There were fewer dark corners and niches, which meant that an incessantly burning light was less impressive. That is to say changes in technology and fashion rather than belief thinned the number of lights in regions which adhered to traditional Catholicism. More will be said about Germany and England where reform taught people to disregard practices that were now classified as 'errors, superstitious ceremonies and human inventions'.[31]

The rapid growth in numbers of guilds and confraternities, the rising prominence of Purgatory in the later medieval thought world, and the indulgences designed to ease Purgatorial pains, the great increase in the amount of wax consumed and the growing numbers of bequests and gifts for the lights were common developments across Europe, but they had a different framing in the various regions. Those differences were essentially historical. In Italy the growth of communal government in the towns was in part at the expense of the power of the bishop. Confraternities mushroomed. In late fifteenth-century Florence there were at least a hundred of them.[32] The importance of the towns is reflected in the increase in numbers of merchant and artisan saints. By contrast, only one priest was sanctified in later medieval Italy.[33] This shift towards lay intitiative left day-to-day religious acts being performed or supervised by lay people, although it was only the priest who could administer the sacrament. A study of San Sepolcro, a town of about five thousand inhabitants in Tuscany, focused on one of its 14 confraternities, that of San Bartolomeo which by the thirteenth century had upwards of a hundred members.[34] San Bartolomeo's 'Book of the Dead', which runs from 1377, recorded deaths and burials, the latter invariably followed by the phrase 'we have the wax'. Since relatives of the dead gave one candle to the confraternity, unless they were poor, this was in effect a mortuary tax. After a funeral service, a member of the confraternity would usually take the remains of one candle. The remnants of candles (termed *moccholi*) were saved until there was enough wax to fashion new ones, and these could be given to the poor or sold.[35] This trade and charity in wax was a defining function of the confraternity, and sums involved in wax sales were high: in 1443, for instance, they sold 400 lb of old wax for 192 lire. Devotion in Italy came in the form of charitable works like these and in the profusion of new groups of lay faithful living lives dedicated to repentance, such as the flagellants, and of course memorialisation remained the focus of a confraternity such as that of San Bartolomeo. Bishops were generally too weak for there to be clashes between cathedral and confraternity. This is an important factor in Italy's unresponsiveness to late medieval teaching on reform. That the latter challenged the authority of Rome was of course another factor in why reformist thinking made little headway in Italy.

France, like Italy, had towns that were old and well established. In the Ile de France, Burgundy and Champagne many towns were under royal control and there was less tension between citizens and bishops. France was more responsive to reform but reformers were blocked by the rulers and threatened with violence, as in the case of John Calvin who was forced to flee to Switzerland in 1536. The French claimed for themselves freedoms and liberties within the Catholic Church in a doctrine later known as 'Gallicanism'.[36] There was, in short, no need for reform that came from challenging the authority of Rome, and no drive, at least for some while, to challenge the culture of venerating the dead through the burning of lights. Spain is slightly different again, but here too the confraternity culture was not challenged. Indeed, confraternities became essential to the organisation of parishes as the Christian kingdoms expanded southwards.[37] Many of the confraternities were closely linked with the military orders before their suppression, and to Christ, Mary and sundry saints after this. Again, reform was apparently not on the agenda in an age of expansion. In all of these areas, the maintenance of lights on the altar, before shrines and at tombs continued to attract funds from lay persons and from religious associations. Candelabra and oil lamps became highly decorated and many survive in museum collections as valuable objects of high art. In fact some of the glass lamps of the Renaissance period were so finely crafted and decorated that centuries later their original function was not recognised, and in the nineteenth century some were given metal bases and were treated as goblets.[38] As Figure 8 shows, these hanging lamps could be used in tandem with altar candles to create a spectacular display of light.

England provides what seems to be the strongest contrast between practices in the early and in the later Middle Ages. In the Introduction and in Chapter 4 of this work it was noted that from the entire Anglo-Saxon period

**8** *The Presentation in the Temple*, copy of Cort's engraving after Frederico Zuccaro, 1568

there is only one document (a will) that recorded a gift for the lights. There were, however, references in normative sources (laws and church canons) to the levying of a common due for the lights. This was known as 'light-scot' or 'wax-scot'. In addition, the English paid for lights in Rome in the form of 'Peter's Pence'.[39] England also legislated for the collection of tithes, a proportion of which should have gone to the lights according to continental practice. But from England before the year 1066 there is simply no evidence that any of these dues were actually collected. There were guilds in England before 1066 but, as we have seen, their regulations have very little to say about lights.[40] After the Norman Conquest of England the picture seems to change greatly. There were, at least from about 1100 onwards, grants for lighting in charters much as might be found in continental Europe.[41] Provision for the lights thereafter became a common element in wills, and guilds and confraternities proliferated and provided wax for funerals and commemoration as they did elsewhere in Europe. The question of how the Norman Conquest changed England is a staple of undergraduate study, but it is not a question asked of this change, perhaps because the answer is too elusive, hence the use here of the term 'seems'. On the face of it, the Normans brought England sharply into line with continental practices, but general levies only slowly died out, and Peter's Pence was collected, if only sporadically, into the sixteenth century. The rapid growth of confraternities and guilds in England after 1066 mirrors their growth elsewhere in Europe and may not have been a consequence of conquest. As noted above, the development of a belief in Purgatory, and the remission at which the indulgences were aimed, were key factors in the increasing number of donations for the lights. Concern with Purgatory became firmly established only relatively late in the twelfth century, thus long after the Norman Conquest. It was a phenomenon common to all the regions of Europe, and thus no less of a driver of change in England than elsewhere. Likewise, England was subject to the same patterns of demographic change, increasing prosperity and urban growth as other regions. Any 'effects of the Norman Conquest' must therefore be set against the wider picture of change across Europe. Although where lights were concerned, the argument from the silence before 1066 compared to the busy documentation after 1100 seems compelling, even that contrast may be partly explained by differences in diplomatic style, and by the poorer survival rate of documents from Anglo-Saxon England. But whatever the reasons for the record of English practices coming to resemble those of other regions, the fact remains that they did do so. By the late fourteenth century there were guilds at parish level in England. They repaired churches, organised festivals and maintained lights in honour of patron saints. In 1388 Parliament ordered an inquiry into the foundations, statutes and properties of guilds.[42] There were more than five hundred returns from craft and parish guilds, but, since there were more than nine thousand parish churches to support, this can only be a fraction of the total number of guilds in later medieval England. One feature that does seem to be particularly prevalent in England was the formation of guilds for women only.[43] The lights they maintained were called 'maiden lights' and they tended to honour female saints. This movement continued into the 1530s until the Henrician Reformation put an end to the veneration at saints' shrines in England.

In Germany, as already noted, bishops were generally under pressure where townspeople stood to gain rights at their expense. This remains generally true despite regional variation, and despite differences in the nature and history of towns in Germany: many towns were 'new', but some were ancient. Others had privileges derived from status as 'imperial towns', yet others were run by bishops of princely status, and some were under the control of lay princes.[44] The Hanseatic town of Lübeck, now a World Heritage Site, provides a good example of how new and old might be linked from one trading centre to another through a devotional concern which merchants brought with them when they moved to establish themselves in new centres. Thanks to the very high number of Wills from Lübeck (over a thousand of them survive for the period up to 1530) it is possible to see these devotional activities in some detail. They focus on the cult of Mary, to which large sums were given for eternal lights. The merchant Albert Bisschop, for instance, in 1459 left 100 marks for an inscribed lamp to burn day and night in Lübeck cathedral. The inscription recalled that Bisschop was originally from Bruges where he had been on the town council. He left another 2,716 marks to relatives in towns around the Baltic, including Riga, as well as supporting several ecclesiastical institutions in Lübeck itself. The inscribed lamp was an eternal and very public commemoration of his success.[45]

The variation in the status and history of its episcopal centres means that Germany was unevenly divided up into parishes. Imperial and royal towns, like Frankfurt for example, tended to have fewer parishes than trading towns which grew rapidly and added parishes as the population grew.[46] Everywhere, however, the responsibility to provide for the lights, as well as to maintain the fabric of the church, lay with the parish.[47] Quite apart from a change in belief in the Reformation, it was the declining power of the bishops in the face of the rising influence of the parish that would place lights at the centre of struggles to control cathedrals. In a series of studies published over the last fifty years, Rolf Kiessling has shown in detail how parish organisations rose to challenge the senior clergy in Augsburg.[48] In common with so many German towns, Augsburg received a town law in the mid-twelfth century. The *censuales* of Augsburg merged with the citizens (*Bürger*) and a superior class of *ministeriales* in turn merged with the *Bürger* over the course of the thirteenth century. The bishop lost control over Augsburg's advocate and was forced to concede rights over market and mint. From the mid-thirteenth century a town seal, a town council, a town hall (*Rathaus*), *Bürgermeister*, consuls, councillors and other officials are all documented. By the fourteenth century Augsburg had two separate legal bodies, the *Bürgerstadt* and the cathedral foundation (*Hochstift*). The next century would see conflict between the two, as was the case across southern Germany. In Augsburg there were in addition to the various confraternities parish organisations known as *Zechen*, first documented in 1284 for the parish of Saint Ulrich.[49] The origins of the *Zeche* lay in the provision of lights for the altar, for family graves and for the chancel. The *Zechen* also provided furniture for the parish churches and cathedral. By the end of the fourteenth century there was a *Zeche* for every parish in Augsburg. Each had a *Zechmeister* who recorded the organisation's accounts, the first records being from 1430–31. The point was to show the income and expenditure from each *Zeche*. Kiessling shows how the *Zechen* came into conflict with the ecclesiastical authorities as they demanded a greater say over how the funds they raised were spent. This is particularly clear in the case of Saint Moritz, a foundation of canons which was second in importance only to the cathedral.[50] Saint Moritz is first recorded as having a parish in 1129. By 1288 it was being part-funded by a parish *Zeche*, but the grant associated with the funds stipulated that the clergy should not have control of them. The main purpose of the funds was for prayers for the dead and for lights. By 1338 the Saint Moritz *Zeche* had pledged to maintain seven lights on the altar. In addition there were eternal lights for commemoration. By 1469 there were 16 eternal lights in Saint Moritz. The Saint Moritz *Zeche* was powerful because the parish was the richest in Augsburg and was backed by the Fuggers, the leading banking family. Conflict, as one might expect when funding was involved, was rather prosaic. It was about the cost of building works, about who should appoint the sacristan and about keyholders. Each time Saint Moritz backed down, and since it involved leading citizens, the *Zeche* tended to get the backing of the town council.[51] So, by the beginning of the sixteenth century the Saint Moritz *Zeche* had influence over church services, church building and the cemetery. They owned the priest's house and ran a parish school.[52] This high level of parish involvement would set the scene for the Reformation in Augsburg, for funding followed belief, although in Augsburg there was actually a plurality of beliefs: Martin Luther remarked that the town was divided into six tendencies or sects.[53] It is to the effect of reform teaching on the lights that I now turn.

Luther famously began his attack on the authority of Rome by protesting against the sale of indulgences. There had in fact been unease about the way in which indulgences were marketed and sold for well over a century before Luther posted his call for reform in 1517.[54] Geoffrey Chaucer, writing at the end of the fourteenth century, certainly thought the practice ripe for ridicule as can be seen from his depiction of the 'Pardoner' in the Prologue to the *Canterbury Tales*. The Pardoner was an indulgence salesman. He had a knapsack full of pardons 'hot from Rome', and he used fake relics to induce people to buy them:

> But with thise relikes, whan that he fond
> A povre person dwellynge upon lond
> Upon a day he gat hym moore moneye
> Than that person gat in months tweye,
> And thus, with feyned flaterye and japes
> He made the person and the peple his apes.[55]

The key change in the thought of Luther was that he saw the concept of Purgatory as an invention of the papacy driven by money-mindedness. It was thus a product of human artefact and did not arise from a divine mandate. In his view salvation was conferred by the Grace of God, for only God could judge. To attempt to buy salvation through an indulgence was not just wrong (it was a form of simony) but also offensive. The money could be spent in better ways, on charity rather than candles.[56] There is some evidence to suggest that this shift took place against a background of coin hoarding and silver debasement in Germany. It was conventional to decry avarice and hoarding, and burying money had been condemned in Scripture. Luther knew well a fourteenth-century text by Nicholas Oresme referring to King Theoderic of Italy (ruled 493–521) who was said to have forbidden the placing of gold and silver in tombs when that wealth could be used for the public good.[57] So, apart from an immediate need to save money, there was a strong moral and historical case for ceasing to waste it on candles. It was, further, pointless for the living to pray for the dead, or to commemorate themselves in ways meant to attract God's attention. God knew perfectly well who should be saved and who should be damned. Saints' relics and shrines should not be venerated. They could not influence the saving of souls any more than could the deceased's relatives. This way of thinking was shared by Zwingli in Switzerland and the effect was at a stroke to cut lights out of the picture.

In Zurich, Basel and Strasbourg, areas particularly influenced by the more iconoclastic Zwingli, the antipathy towards the lights culminated in 1524 in attacks on lamps. Lay supporters of Zwingli who were in the main craftsmen, thus likely to belong to social organisations which had formerly funded the lights, now attacked the practice of burning lights as idolatry (*Abgötteri*). Oil lamps and candles were seen as evil consumers of pious bequests and of tithe income. The lamps were referred to as *Ölgötzen*, 'oil-guzzling idols', and sometimes they were smashed.[58] It was apparently the oil rather than the lamps themselves which was offensive. Funding for oil tended to come from the tithe rather than from donations, and it was the tithe that was the form of ecclesiastical income that laypeople found most onerous.[59] The Zurich lamp-smashers were treated leniently, for they received only three days in prison as punishment. The authorities seemed to take the violent action rather lightly, and the town council to more or less validate it.[60] They allowed images to remain in the churches, but candles could not be burned before them. Then a new council ordered all 'idols' to be removed and broken up. They were to be melted down and the proceeds given to the poor. In Strasbourg in 1525 the council was requested to remove all idols, and this included a lamp that burned before an image of the Mount of Olives, for the lamp 'burns more than ever and during the day, in defiance of God and pious Christians'.[61] The idea that burning light in the day was stupid takes us back to the beginning of this study, where the same thought that lighting candles in the day was pointless and should be excluded from Christian practice was expressed at the Council of Elvira in the late fourth century.[62] The rather uncomfortable fit between Old and New Testaments which had been an issue in early Christianity resurfaced here. The point is that the original decision to adopt the Mosaic injunction to burn an eternal light was tied up in the design of a Christian priesthood, the priesthood being seen to descend from the sons of Aaron who were given the charge of maintaining an eternal flame.[63] This the sixteenth-century reformers were trying to unravel. One can see why they might have wished to do so, given the growing lay control of church income and expenditure. The historical irony is that the same lay enthusiasm which had been nurtured for so long had led to a profusion of light which suddenly seemed excessive when light was disassociated from eternity. The growing involvement of parish guilds had also helped lay people gain control of church funds, church furniture and church appointments.

So far I have been discussing reform in German-speaking lands. As might be expected, given the great variety of towns, the relative strengths and weaknesses of the bishops, and the complex political history of Germany, the pace and permanency of reform differed greatly from region to region. Each place had a local history that determined the relationship between lay and ecclesiastical, between reform and orthodoxy.[64] The lights would eventually be back in Augsburg, but not in Zurich. In England the picture is somewhat different, but with the same effect upon the lights. There, reform was brought about by a series of acts promulgated by central government through Parliament, albeit the reformers were trying to put into practice ideas that came from the German-speaking areas. This means the same crucial challenge to the concept of Purgatory and the banning of lights before shrines, eternal lights on the altar and commemorative lights. These were 'works devised by men's fantasies' and were 'things tending to idolatry and superstition': an ancient belief was now reclassified as 'superstition'. As an act which shows the political weight behind the reform, one could point to the destruction of the shrine of Saint Thomas à Becket at Canterbury, the very place towards which Chaucer's Pardoner and the other pilgrims had been heading. In 1538 King Henry VIII arrived at Canterbury, destroyed the shrine and scattered the bones of England's premier saint.[65] Thomas's sanctity had of course derived from the fact that he was martyred for defending the Catholic church and Rome against Henry's twelfth-century namesake. But at the same time, Henry outlawed the entire cult of the saints which had been a focus of mortuary piety. No longer could lights be set before images, and soon the images themselves would be removed from churches. Any money that could be made by melting down precious metals they contained was to go towards the cost of producing a bible for every church. The symbolic importance of candles for both traditionalists and reformers can be seen from two episodes involving queens. Queen Anne Boleyn was executed in 1536, just after attacks on the cult of intercession had begun. Anne had been strongly associated with Protestantism and her death was welcomed by traditionalists. A rumour then started in Dover that at the moment she was beheaded the candles surrounding the grave of her Catholic predecessor had spontaneously ignited as a token of the restoration of the old order. In 1558 Anne Boleyn's daughter Elizabeth became queen, following the death of her sister Mary who had tried to restore Catholic practices in England. Elizabeth had to walk a tightrope between traditionalists and reformers. In 1559 when she attended Westminster Abbey for the opening of Parliament she was met by the abbot and a procession bearing candles. In order to show her credentials

*Eternal light and earthly concerns*

as a reformer she turned on the procession and called out 'away with those torches, for we see very well'.[66] Here again was the notion that burning lights in daylight was pointless and even superstitious. So this public attack on them was political. At the other end of the tightrope, Elizabeth had candles and a cross set up in her private chapel, something that was frowned on by the reformers, much to the comfort of the traditionalists. Those in power could not avoid commenting on the lights, whether they were for or against them. Fittingly, to the very end, the subject of lights was one germane to a discourse of power, something this study has traced forward from the time of Charlemagne.

In his pathbreaking work *The Stripping of the Altars*, Eamon Duffy was concerned to counter the Protestant narrative of the Reformation, which began with an exhausted and decaying church run by a venal clergy. In Duffy's view late medieval Catholicism 'exerted an enormously strong, diverse and vigorous hold over the imagination and the loyalty of the people up to the very moment of the Reformation'.[67] Though his approach has been criticised for being too much an *apologia* for medieval Catholicism, and for wilfully refusing to explore the notion of popular religion, Duffy was surely right to emphasise the suddenness and shock of the change.[68] It was shocking because it marked a sharp change in a sphere that was supposedly immutable. In a second, and less contentious, work, *The Voices of Morebath*, Duffy followed the effects of the Reformation on one small Devonshire village, Morebath.[69] This could be done because the long-lived priest at Morebath kept parish records for the whole period 1520–74. They begin with a parish organised around various saints' cults, including the cult of Saint Sidwell which the pastor had introduced and painstakingly built up. The records detail the holdings of 'stores' which were the funds collected for each saint. These stores look rather like the Augsburg *Zechen*. Their main income was from sheep, each household having one sheep to rear, and from brewing and selling ale. The income was primarily for the lights. In 1538 it was forbidden to burn lights before images, and the accounts for 1538 show that no more was spent on them.[70] In the record for 1539 the stores were no longer mentioned, and the sheep were amalgamated into a single church flock. The income now went towards buying a bible and other books. By now the images in the church had been taken down and other decorations removed. Next, after 1547 the church flock was sold, and all moneys now went to the poor box in the church. To quote Duffy: 'by the early summer of 1549 the parish of Morebath had been stripped to the bone. Its images and many ritual furnishings were gone, vestments concealed. Its social life was suspended as the church house lay locked and empty, and every one of its parish organisations had been dissolved'.[71]

Duffy noted with surprise the promptness of obedience to these orders to drop acts of intercession and to get rid of precious images, and otherwise to change age-old practices. For this was a very traditional region of England.[72] The swift obedience must relate in part to the coercive power of Tudor government, for attempted risings against the changes were met with brutal force. But in many areas of England, and in most of Germany too, these sudden changes were carried through without force. One cannot imagine many people feeling threatened by the lamp-smashers of Zurich. Much of the obedience must relate to the way in which this massive change in belief seems to have been readily accepted, possibly because the argument that Purgatory and intercession were human inventions was irrefutable once it was shown that these beliefs and practices had no scriptural support. Once the belief that it was possible to intercede with God through ritual practices fractured, those practices would immediately become redundant. This might help explain the suddenness of the change. Once parish organisations had acquired the images and provided the candles, and paid the priest to say masses for individuals, they were in a position to halt the machinery of intercession. A first step that was symbolically important in breaking the material link with eternity was snuffing out the lights. It was a highly visible and venerable act that went to the heart of the new.

### Notes

1 D. Postles, 'Lamps, Lights and Layfolk: Popular Devotion before the Black Death', *Journal of Medieval History* 25.2 (1999), 97–114, at 98.
2 R. Swanson, *Religion and Devotion* in Europe c. 1215–1515 (Cambridge, 1995), p. 122.
3 A. Vauchez, *The Laity in the Middle Ages*, trans. B. Schneider (Notre Dame, Ind., 1993), p. 25. A phrase that evokes the same phenomenon, *gezählte Frömmigkeit* (literally, 'calculated piety'), is common in German-language scholarship: see, for instance, A. Angenendt, T. Brauks, R. Busch, T. Lentes and H. Lutterbach, 'Gezählte Frömmigkeit', *Frühmittelalterliche Studien* 29 (1995), 1–75.
4 The classic work is J. Le Goff, *The Birth of Purgatory*, trans. A. Golhammer (Chicago, 1984). The definitive statement on the shortening of Purgatory came from the Second Council of Lyons, held in 1274: 'Repentant souls cleansed after death by purgatorial or purifying punishment ... to relieve punishment of this kind, the offerings of the living faithful are of advantage to these, namely, the sacrifice of Masses, prayers, alms, and the other duties of piety which have customarily been performed by the faithful for the other faithful according to the regulations of the Church'. For a very clear explanation for the growing

importance of Purgatory and of the willingness to buy indulgences to shorten the time spent there, P. Marshall, *Heretics and Believers. A History of the English Reformation* (New Haven and London, 2018), pp. 16–22.

5   Postles, 'Lamps, lights and layfolk', 105. More sinister was the 40 days' indulgence offered to people who would carry a faggot to the burning of a heretic.
6   C. Vincent, *Fiat lux. Lumière et luminaires dans la vie religieuse du XIIe au XVI siècle* (Paris, 2004), p. 71.
7   R. Swanson. *Religion and Devotion*, pp. 219–20, 227.
8   On the temple cattle see above, Chapter 1.
9   R. Kiessling, *Bürgerliche Gesellschaft und Kirche in Augsburg im Spätmittelalter* (Augsburg, 1971), pp. 102–8.
10  A. Sapoznik, 'Bees in the Medieval Economy: Religious Observance and the Production, Trade, and Consumption of wax in England c. 1300–1500', *Economic History Review* 72.4 (2019), 1152–74, at 1157.
11  G. Copus (ed.), *Chelsfield Chronicles 1450–1920's. Annals of a Kentish Parish* (Tunbridge Wells, 2003), p. 33. In the early sixteenth century in the village of Morebath in Devon each household in the parish was required to look after one sheep, the wool going to the parish church: E. Duffy, *The Voices of Morebath. Reformation and Rebellion in an English Village* (New Haven and London, 2001).
12  See above, p. 143.
13  Vincent, *Fiat lux*, p. 159.
14  Vincent, *Fiat lux*, p. 154.
15  Note that the modern French word for a candle, *bougie*, derives from the bay of Bougie on the Algerian coast. For the increase in wax consumption and the import of wax, A. Sapoznik, 'Bees', 1160–7.
16  Sapoznik, 'Bees', 1158, 1166. She also shows that the price of wax was falling over the later period: in the year 1300, five days' work was what it took to earn enough to buy a pound of wax. By 1400 this had fallen to 1.5 days, 'Bees', 1164. For a selection of parish records which show how much wax was donated for funerals and festivals, R. Swanson, *Catholic England. Faith, Religion and Observance before the Reformation* (Manchester, 1993, reissued 2014), pp. 150–63.
17  These points are made by B. Graham, 'Olives and Lighting in Dark Age Europe', *Early Medieval Europe* 28.3 (2020), 344–66.
18  See above, Chapter 4.
19  For the wording of that injunction, Chapter 1 above.
20  C. de Miramon, *Les donnés au Moyen Age. Une forme de vie religieuse laïque v. 1180 – v. 1500* (Paris, 1999), p. 97.
21  De Miramon, *Les donnés*, pp. 274–80.
22  The *se et sua* donation is here like the English *corrody*, a point de Miramon finally came to on p. 332 of *Les donnés*.
23  J. van Engen, *Sisters and Brothers of the Common Life. The Devotio Moderna and World of the later Middle Ages* (Philadelphia, 2008).

24 U. Grieme, N. Kruppa and S. Patzold (eds), *Bischof und Bürger. Herrschaftsbeziehungen in den Kathedralstädten des Hoch- und Spätmittelaltern* (Göttingen, 2004). This collection consists of 12 papers each of which examines the pressures on bishops from different angles.
25 The classic work is J. Huizinga, *The Waning of the Middle Ages* (Eng. trans., London, 1924).
26 Note 23 above.
27 Vincent, *Fiat lux*, pp. 406–33, for a clear account of the spread of lighting provision in the later Middle Ages.
28 *Calendar of the Liberate Rolls*, ed. H. Maxwell Lyte, 6 vols (Public Records Office, London, 1916–64). These documents are basically writs ordering expenditure. The volumes are well indexed. Wax and lights appear under heading 'Ecclesiastical matters'.
29 See above, Chapter 2.
30 Above, Chapter 5 for the recall of the Braga canons in Germany. Gratian, *De consecratione* 1.9: *Nemo ecclesiam edificet ante quam civitatis episcopus veniat et ibidem crucem figat, publice atrium designet et ante prefiniat, qui edificare vult, que ad luminaria, et ut ad custodiam, et stipendia custodum sufficiat, et ostensa donatione sic domum edificet.* Quoted from Vincent, *Fiat lux*, pp. 48–9.
31 The phrase comes from the opening of *Fox's Book of Martyrs*.
32 Swanson, *Religion and Devotion*, p. 118.
33 Vauchez, *The Laity*, pp. 103–5.
34 J. Banker, *Death in the Community. Memorialization and Confraternities in an Italian Commune in the Late Middle Ages* (Athens, Ga, and London, 1998).
35 Banker, *Death in the Community*, pp. 95–8.
36 P. Fouracre, 'Francia and the History of Medieval Europe', *Haskins Society Journal* 23 (2011, pub. 2014), 1–21, at 3–5.
37 A. Durán Cudiol, *El hospital de Somport entre Aragón y Bearn (siglos XII–XIII)* (Zaragoza, 1986) for the study of how one confraternity expanded until it had 21 parishes dependent upon it.
38 E. Sani, 'Renaissance Light: a Glass *Cesendello* (Hanging Lamp) Rediscovered', *Journal of Glass Studies* 59 (2017), 193–205.
39 Above, p. 118.
40 See above, Chapter 5, p. 116.
41 Postles, 'Light, lamps and layfolk', 97–8, for an early example, a charter from between 1109 and 1114.
42 B. Hanawalt, 'Keepers of the Lights: Late Medieval Parish Gilds', *Journal of Medieval and Renaissance Studies* 14 (1984), 21–37.
43 K. French, 'Maiden's Lights and Wives' Stores: Women's Parish Guilds in Late Medieval England', *The Sixteenth Century Journal* 29 (1998), 399–425.
44 For the range of towns in Germany and common pressures on bishops, H. Flachenecher, 'Eine vertane Chance? Die Rolle der bischöflichen *civitates* in hochmittelalterlichen Spannung zwischen Raumerfassung und

Herrschaftsausbildung', in U. Grieme, N. Kruppa and S. Patzold (eds), *Bischof und Bürger. Herrschaftsbeziehungen in den Kathedralstädten des Hoch- und Spätmittelaltern* (Göttingen, 2004), pp. 11–26.

45 H. Dormeier, 'Das laikale Stiftungsgewesen in spätmittelalterliche Pfarrkirchen: Kaufleute, Korporationen und Marienverehrung in Lübeck', in E. Bünz and G. Fouquet (eds), *Die Pfarrei im späten Mittelalter, Vorträge und Forschungen 77* (Ostfildern, 2013), pp. 279–340. Extracts from the wills are on pp. 323–37, and a list of members of the Marian confraternity at pp. 337–40.

46 F. Schmieder, 'Die Pfarrei in der deutschen städtischen Kirchenlandschaft', in E. Bünz and G. Fouquet (eds), *Die Pfarrei im späten Mittelalter, Vorträge und Forschungen 77* (Ostfildern, 2013), pp. 131–56.

47 W. Petke, 'Die Pfarrei in Mitteleuropa im Wandel vom Früh-zum Hochmittelalter', in E. Bünz and G. Fouquet (eds), *Die Pfarrei im späten Mittelalter, Vorträge und Forschungen 77* (Ostfildern, 2013), pp. 21–60, at pp. 58–9.

48 The seminal work is R. Kiessling, *Bürgerliche Gesellschaft und Kirche in Augsburg im Spätmittelalter* (Augsburg, 1971).

49 *Zeche* (pl. *Zechen*) means 'account' in modern German, but the verb *zechen* means to drink alcohol. Whether the Augsburg *Zechen* had a drinking culture is not clear. If they had, then the *Zechmeister* might have been a kind of master of ceremonies as well as the head of accounts. In late Middle High German *Zeche* had the meaning of 'accounting organization'. The term is seen very rarely outside of Augsburg.

50 R. Kiessling, 'Pfarrgemeinde und Zeche bei Saint Moritz. Die Mitwirkung der Laien in einer zentralen Pfarrei der Stadt', in G. Müller (ed.), *Das ehemalige Kollegialstift Saint Moritz in Augsburg (1019–1803)* (Lindenberg, 2006), pp. 185–208.

51 Kiessling, *Bürgerliche Gesellschaft*, p. 103. In 1511 the cathedral *Zeche* even attempted to paint the town arms on to the chests they held in the church: Kiessling, *Bürgerliche Gesellschaft*, p. 117

52 Kiessling, 'Saint Moritz', pp. 189–90.

53 Kiessling, 'Saint Moritz', pp. 194–6.

54 For works generally critical of the culture of cost and calculation, Angenendt et al., *Gezählte Frömmigkeit*, 57–79.

55 *The Canterbury Tales, General Prologue*, ll. 701–6, *The Riverside Chaucer* (Oxford, 1987), p. 34.

56 Note Swanson's comment, quoted above, that before this candles predominated over charity.

57 P. Rössner, 'Luther – ein tüchtiger Ökonom? Über die monetären Ursprünge der Deutschen Reformation', *Zeitschrift für Historische Forschung* 42 (2015), 37–74, at 55–9.

58 L. Wandel, *Voracious Idols and Violent Hands. Iconoclasm in Reformation Zurich, Strasbourg and Basel* (Cambridge, 1995), pp. 67–75. Candles may have been included in the term *ölgötzen*: in a fictional dialogue of 1523 an old mother figure (*Mütterlein*) boasted of burning seven pence worth of candles a week ('*ich*

*verprenne all wuchen 7 pfenbart liecht*'). This, she was told, was to serve *abgoettern* and *oelgoetzen*. See Rössner, 'Luther', 58.
59 Wandel, *Voracious Idols*, pp. 69–70.
60 Wandel, *Voracious Idols*, p. 76.
61 Wandel, *Voracious Idols*, p. 119.
62 See above, p. 23.
63 See above, Chapter 1.
64 A good example of how background affected the reception of reform in one town, Erfurt, R. Scribner, 'Civic Unity and the Reformation in Erfurt', *Past and Present* 66 (1975), 29–60, noting that by 1664 Catholicism had been re-established as the sole creed in Erfurt.
65 Marshall, *Heretics and Believers*, p. 264.
66 Marshall, *Heretics and Believers*, p. 425.
67 E. Dufffy, *The Stripping of the Altars. Tradition and Religion in England c. 1400 – c. 1580* (New Haven, 1992), p. 4.
68 For a critical review of *Stripping the Altars* on these grounds, see the review by P. Griffiths, *Continuity and Change* 9.2 (1994), 354–7.
69 See note 11 above.
70 Duffy, *The Voices of Morebath*, pp. 88–101.
71 Duffy, *The Voices of Morebath*, p. 127.
72 Duffy, *The Voices of Morebath*, p. 103.

# Conclusions

This study began with the Old Testament instruction to keep a flame burning before the tabernacle at all times. It charted the adoption of this injunction by the early Christian Church, and showed how the practice of keeping a light burning in churches spread and became the concern of rulers, before becoming a normal part of religious practice at all levels of society. The study ended with the rejection of the belief that burning a light in a church had any spiritual efficacy. As Benjamin Graham has pointed out, Christians were not *bound* to accept all, or even any, of the Mosaic injunctions, and the early books of the Old Testament contained plenty of rules and vetoes that the Christians did not in fact adopt.[1] Jewish dietary laws are a good example. So why adopt the instruction to keep a flame alight? The answer in part is surely that the injunction to keep a flame burning was tied up with the design of the priesthood. The sons of Aaron (who was Moses' brother) were charged with keeping the flame alight, and there were dire consequences when they failed to do so. The sons of Aaron were imagined as the progenitors of the Christian priesthood and their duty of keeping the light aflame was passed on to the priests. According to the Old Testament example, tending the flame was the first duty of the priesthood. It was a duty that was at the base of their spiritual authority, and it gave the priests a measure of social authority too as the sons of Aaron were charged with collecting from the Israelites the oil for the eternal flame. What propelled concern for the lights into the mainstream of Christian culture was the support for it that came from a combination of secular and religious leaders. This was despite others voicing doubts about the spiritual usefulness of burning lights, especially in the daytime. Honouring God, the saints and other dead with lights may also have been made more acceptable and attractive because of a pre-existing culture of veneration through

## Conclusions

the creation of light. The early grafting of pre- or non-Christian practices onto a fairly weak Old Testament base (and no base at all in the case of the New Testament), would allow reformers at the end of the Middle Ages to argue that the practice of burning lights in churches had no scriptural justification. It was a mere human invention that was spiritually useless.

As early medieval rulers came to claim a religious mandate for the exercise of power, so they came to express concerns over the conduct of religion, and they strove to ensure that priests discharged their duties properly: these included the maintenance of the lights. Constantine, the first Christian Roman emperor (ruled 306–37), set the pace in donating property to the church for the provision of lights, especially in Rome itself. But what this study shows is that Constantine's giving was at a pace and across a range impossible to match, for not only did political power become fragmented over the course of the fifth and sixth centuries but also supplies of oil, the preferred lighting fuel, began to dry up. Other forms of oil such as nut oil in the Basque country, or whale oil in Normandy, or even tallow, could be used for lighting the church in general, but it was specifically olive oil that was required for the light before the tabernacle. Apart from the Mosaic injunction to use it, olive oil was preferred for its slow and near-smokeless burning. Getting hold of such oil north of the Alps and Pyrenees, however, became harder, so that by the mid-seventh century it was only the major churches and monasteries that were able to obtain it, and they were able to do so only with the help of the rulers. This is the context in which royal immunities developed in Francia.

The immunity was an instrument for taking from the 'fisc' (the treasury, which included a variety of public assets) and giving to the Church, for 'whatever the fisc had formerly been able to obtain' from the lands in question was now to go to a favoured ecclesiastical institution for the lights, for alms and for the support of the monks or clergy. The immunity was the device particularly favoured by the Frankish rulers, and it was possible to show that the northern Frankish institutions which benefited from immunities did actually travel to the south to obtain oil. Evidence from outside of Francia shows that in southern Europe oil for lighting was available on a more local level. In Italy especially it is possible to see local production replacing bulk imports of oil, and, as a consequence of small-scale local production, a greater range of people were able to donate for the provision of lighting. England shows another variation in that as early as the mid-seventh century, that is, not long after conversion to Christianity, Anglo-Saxons visited Rome and were aware of the splendid lighting in the churches there, and they were also aware of why churches should be shining with lights, but there was virtually no oil to be had in England. England, not surprisingly, shows early indications of a veneration of beeswax, which became not only an acceptable substitute for oil but also the preferred fuel for the lights, not just in the north but also by the central Middle Ages in southern Europe too. Since wax could be obtained locally and by peasants, the preference for it amounted to a kind of democratisation of this form of piety. At the same time, the church was pushing to make sure that every church had a light burning at all times on the altar, a requirement seen in two late sixth-century Church Councils from Spain, the canons of these councils being repeated down through the Middle Ages. Evidence from Italy, Spain and Francia showed that there was a spontaneous desire to provide lights before saints' shrines, and, slightly later, to maintain lights before the tombs of ancestors as a form of commemoration.

For the early period, that is up to the mid-ninth century, the evidence for those both inside and outside the elites giving for the lights is consistent, but patchy, across Europe. With the exception of England, charters which mentioned lights ran at around 7 per cent of the total issued in the period 750–950. It is perhaps the scattered nature of such evidence, plus its rather low-level intensity (with lighting often mentioned *en passant*), that has resulted in modern historians having little to say on the subject. It is to be hoped that the present study has demonstrated that there is sufficient early evidence to say a great deal, not least to explain how giving for the lights moved from the periphery to the centre of religious activity from the central Middle Ages onwards. On the face of it, that move to centre stage was the result of steady pressure from the top, and above all from Carolingian rulers who dealt with the provision of lighting and the abuses that came from the management of resources for the lights. They repeated the canons of earlier councils, pressed for the levying of the tithe, and ordered bishops to make sure that the clergy, the latter-day sons of Aaron, were fulfilling their duties. This is what I termed 'the Carolingian moment'. In that time, from the late eighth to the end of the ninth century, concern for the lights was manifested in a steady stream of capitularies, charters, conciliar canons, episcopal statutes, letters and polyptychs. They reveal a slightly different face too, in that one can deduce from them that some of the pressure for adherence to 'correct' practices may have come from below. What is more certain, however, is that it was seen as the duty of rulers to ensure that churches were appropriately provided with lights, and that the responsibility for keeping them burning was ultimately that of the ruler. As rulers justified their exercise of power on the basis that they had a divine mandate to do so, concern for the lights became part of political discourse. Notably this was seen in a letter sent to Pippin of Aquitaine from the Council of Aachen in 836, where the Council reminded Pippin of the duties of the sons of Aaron, and of the dire consequences of letting the eternal flame die. It was ultimately Pippin's responsibility to keep it alight. Light sparked a series of metaphors in political discourse. It stood for the church as a whole, for the property of the church, for truth and for justice. Providing for the lights could also be an expression of power in a much more practical and prosaic way. This was the case with Charlemagne's conquest in 774 of the Lombard kingdom, which was followed by grants of Italian oil to Frankish monasteries. The practical and the moral might come together, as was seen in the series of documents issued by King Lothar II in his bid to divorce his wife Theutberga and to marry Waldrada, the mother of his son. Early negotiations for this divorce, taking place between 860 and 863, were bound up with grants for lighting, for these showed Lothar's good intentions and worthiness as a ruler. Supporting the church in this way was something with which it was impossible to disagree, and rulers emphasised their ancestry and legitimacy by confirming the grants their predecessors had made for the lights.

Increasing amounts of evidence from the Carolingian period onwards allow one to begin to investigate the social and economic consequences of devoting resources to the lights, or, to put it another way, to try and gauge the material consequences of adhering to the belief that all churches should have lights. To light a candle or a lamp, it was believed, would aid salvation. That all Christians should contribute to the costs of lighting was made clear in Carolingian legislation that urged people to pay tithes, for a quarter of the tithe was earmarked for the lights. That some people had a special duty to provide for the lights was evident from the polyptychs (surveys of church estates) in which people were said to owe tribute to a particular church or monastery in support of the lights. The most obvious example of such people were the *luminarii*, 'light payers', who appeared in the polytptych of Saint Bertin. There were also ecclesiastical tributaries in Italy, and a few (but actually very few) people in tenth-century Spain who looked as if they were bound to churches in this way. This pool of people whose social distinction was that they paid for lights should also include those who paid a rent to the church because they held, or lived or worked on, lands occupied in precarial tenure. This was when people gave lands to a church and then received them back to enjoy 'in usufruct' (that means, taking the produce or revenues from the land) until they died, at which point the tenure of the land might well have been passed on to an heir. These tenants usually paid a small rent (the *census*) to the church, and, to signify that the church was now the ultimate owner of the land in question, the rent was meant to be used for ecclesiastical purposes, and prominent amongst these was the maintenance of the lights. There were thousands of these precarial agreements in Francia, and I have argued that they were particularly prevalent in East Francia, the area that became Germany. This was because the church had played a key role in organising the eastern region after its conquest by Charlemagne. So alongside the dedicated tributaries like the *luminarii*, there were an indeterminate number of people paying *census* by virtue of holding precarial tenancies, and a growing number of people, especially in Germany, who gave themselves into the service of churches and then paid *census* to them. Yet more people who were under the control of others could simply be given to a church in order to pay *census*. Both the given and self-givers and their descendants would remain as a part of the church's *familia*, or group of dependants. Since there was virtually no way out of this condition, one must assume that the numbers in service to the Church in this way would have grown over the generations. Starting with the early Frankish *precariae* of the mid-eighth century, it was clear that the link between the payment of *census* and the lights was strong. The payers were termed *censuales* and often *cerocensuales* which means 'payers of *census* in wax'. There were also normative statements to the effect that *census* was for the lights and nothing else. The *censuales* or *cerocensuales* should have no other burdens. The statement made in a charter of 1153 by the abbot of Stavelot-Malmedy to this effect (discussed in Chapter 5) is very clear. It is also noteworthy that the abbot was backed up by the emperor, Frederick Barbarossa.

Taking into account the various ways in which people could become light payers, and noting the apparently high numbers of such people, it was important to ask whether this way of collecting revenues for the lights had the effect of structuring the social and economic landscape. A comparison with the Islamic institution of the *waqf* (or *hubs* as this was known in Spain) reveals a device for preserving inheritance known as the *mu'aqqab*. This form of family endowment looks very similar to the Frankish *precaria*. In both cases land was donated to a religious institution and received back in usufruct, and could be passed on to heirs. The difference was that lights did not feature in the Islamic *waqf*. It could be argued therefore that this form of social organisation was determined not by the need to provide for the lights but by the need to build a secure path to inheritance. That the precariat *did* pay *census* for the lights, relates, however, to the fact that providing for the lights was an important obligation in Christian culture, and, if it did not actually call this form of landholding into being, it certainly lent to it a justification and a purpose, this being the salvation of the original donor.

*Censuales* may have been created by different means (by tenure, by manumission, by gift and by gift of self), but they were consolidated as a group by common conditions and obligations. They were, moreover, recognised as a distinct category of people, as the abbot of Stavelot-Malmedy said, by their payment of *census* for the lights, and by common customs around inheritance and marriage. They would eventually have their own 'law', and German historians have in the main been helpful in giving the *censuales* a modern noun, the *Zensualität*, which evokes a collective identity and common status. Given that *censuales* or *cerocensuales* were to be found above all in Germany, it was essential to ask whether they had equivalents in other regions: whether or not providing for the lights did have an effect on social structure more widely in Europe turns on the answer to this question. The focus of the inquiry was a comparison between the *censuales* in Germany and people referred to as *colliberti* in what had become France. The comparison was inviting because both France and Germany had been ruled as kingdoms which were parts of the same Frankish empire. They shared a legacy of laws, both secular and ecclesiastical, which suggests that they may have had a common approach to meeting the needs of the Church. Comparison, however, proved difficult as it had to comprehend differences in modern historiography and different ways of thinking about post-Carolingian development. The result was a chapter (Chapter 5) that was something of a historiographical and comparative excursus, and which drew a blank when it came to the *colliberti*. The problem was that there was not enough evidence to decide upon the nature of these people. Scholars have been divided over the origins of the *colliberti*, and over their exact status. The term *colliberti* itself suggests people who had been freed from a greater servitude, but in surviving documents they were treated just as if they were serfs. There is no evidence at all that they were people who were linked to service to the Church, but this was something that was important to establish. The conclusion to the comparative discussion was that the *censuales* had in effect been called into being as a distinct group in order to provide the wherewithal for churches to maintain lights and to support the religion more generally, but that by the time of the central Middle Ages this category of persons or group was one that did not have equivalents in other parts of Europe.

Following through on the history of the *Zensualität* led to a focus on towns in the central medieval period, for it was in towns that *censuales* acquired privileges and merged with other citizens, so that eventually one law covered all townspeople. At the same time emphasis was given to the emergent confraternities and guilds, for the records show that they played an increasing part in the supply of materials to the Church, not least at parish level. The guilds did this in the course of furnishing candles for funerals, commemorating their members with lights, by providing lights for the shrines of their patron saints and by maintaining eternal lights at various points in the churches they supported. The background to the mushrooming of guilds and confraternities was a belief in Purgatory which became more or less universal from the end of the twelfth century onwards. To perform good works, either individually or through the guild, was in effect to buy time off the sufferings of Purgatory, and time off could in the later Middle Ages be purchased as a commodity through an 'indulgence'. There was in this later period a strong mortuary culture, as one might expect given the incidence of famine and then plague. More and more resources were devoted to funerals and commemoration, and this meant burning ever more lights. Guilds, it was suggested, spent rather more on candles than they did on charity. This was exemplified by the history of the confraternity of Sant Bartolomeo in San Sepulcro in Tuscany.

By the mid-fifteenth century so much was being consumed by the lights that wax had to be imported from areas outside Western Europe. At this point it could be said that feeding the lights did have a significant impact upon economic activity. Later records, primarily from the village of Morebath in Devon (England), show that all the parishoners were involved in making contributions towards the lights. One can see how the contributions meshed with the local pastoral economy as people generated wealth for the church by pasturing sheep and cattle. Such activities cannot be said to have led to new social formations, but they certainly shaped older forms such as the parish, the guild and the confraternity, the origins of all of which can be traced back to the early Middle Ages.

The Reformation in Europe has been characterised as 'the stripping of the altars'.[2] Reformers sought to return churches to simplicity, a space around the bible rather than one studded with shrines and bright with lights and decoration. One could with equal justification characterise the reform as 'turning out the lights', for the reformers were set against the lights as a symbol of archaic and (to them) misguided belief. Once the existence of Purgatory had been challenged as a mere human invention, the lifeline to the lights was cut. It was, ironically, the increasing involvement of parish organisations, guilds and confraternities in maintaining the lights that facilitated the iconoclasm of the early Reformation. As was shown in the discussion around the Augsburg *Zechen*, lay persons had acquired a large measure of control over church buildings and church furniture. It was thus in their power to extinguish the lights. What made them do so was the change in belief. The study thus ends where it began, with doubts about the value of eternal lights. The belief that they *were* useful lasted from the early fourth to the early sixteenth century, a period of over twelve hundred years, and it continues to this day in areas which did not experience the Protestant Reformation.[3]

The overall conclusion to this study is that it is not only possible but also richly rewarding to follow the history of the use of lights in worship across the whole medieval period. The use of lights, and the gathering of resources to fuel them, did not generally shape society, but it did affect the lives of many people. In Germany, however, it can be said to have resulted in the formation of a distinct social group, the *censuales* or *cerocensuales*. There are two elements in this history. The first element is the belief that burning lights in churches had spiritual value which was followed by the incorporation of the practice into religious life everywhere, and the second element is the material consequences of putting that belief into practice. The belief was strong, and grew stronger at the end of our period, and the cost was great, and rising. In this way the history of the lights roughly follows the contours of social and political change across the period. That is one benefit of following this *longue-durée* narrative, but another is that it allows one to see those changes from another angle. The use of light and the provision of light in political discourse is one example of this. Another is the fading away of tributary groups to be replaced with parish, guild and confraternity organisations. To study the means by which the lights were provided for furnishes in particular a new way of looking at the social transformations of the central Middle Ages. Such examples could be multiplied for every turn in the evolution of West European society. As important is the fact that there was no gender difference when it came to giving for the lights. The subject is one which allows us to see women participating alongside men on what seem to be equal terms. The history of the lights thus acts as a kind of *vade mecum* to medieval history. The end of the story in what became Protestant areas is equally revealing. What the early sixteenth-century reformers said, effectively, was that those who paid for the lights, and those who sold and bought indulgences, were trying to commodify eternity. In defence of the medieval practice, it must be said that wax and oil *were* commodities. They had uses beyond the religious: wax was also used for seals and for writing tablets, or oil had medicinal uses. Belief in the flame as a portal to eternity came first, ways of paying for access to it came second. This was as much driven by necessity as it was

*Eternal light and earthly concerns*

a move towards commodification. All beliefs have material consequences. This is one area in which the two can be studied together over a period of well over a thousand years.

I will close on a near contemporary note, concerning reaction to the death of Diana, Princess of Wales, in August 1997. There was a mass outpouring of grief after her sudden death at the age of 36. People in their thousands lit candles, many of which were placed on the Mall, the road leading up to Buckingham Palace in London. George Carey, the archbishop of Canterbury, lit one too (Figure 9).

The caption reads 'the Archbishop of Canterbury lights a candle in memory of Diana Princess of Wales'. As leader of a Protestant Church he could do so only 'in memory of', not as intercession for. The Church of England found it necessary to point this out, leaving the impression that the bulk of their congregations did not understand the difference between memorial and intercession. The wish to light a candle, it seems, overrode any theological considerations. Diana was personified in song as 'a candle in the wind', though this song was actually written about Marilyn Monroe and

9 The Archbishop of Canterbury lights a candle in memory of Diana, Princess of Wales

## Conclusions

adapted for the occasion. A guttering candle represented a fragile life. If candles today can have such significance, and lighting them can be a means of expressing emotion, then much more so in the Middle Ages where the effect of burning them in dark buildings, and through the night, must have been all the more impressive. That candles and lamps should have been taken to the heart of Catholic Christianity, and to have been so important to worshippers for so long, may well owe much to how they looked and how they converted material into flame. Light stood for truth and eternity, and it came from a familiar object fashioned from material produced by hard-working, chaste and disciplined bees. That material, furthermore, was readily available. Belief and the material through which that belief could be expressed were a match made if not in heaven, then for heaven.

### Notes

1. B. Graham, 'Olives and Lighting in Dark Age Europe', *Early Medieval Europe* 28.3 (2020), 344–66.
2. The phrase is taken from the title of E. Duffy's work *The Stripping of the Altars. Tradition and Religion in England c. 1400 – c. 1580* (New Haven, 1992).
3. The author was able to purchase a litre of 'Holy Light Lamp Oil' near a shrine in Cyprus. It cost only €2.25, but since the label also warned 'May be fatal if swallowed' it was clear that this was not olive oil.

# Bibliography

## Primary sources

Note that works in the *Monumenta Germaniae Historica* (*MGH*) series are cited by volume number within main sections and do not reference the full section and subsection headings. For these, and for the texts that are contained within them, there is access via the *MGH* website: www.dmgh.de.

*Anglo-Saxon Wills*, ed. and trans. D. Whitelock, Cambridge, 1930.

*The Annals of Saint-Bertin*, trans. J. Nelson, Manchester, 1991.

*Antifonaria Visigotica Mozarabe de la Catedral de Léon*, ed. L. Brou and J. Vives, Barcelona and Madrid, 1959.

*Appendix ad Hrabanum, Epistolarum Fuldensium Fragmenta*, ed. E. Dümmler, *MHG Epistolae* V, *Epistolae Karolini Aevi* 3, Berlin, 1899.

Baraut, C., 'Les actes de consagracions d'esglésies del bisbat d'Urgell (segles IX–XII)', *Urgellia* 1 (1978), 11–182.

Baraut, C., *Les actes de consagracions d'esglésies de l'antic bisbat d'Urgell (segles IX–XII)*, La Seu d'Urgell, 1986.

*Bechbretha*, ed. and trans. T. Charles-Edwards and F. Kelly, *Early Irish Laws Series* 1, Dublin, 1983.

Bede, *The Reckoning of Time*, trans. F. Wallis, Liverpool, 1999.

*Calendar of the Liberate Rolls*, ed. H. Maxwell Lyte, 6 vols, Public Records Office, London, 1916–64.

*MGH Capitula Episcoporum*, 3 vols, ed. P. Brommer and R. Pokorny, Hanover, 1985–95.

*MGH Capitularia regum Francorum* I, ed. A Boretius, Hanover, 1883.

*MGH Capitularia regum Francorum* II, ed. A. Boretius and V. Krause, Hanover, 1897.

*Le carte del decimo secolo nell'archivio arcivescovile di Ravenna* I, ed. Ruggero Benericetti, Ravenna, 1999.

*Le carte Ravennati del secolo undecismo* I (1001–1024), ed. Ruggero Benericetti, Bologna, 2003.

*Cartulario de Valpuesta*, ed. M. Desamparados Perez Soles, Valcencia, 1970.

# Bibliography

*Cartulaire del'Abbaye de Gorze*, ed. A. D'Herbomez, 2 vols, Paris, 1898.
*Catalunya Carolingia II. Els diploms Carolingis a Catalunya*, ed. R. Abadal and I. de Vinyals, Barcelona, 1926–50.
*Catalunya Carolingia IV. Els comtats de Rosselló, Conflent, Vallespir I Fenollet*, ed. Ramon Ordeig Mata, Barcelona, 2006.
*Charters of Christ Church Canterbury*, ed. N. Brooks and S. Kelly, Oxford, 2013.
*Chartes et documents de l'abbaye de Saint-Pierre au Mont-Blandin à Gand*, ed. A. van Lockeren, 2 vols, Ghent, 1868, 1871.
*Chartes et documents pour server à l'histoire de l'abbaye de Saint-Maxient de Poitiers*, ed. A. Richard, Poitiers, 1886.
Chaucer, G., *The Canterbury Tales, The Riverside Chaucer*, Oxford, 1987.
*Chelsfield Chronicles 1450–1920's*, ed. G. Copus, *Annals of a Kentish Parish*, Tunbridge Wells, 2003.
*Codice Diplomatico del Monasterio di S. Columbano di Bobbio*, vol. 1, ed. C. Cipolla, Rome, 1918.
*Codice Diplomatico Langobardo*, vols I and II, ed. L. Schiaparelli, *Fonti per la Storia d'Italia* 62, Rome, 1929 and 1933.
*Coleccion Diplomatica del Monasterio de Sahagun*, vol. 1 (*siglos IX y X*), ed. José María Minguez Fernández, Léon, 1976, vols 2 and 3, ed. M. Herrero de la Fuente, Léon, 1988, *Index verborum dela documentación Leonensa*, vols 2 and 3, *Monasterio de Sahagun*, ed. José María Fernández Catón, Léon, 1999.
*Coleccion documental del archive de la Catedral de Léon (775–1230)*, ed. E. Saez, Léon, 1987, vol. VII, *Apéndices e indices*, ed. José M. Fernández Catón and José Manuel Ruiz Ascensio, Léon, 2002.
*MHG Concilia II*, ed. A. Werminghof, Hanover and Leipzig, 1908.
*MGH Concilia III*, ed. W. Hartmann, Hanover, 1984.
*MGH Concilia IV*, ed. W. Hartmann, Hanover, 1998.
*Concilium Liftinense*, ed. A. Werminghof, *MGH Concilia Ii*, Hanover and Leipzig, 1906.
Council of Elvira, ed. J. Vives, *Concilios Visigóticos et Hispano-Romanos*, Barcelona and Madrid, 1963.
Council of Toledo 597, ed. J. Vives, *Concilios Visigóticos et Hispano-Romanos*, Barcelona and Madrid, 1963.
Councils of Braga I and II, ed. J. Vives, *Concilios Visigóticos e Hispano-Romanos*, Barcelona and Madrid, 1963.
*Councils and Synods with Other Documents Relating to the English Church*, part I, 871–1066, ed. D. Whitelock, M. Brett and C. N. L. Brooke, Oxford, 1981.
Davis, R., *The Lives of the Eighth-Century Popes (Liber Pontificalis): The Ancient Biographies of Nine Popes from AD 715 to AD 817*, Liverpool, 1992.
Davis, R., *The Lives of the Ninth-Century Popes (Liber Pontificalis): The Ancient Biographies of Ten Popes from AD 817–891*, Liverpool, 1995.
Davis, R., *The Book of Pontiffs (Liber Pontificalis): The Ancient Biographies of the First Ninety Roman Bishops to AD 715*, 2nd rev. edn, Liverpool, 2000.

# Bibliography

*Diplomata Belgica ante Annum Millesimum Centesimum Scripta*, ed. M. Gysseling and A. Koch, Brussels, 1950.
*MGH Diplomata Karolinorum* I, ed. E. Mühlbacher, Hanover, 1906.
*MGH Diplomata Karolinorum* III, ed. T. Schieffer, Berlin, 1966.
*MGH Diplomata Regum Francorum e stirpe Merovingicarum*, ed. T. Kölzer, *Die Urkunden der Merowinger*, Hanover, 2001.
*MGH Diplomata Regum et Imperatorum Germaniae* I, Hanover, 1879–84.
*MGH, Diplomata Regum* IV (*Die Urkunden der deutschen Könige und Kaiser* IV), ed. H. Bresslau, Hanover and Leipzig, 1909.
*MGH Diplomata Regum et Imperatorum Germaniae* X, *Friderici* I, 4, Hanover, 1990.
*Diplomatarium Islandicum I*, ed. J. Sigurdsson, Copenhagen, 1857–1876.
*Documentación medieval de Leire (siglos IX a XII)*, ed. A. J. Martin Duque, Pamplona, 1983.
'Donation of Constantine' (*Constitutum Constantini*), ed. H. Fuhrmann, Hanover, 1968.
*Les Dotalies de les Església de Catalunya (segles IX–XII)*, ed. Ramon Ordeig I. Mata, 7 vols, Vic, 1993–2000.
*Edictum Pistense*, *MGH Capitularia* II, ed. A. Boretius and V. Krause, Hanover, 1897, pp. 310–28.
*Edictus Rothari*, ed. G. Pertz, *MGH Legum* III, Hanover, 1868, pp. 300–3, trans. K. Fischer-Drew, *The Lombard Laws*, Philadelphia, 1973.
*MGH Epistolae* 4, ed. E. Dümmler, Berlin, 1895.
*Formuale Visigothicae*, ed. K. Zeumer, *MGH Formulae Merowingici et Karolini Aevi*, Hanover, 1882–6, pp. 572–95.
*Formula Bituricensis*, ed. K. Zeumer, *Formulae Merowingici et Karolini Aevi*, Hanover, 1886.
*The Formularies of Angers and Marculf: Two Merovingian Legal Handbooks*, trans. A. Rio, Liverpool, 2008.
*Gesta Dagoberti* I, ed. B. Krusch, *MGH SRM* II, Hanover, 1888, pp. 399–425.
*Gesta sanctorum patrum Fontanellensis coenobii*, ed. and French trans. P. Pradié, *Chronique des abbés de Fontanelle (Saint Wandrille)*, Paris, 1999.
*Grágás: Elzta lögbók Íslendiga. Útgefin eptir skinnbókini í bókasafini konungs*, 2 vols, ed. V. Finsen, Copenhagen, 1852, repr. Reykjavik, 1945.
Gratian, *De consecratione*, Gratian, *Decretum*, part III, ed. E. Richter and E. Friedberg, Leipzig, 1879, repr. Graz, 1959.
*Gregorii Magni, Opera Registrum Epistularum*, ed. D. Norberg, *Corpus Christianorum, series Latina* cxl–cxlA, Turnhout, 1982.
Gregory of Nazianzen, *Select Orations*, ed. C. Brown and J. Swallow, *Nicene and Post Nicene Fathers of the Christian Church*, vol. 7, Grand Rapids, 1893.
Gregory of Tours, *Decem Libri Historiarum*, ed. B. Krusch and W. Levison, *MGH SRM* 1.i, Hanover and Leipzig, 1937–51, trans. L. Thorpe, *Gregory of Tours, The History of the Franks*, Harmondsworth, 1974.
Gregory of Tours, *Liber in gloria martyrum*, ed. B. Krusch, *MGH SRM* 1 Hanover and

*Bibliography*

Leipzig, 1888, trans. R. van Dam, *Gregory of Tours. Glory of the Martyrs*, Liverpool, 1988.
Gregory of Tours, *Libri de virtutibus sancti Martini episcopi*, ed. B. Krusch, *MGH SRM* 1, Hanover and Leipzig, 1885, pp. 584–661, trans. R. van Dam. *Saints and Their Miracles*, Princeton, 1993, pp. 199–303.
Ibn al-'Attār, *Formulario notarial y judicial andalusí del alfaquíy notario cordobés*, ed. and trans. with commentary P. Chalmeta and M. Marugán, Madrid, 2000.
Isidore of Seville, *De Ecclesiasticis Officiis*, ed. C. Lawson, *Corpus Christianorum*, Series Latina 113, Turnhout, 1989.
*Islandske annaler indtil 1578*, ed. G. Storm, Chria, 1888.
*Islenzk fornrit* XVII, ed. Gudrun Asa Grimsdottir, Reykjavik, 1998.
Jerome, *Contra Vigilantium*, *Patrologia Latina* 22, col. 339.
King, P. D., *Charlemagne. Translated Sources*, Lambrigg, 1987.
*The Koran*, trans. N. J. Dawood, Penguin Classics, 4th edn, Harmondsworth, 1974.
*Laws of Ine*, trans. D. Whitelock, *English Historical Documents* I, London, 1968, pp. 364–72.
*Leges Visigothorum*, ed. K. Zeumer, *MGH Legum* I.i, Hanover and Leipzig, 1902, pp. 35–456.
*Liber de Servis Majoris Monasterii*, ed. Ch. L. Grandmaison, Tours, 1864.
*Liber largitorius vel notarius Parphanensis* I, ed. G. Zucchetti, Rome, 1913.
'The Life of Saint Aemilian', trans. A. Fear, *Lives of the Visigothic Fathers*, Liverpool, 1997, pp. 15–43.
*Marculfi Formularum Libri Duo*, ed. A. Uddholm, Uppsala, 1962, trans. A. Rio, *The Formularies of Angers and Marculf: Two Merovingian Legal Handbooks*, Liverpool, 2008.
*Il Museo Diplomatico dell'Archivio di Stato di Milano*, ed. with facsimile A. Natale, Milan, c. 1970.
*La Notitia Dignitatum. Nueva edición crítica y commentario histório*, Concepción Niera Faleiro, Madrid, 2005.
Origen, *De Principiis*, trans. J. Behr, *Origen on First Principles*, Oxford, 2017.
*Pals saga biskups*, ed. Asdis Egilsdottir' *Izlenzk fornrit* XVI, Reykjavik, 2002.
*The Paterik of the Kievan Caves Monastery*, trans. M. Heppell, *Harvard Library of Early Ukrainian Literature, English Translations* 1, Cambridge, Mass., 1989.
*Las Pizzaras Visigodas*, ed. Isabel Velázquez Soriano, Madrid and Burgos, 2004.
*The Poems of Saint Paulinus of Nola*, trans. P. G. Walsh, New York, 1975.
*Le polyptyque de l'abbaye de Saint Bertin (844–859)*, ed. F. L. Ganshof, Paris, 1975.
*Le polyptyque et les listes de biens de l'abbaye de Saint-Pierre de Lobbes (IXe–XIe siècles)*, ed. J.-P. Devroey, Brussels, 1986.
*Le polyptyque et le listes de cens de l'abbaye de Saint-Remi de Reims (IXe–XIe siècles)*, ed. J.-P. Devroey, Reims, 1984.
*Das Polyptychon von Saint-Germain-des-Prés*, ed. D. Hägermann, Cologne, Weimar and Vienna, 1993.
*Recueil des actes de Charles III le simple*, vol. 1, text, ed. F. Lot and Ph. Lauer, Paris, 1940.

*Recueil des actes de Louis IV*, ed. M. Prou and Ph. Lauer, Paris, 1914.
*Recueil des chartes de Charles II Le Chauve*, ed. G. Tessier, *Chartes et diplômes relatifs à l'histoire de France*, 3 vols, Paris, 1941, 1952, 1955.
*Recueil des chartes de l'abbaye de Stavelot-Malmedy*, ed. J. Halkin and C. Roland, 2 vols, Brussels, 1909.
*Regesta Chartarum Pistorensium* (no editor given), *Fonti Storiche Pistoeisi* 2, Pistoia, 1973.
*Il Regesto di Farfa compilato da Gregorio di Catino*, 5 vols, ed. I. Giorgi and V. Balzani, Rome, 1879–1914.
*The Rights and Ranks of People*, trans. D. C. Douglas, *English Historical Documents* II, London, 1961, pp. 813–16.
Sawyer, P., *Anglo-Saxon Charters. An Annotated List and Bibliography*, London, 1968.
*Sturlunga saga*, ed. Jon Johannesson, Magnus Finnbogason and Kristjan Eldjarn, Reykjavik, 1946.
Swanson, R., *Catholic England. Faith, Religion and Observance before the Reformation*, Manchester, 1993, reissued 2014.
Tertullian, *Apology*, trans. T. R. Glover, London, 1931.
Tertullian, *De Idolataria*, ed. and trans. with commentary J. Wascinc and J. M. C. Van Winden, Leiden, 1987.
*O Tombo de Celanova*, vol. 1, ed. José M. Adrade, Santiago de Compostello, 1995.
*Tractate Menachot* 86a, sefania.org/william-davidson-talmud.
*Die Traditionen des Hochstifts Regensburg und des Klosters S. Emmeram*, ed. J. Widemann, Munich, 1943, repr. Aalen, 1969.
*Traditiones Wizenburgenses. Die Urkunden des Klosters Weissenburg 661–864*, ed. K. Glöckner and A. Doll, Darmstadt, 1979.
*Die Urkunden Karls III*, ed. P. Kehr, *MGH Diplomata Regum Germaniae ex stirpe Karolinorum* II, Berlin, 1936.
*Vercelli Homily* XVI, ed. D. Scragg, *Old English Text Series* O.S. 300, 1992.
*Visio Baronti*, ed. W. Levison, *MGH SRM* V, Hanover 1910, pp. 377–94.
*Vita Ansberti*, ed. W. Levison, *MGH SRM* V, Hanover, 1910.
*Vita Balthildis*, trans. with commentary P. Fouracre and R. Gerberding, *Late Merovingian France. History and Hagiography 640–720*, Manchester, 1996, pp. 95–132.
*Vita Filiberti*, ed. W. Levison, *MGH SRM* V, Hanover, 1910, pp. 583–612.

## Secondary works

Adams, N. 'Hanging basins and the wine-coloured sea. The wider context of early medieval hanging bowls', in A. Reynolds and L. Webster (eds), *Early Medieval Art and Archaeology in the Northern World: Studies in Honour of James Graham-Campbell* (Leiden and Boston, 2013), pp. 3–49.
Airlie, S. 'Private Bodies and the Body Politic in the Divorce Case of Lothar II', *Past and Present* 161 (1998), 3–38.

# Bibliography

d'Allemagne, H. R. *Histoire du luminaire depuis l'époque romaine jusqu'au xix siècle*, Paris, 1891.
Andermann, K. 'Bürgerrecht. Die Speyer Priviligien von 1111 und die Anfänge persönlicher Freiheitsrechte in deutschen Städten des hohen Mittelalters', *Historische Zeitschrift* 296 (2012), 593–624.
Angenendt, A., Brauks, T., Busch, R., Lentes, T., and Lutterbach, H. 'Gezählte Frömmigkeit', *Frühmittelalterliche Studien* 29 (1995), 1–75.
Archetti, G. 'Infundit vinum et oleum. Olio e vino nella traditzione monastica', *Settimane di Spoleto* 54 (2007), 1098–203.
Balzaretti, R. *Dark Age Liguria. Regional Identity and Local Power c. 400–1020*, London, 2013.
Balzaretti, R. *The Lands of Saint Ambrose. Monks and Society in Early Medieval Milan*, Turnhout, 2019.
Balzaretti, R., Barrow, J., and Skinner, P. (eds), *Italy and Early Medieval Europe. Papers for Chris Wickham*, Oxford, 2018.
Banker, J. *Death in the Community. Memorialization and Confraternities in an Italian Commune in the Late Middle Ages*, Athens, Ga, and London, 1998.
Barthélemy, D. *La société dans la comté de Vendôme de l'an mil au XIVe siècle*, Paris, 1991.
Barthélemy, D. *The Serf, the Knight and the Historian*, trans. G. Edwards, Ithaca and London, 2009.
Bartlett, R. *Why Can the Dead Do Such Great Things?*, Princeton, 2013.
Benjamin, W. *The Arcades Project*, trans. H. Elland and K. McLaughlin, Cambridge, Mass., 1999.
Bijsterveld, A.-J. 'Looking for common ground: from monastic *fraternitas* to lay confraternity in the southern Low Countries in the tenth to twelfth centuries', in E. Jamroziak and J. Burton (eds), *Religious and Laity in Western Europe 1000–1400. Interaction, Negotiation and Power*, Turnhout, 2006, pp. 287–309.
Bisson, T. 'The Feudal Revolution', *Past and Present* 142 (1994), 6–42.
Blancard, L. 'Rôle de la confrèrie de Saint-Martin de Canigou', *Bibliothèque de l'École des Chartes* 42 (1881), 5–7.
Blair, J. *The Church in Anglo-Saxon Society*, Oxford, 2005.
Bloch, M. 'Les *colliberti*. Étude sur la formation de la classe servile', *Revue Historique* 57 (1928), pp. 1–48, 225–63 [repr. M. Bloch, *Mélanges historiques I* (Paris, 1963), pp. 385–451].
Bloch, M. *Feudal Society*, trans. L. Manyon, London, 1961.
Bloch, M. *Mélanges historiques I*, Paris, 1963.
Bolens, L. 'Al-Andalus: la vigne et l'olivier, un secteur de pointe (xe–xiiie siècles)', *Settimane di Spoleto* 37 (1990), 423–8.
Bonnassie, P. 'Rural communities in Catalonia and Valencia (from the ninth to the mid-fourteenth centuries)', in P. Bonnassie, *From Slavery to Feudalism in South-western Europe*, trans. J. Birrell, Cambridge, 1991, pp. 243–87.
Bose, E. J. 'A Medieval Lamp from Peter Street, Bristol', *Transactions of the Bristol and Gloucestershire Archaeological Society* 199 (2001), 179–82.

# Bibliography

Bourasse, M. 'Le testament de S. Perpetue, évêque de Tours', *Bulletin de la Société Archéologique de Touraine* 2 (1871–73), 256.

Bresc, H. 'Mer morte et oliviers perdus. Repli et survie de l'olivaie Méditerranéenne (ive–xiie siècle)', in *Olio e vino nell'alto medioevo*, Settimane di Spoleto 54 (2007), 55–106.

Brown, E. A. R. 'The Tyranny of a Construct: Feudalism and the Historians of Medieval Europe', *American Historical Review* 79 (1974), 1063–88.

Brown, W. *Unjust Seizure: Conflict, Interest and Authority in an Early Medieval Society*, Ithaca, 2001.

Brugnoli, A. 'Del Mediterraneo all'Europa: l'olivocultura di frontier nell'alto medioevo', *Settimane di Spoleto* 54 (2007), 107–54.

Bührer-Thierry, G. 'Lumière et pouvoir dans le haut moyen âge occidental. Célébration de pouvoir et metaphors lumineuses', *Mélanges de l'École Française de Rome. Moyen Age*, 116.2 (2004), 521–56.

Bünz, E. and Fouquet, G. (eds). *Die Pfarrei im späten Mittelalter*, Vorträge und Forschungen 77, Ostfildern, 2013.

Campbell, J. 'Observations on English Government from the Tenth to the Twelfth Century', *Transactions of the Royal Historical Society* 5th series 25 (1975), 39–54 [reprinted J. Campbell, *Essays in Anglo-Saxon History*, London, 1986, no. 10].

Canetti, L. '*Olea sanctorum*: reliquie e miracoli fra tardoantico e alto medieoevo', *Settimane di Spoleto* 54 (2007), 1335–415.

Cassiday, A. 'Saint Aldhelm's Bees (De virginitate prosa, cc. iv–vi): Some Observations on Literary Tradition', *Anglo-Saxon England* 33 (2004), 1–22.

Castellanos, S. 'The Significance of Social Unanimity in a Visigothic Hagiography: Keys to an Ideological Screen', *Journal of Early Christian Studies* 11 (2003), 387–420.

Castellanos, S., and Martin Viso, I. 'The Local Articulation of Central Power in the North of the Iberian Peninsula (500–1000)', *Early Medieval Europe* 13 (2005), 1–42.

Clark, C. 'Cultural Landscapes of Burial in Gaul 450–900', PhD thesis, Birkbeck College, London, 2017.

Claude, D. 'Freedmen in the Visigothic kingdom', in E. James (ed.), *Visigothic Spain. New Approaches*, Oxford, 1980, pp. 159–88.

Claude, D. 'Der Handel im westlichen Mittelmeer während des Frühmittelalters', in K. Düwel, H. Jankhun, H. Siems, and D. Timpe (eds.) *Untersuchungen zu Handel und Verkehr der vor- und frühgeschichtlichen Zeit im Mittel- und Nordeuropa*, Göttingen, 1985, II, pp. 74–86.

Comet, G. 'Le vin et l'huile en Provence médièvale, essai de bilan', in *L'Ambiente Vegetale nell'alto Medioevo*, Settimane di Spoleto 37 (1990), 343–58.

Constable, G. 'Nona et Decima', *Speculum* 35 (1960), 224–50.

Costambeys, M. 'Settlement, Taxation and the Condition of the Peasantry in Post-Roman Central Italy', *Journal of Agrarian Change* 9 (2009), 92–119.

Costambeys, M., Innes, M., and MacLean, S. *The Carolingian World*, Cambridge, 2011.

*Bibliography*

Crook, J. *The Architectural Setting of the Cult of Saints in the Early Christian West*, Oxford, 2000.

Cushing, K. *Reform and the Papacy in the Eleventh Century. Spirituality and Social Change*, Manchester, 2005.

Czock, M. *Gottes Haus. Untersuchungen zur Kirche als Heiligem Raum von der Spätantike bis ins Frühmittelalter*, Göttingen, 2012.

Dam, R. van. *Saints and Their Miracles in Late Antique Gaul*, Princeton, 1993.

Daryaee, T. 'Honey: a Demonic Food in Zoroastrian Iran?', *Studia Litteraria Universitatis Iagellonicae Cracoviensis*, Special Issue (2019), 53–7.

Davies, W. *Acts of Giving. Individual, Community and Church in Tenth-century Christian Spain*, Oxford, 2007.

Davies, W. 'Free persons and large landowners in the West', in J.-P. Devroey and A. Wilkin (eds), *Autour de Yoshiki Morimoto. Les structures agricoles en dehors du monde caroligien, forms et genes, Revue Belge de Philologie et d'Histoire* 90 (2012), 381–90.

Davies, W. *Windows on Justice in Northern Iberia*, London, 2016.

Davies, W., and Fouracre, P. (eds), *The Settlement of Disputes in Early Medieval Europe*, Cambridge, 1986.

Davies, W., and Fouracre, P. (eds), *Property and Power in the Early Middle Ages*, Cambridge, 1995.

Davies, W., and Fouracre, P. (eds), *The Languages of Gift in the Early Middle Ages*, Cambridge, 2010.

Delehaye, H. *The Legends of the Saints*, 4th edn, trans. D. Attwater, London, 1962.

Delmaire, R. *Les institutions du Bas-Empire romain, de Constantin à Justinien*, Paris, 1995.

Dendy, D. R. *The Use of Lights in Christian Worship*, London, 1959.

Devroey, P. 'Réflexions sur l'économie des premiers temps carolingiens (768–877). Grands domaines et action politique entre Seine et Loire', *Francia* 13 (1986), 475–88.

Devroey, P. *Études sur le grand domaine carolingien*, Aldershot, 1993.

Devroey, J.-P. *Puissants et misérables. Système social et monde paysan dans l'Europe des Francs (vi–ix siècles)*, Brussels, 2006.

Dormeier, H. 'Das laikale Stiftungsgewesen in spätmittelalterliche Pfarrkirchen: Kaufleute, Korporationen und Marienverehrung in Lübeck', in E. Bünz and G. Fouquet (eds), *Die Pfarrei im späten Mittelalter, Vorträge und Forschungen* 77 (Ostfildern, 2013), pp. 279–340.

Duby, G. *La société aux XIe et XIIe siècles dans la region mâconaise*, Paris, 1953.

Duffy, E. *The Stripping of the Altars. Tradition and Religion in England c. 1400 – c. 1580*, New Haven, 1992.

Duffy, E. *The Voices of Morebath. Reformation and Rebellion in an English Village*, New Haven and London, 2001.

Durán Cudiol, A. *El hospital de Somport entre Aragón y Bearn (siglos XII–XIII)*, Zaragoza, 1986.

Durliat, J. *Les finances publiques de Dioclétian aux Carolingiens*, Sigmaringen, 1990.

# Bibliography

Eldevik, J. *Episcopal Power and Ecclesiastical Reform in the German Empire. Tithes, Lordship and Community 950–1150*, Cambridge, 2012.

*Encylopaedia of Islam* VI, Leiden, 1986.

Engen, J. van. *Sisters and Brothers of the Common Life. The Devotio Moderna and World of the Later Middle Ages*, Philadelphia, 2008.

Ermine Pani, L., and Stasolla, F. R. 'Le strade del vino e dell'oliio: commercio, transporto e conversazione', *Settimane di Spolteo* 54 (2007), 539–97.

Escalona, J. 'Mapping scale change: hierarchization and fission in Castilian rural communities in the tenth and eleventh centuries', in W. Davies, G. Halsall and A. Reynolds (eds), *People and Space in the Middle Ages 300–1300* (Turnhout, 2006), pp. 143–66.

Esders, S. *Die Formierung der Zensualität, Vorträge und Forschungen*, Sonderband 54, Ostfilde, 2010.

Everett, N. *Literacy in Lombard Italy c. 568–774*, Cambridge, 2003.

Fanciulli, L. *De Lucernis sive Lampadibus Pensilibus*, Macerate, 1802.

Flachenecher, H. 'Eine vertane Chance? Die Rolle der bischöflichen *civitates* in hochmittelalterlichen Spannung zwischen Raumerfassung und Herrschaftsausbildung', in *Bischof und Bürger. Herrschaftsbeziehungen in den Kathedralstädten des Hoch- und Spätmittelalters*, ed. U. Grieme, N. Kruppa and S. Patzold (Göttingen, 2004), pp. 11–26.

Flechner, R. 'Identifying Monks in Early Medieval Britain and Ireland: a Reflection on Legal and Economic Aspects', *Settimane di Spoleto* 64 (2017), 805–44.

Fouracre, P. '"Placita" and the settlement of disputes in later Merovingian Francia', in W. Davies and P. Fouracre (eds), *The Settlement of Disputes in Early Medieval Europe*, Cambridge, 1986, pp. 23–43 [repr. Fouracre, *Frankish History*, no. X].

Fouracre, P. 'Cultural Conformity anocial Conservatism in Early Medieval Europe', *History Workshop Journal* 33 (1992), 152–61 [repr. Fouracre, *Frankish History*, no. XIV].

Fouracre, P. 'Eternal light and earthly needs: practical aspects of the development of Frankish immunities', in W. Davies and P. Fouracre (eds), *Property and Power in the Early Middle Ages* (Cambridge, 1995), pp. 53–81 [repr. Fouracre, *Frankish History*, no. XII].

Fouracre, P. 'Carolingian Justice: the Rhetoric of Improvement and Contexts of Abuse', *Settimane di Spoleto* 42 (1995), 771–803 [repr. Fouracre, *Frankish History*, no. XI].

Fouracre, P. *The Age of Charles Martel*, Harlow, 2000.

Fouracre, P. 'Marmoutier and Its Serfs in the Eleventh Century', *Transactions of the Royal Historical Society* 6th series 15 (2005), 29–49 [repr. Fouracre, *Frankish History*, no. XV].

Fouracre, P. 'Marmoutier: *Familia* versus family. The relations between monastery and serfs in eleventh-century north-west France', in W. Davies, G. Halsall and A. Reynolds (eds), *People and Space in the Middle Ages 300–1300*, Turnhout, 2006, pp. 255–73.

*Bibliography*

Fouracre, P. 'The use of the term *beneficium* in Frankish sources. A society based on favours?', in W. Davies and P. Fouracre (eds), *The Languages of Gift in Early Medieval Europe* (Cambridge, 2010), pp. 62–88 [repr. Fouracre, *Frankish History*, no. XVI].

Fouracre, P. 'The "Book of Serfs" of Marmoutier (eleventh century): reflections on the development of servitude', in B. Hudson (ed.), *'Familia' and Household in the Medieval Atlantic World*, Penn State Medieval Studies 3, Tempe, Az., 2011, pp. 123–39.

Fouracre, P. *Frankish History. Studies in the Construction of Power*, Farnham, 2013.

Fouracre, P. 'Francia and the History of Medieval Europe', *Haskins Society Journal* 23 (2011, published 2014), 1–21.

Fouracre, P. '"Framing" and lighting: Another angle on transition' in R. Balzaretti, J. Barrow and P. Skinner (eds), *Italy and Early Medieval Europe: Papers for Chris Wickham* (Oxford, 2018), pp. 305–14.

Fouracre, P. 'Lights, Power and the Moral Economy of Early Medieval Europe', *Early Medieval Europe* 28.3 (2020), 1–21.

Freedman, P. 'Peasants, the seigneurial regime and serfdom', in T. F. X. Noble and J. van Engen (eds), *European Transformations. The Long Twelfth Century*, Notre Dame, Ind., 2012, pp. 259–78.

French, K. 'Maiden's Lights and Wives' Stores: Women's Parish Guilds in Late Medieval England', *The Sixteenth Century Journal* 29 (1998), 399–425.

Fumigalli, V., and Rosetti, G. (eds). *Medioevo rurale. Sulle trace della civiltà Contadina*, Bologna, 1980.

Ganshof, F. L. *Feudalism*, trans. P. Grierson, 3rd edn, London, 1964.

Ganshof, F.-L. 'À propos du tonlieu sous les Mérovingiens', in *Studi in onore di Amintore di Fanfani* 1, Milan, 1962, pp. 291–315.

Ganz, D. 'Giving to God in the mass. The experience of the offertory', in W. Davies and P Fouracre (eds), *The Languages of Gift*, Cambridge, 2010, pp. 18–32.

Ganz, D. 'Theology and the organization of thought', in R. McKitterick (ed.), *New Cambridge Medieval History* II, Cambridge, 1995, pp. 758–85.

Garcia Sanjuán, A. *Till God Inherits the Earth. Islamic Pious Endowment in al-Andalus (9th–15th Centuries)*, Leiden and Boston, 2007.

Gaudemet, J. 'Les status épiscopaux de la première decade du IX siècle', *Proceedings of the Fourth International Congress of Medieval Canon Law*, ed. S. Kuttner, Monumenta Iuris Canonici, series C, subsidia 5, Vatican, 1976, pp. 303–49.

Geary, P. *Aristocracy in Provence: The Rhône Basin at the Dawn of the Carolingian Age*, Stuttgart, 1985.

Geary, P. 'Die Provenz zur Zeit Karl Martells', in J. Jarnut, U. Nonn and M. Richter (eds), *Karl Martell in seiner Zeit*, Beihefte der *Francia* 37, Sigmaringen, 1994.

Geertmans, H. 'L'illuminazione della basilica paleocristiana secondo il Liber Pontificalis', *Rivista di Archeologia Christiana* 64 (1988), 135–60.

Gellinger, B. *Icelandic Enterprise. Commerce and Economy in the Middle Ages*, South Carolina, 1981.

## Bibliography

Gem, R. '*Gabatae Saxiscae*: Saxon bowls in the churches of Rome during the eighth and ninth centuries', in A. Reynolds and L. Webster (eds), *Early Medieval Art and Archaeology in the Northern World. Studies in Honour of James Graham-Campbell* (Leiden and Boston, 2013), pp. 87–110.

Goffart, W. 'Old and New in Merovingian Taxation', *Past and Present* 96 (1982), 3–32.

Goffart, W. *The Le Mans Forgeries. A Chapter from the History of Church Property in the Ninth Century*, Cambridge, Mass., 1966.

Graham, B. 'Olives and Lighting in Early Medieval Dark Age Europe', *Early Medieval Europe* 28.3 (2020), 344–66.

Grieco, A. J. 'Olive tree cultivation and the alimentary use of olive oil in Late Medieval Italy', in M. C. Amouretti and J.-P. Brun (eds), *La production du vin et d'huile en Méditerranée* (*Bulletin de Correspondance Hellénique*, Supplément 26), Paris, 1993, pp. 297–306.

Grieme, U., Kruppa, N., and Patzold, S. (eds), *Bischof und Bürger. Herrschaftsbeziehungen in den Kathedralstädten des Hoch- und Spätmittelalters*, Göttingen, 2004.

Grierson, P., and Blackburn, M. *Medieval European Coinage*, I: *The Early Middle Ages (5th to 10th Centuries)*, Cambridge, 1986.

Halsall, G. *The Barbarian Migrations*, Cambridge, 2007.

Hammer, C. *A Large-scale Slave Society of the Early Middle Ages. Slaves and Their Families in Early Medieval Bavaria*, Aldershot, 2002.

Hammer, Carl, I. 'Land Sales in Eighth- and Ninth-Century Bavaria: Legal, Economic and Social Aspects', *Early Medieval Europe* 6 (1997), 47–76.

Hanawalt, B. 'Keepers of the Lights: Late Medieval Parish Gilds', *Journal of Medieval and Renaissance Studies* 14 (1984), 21–37.

Hartung, W. 'Adel, Erbrecht, Schenkung: die strukturellen Ursachen der frühmittelalterlichen Besitzübertragungen an die Kirche', in F. Seibt (ed.), *Gesellschaftsgeschichte. Festschrift für Karl Bosl zum 80 Geburtstag*, 2 vols, Munich, 1988, vol. 1, pp. 417–38.

Head, T., and Landes, R. (eds). *The Peace of God: Social Violence and Religious Response in France around the Year 1000*, Ithaca, 1992.

Heather, P. *The Fall of the Roman Empire*, Basingstoke and Oxford, 2005.

Heinzelmann, M. 'Neue Aspekte der biographischen und hagiographischen Literatur in der lateinischen Welt (1–6 Jahrhundert)', *Francia* 1 (1973), 27–44.

Heinzelmann, M. '"Sanctitas" und "Tugendadel": zur Konzeptionen von "Heilgikeit" in 5 und 10 Jahrhundert', *Francia* 5 (1977), 741–52.

Heinzelmann, M. *Gregory of Tours*, Cambridge, 2001.

Higham, N. (ed.), *Wilfrid. Abbot, Bishop, Saint*, Donington, 2013.

Hilton, R. *Bond Men Made Free. Medieval Peasant Movements and the English Rising of 1381*, London, 1973.

Huizinga, J. *The Waning of the Middle Ages*, Eng. trans., London, 1924.

Iogna-Prat, D. 'Lieu du culte et exégèse liturgique à l'époque carolingienne', in C. Chazelle and B. Van Nam Edwards (eds), *The Study of the Bible in the Carolingian Era*, Medieval Church Studies 3, Turnhout, 2003, pp. 215–44.

## Bibliography

Jahn, J. 'Tradere ad sanctum: politische und gesellschaftliche Aspekte der Traditionspraxis im agilolfingerische Bayern', in F. Seibt (ed.), *Gesellschaftsgeschichte. Festschrift für Karl Bosl zum 80 Gerburtstag*, 2 vols (Munich, 1988), vol. 1, pp. 400–16.

Jarrett, J. *Rulers and Ruled in Frontier Catalonia 800–1010*, Woodbridge, 2010.

Jobert, Ph. *La notion de donation: convergences: 630–750*, Paris, 1977.

Jong, M. de. '"Ecclesia" and the early medieval polity', in S. Airlie, W. Pohl and H. Reimitz (eds), *Staat im frühen Mittelalter*, Vienna, 2006, pp. 113–32.

Jong, M. de. 'The state of the Church: *ecclesia* and early-medieval state formation', in W. Pohl and V. Wieser (eds), *Der frühmittelalterliche Staat. Europäische Perspectiven*, Vienna, 2009, pp. 242–54.

Kaiser, R. 'Royauté et pouvoir épiscopale au Nord de la Gaule vii–ix siècles', in H. Atsma (ed.), *La Neustrie: les pays au nord de la Loire de 650 à 850*, Actes du colloque historique international, 2 vols, Sigmaringen, 1989, I, pp. 141–60.

Kaiser, R. *Trunkenheit und Gewalt im Mittelalter*, Cologne, Weimar and Vienna, 2002.

Kanaka Durgan, P. S., and Sudhakar Reddy, Y. A. 'Kings, Temples and Legitimation of Autochthonous Communities', *Journal of the Economic and Social History of the Orient* 35 (1992), 145–66.

Kiessling, R. *Bürgerliche Gesellschaft und Kirche in Augsburg im Spätmittelalter*, Augsburg, 1971.

Kiessling, R. 'Pfarrgemeinde und Zeche bei Saint Moritz. Die Mitwirkung der Laien in einer zentralen Pfarrei der Stadt', in G. Müller (ed.), *Das ehemalige Kollegiatstift Saint Moritz in Augsburg (1019–1803)*, Lindenberg, 2006, pp. 185–208.

Koziol, G. *Politics of Memory and Identity in Carolingian Royal Diplomas. The West Frankish Kingdom (840–987)*, Turnhout, 2012.

Kroell, M. *L'immunité franque*, Paris, 1910.

Kuchenbuch, L. *Bauerliche Gesellschaft und Klosterherrschaft im 9 Jahrhundert, Vierteljahrschrift für social und Wirtschaftsgeschichte*, Beiheft 61, Wiesbaden, 1978.

Kuchenbuch, L. '*Porcus donativus*: language use and gifting in seigniorial records between the eighth and tenth centuries', in G. Algazi, V. Groebner and B. Jussen (eds), *Negotiating the Gift: Pre-modern Figurations of Exchange*, Veröffentlichungen des Max-Planck-Instituts für Geschichte 188, Göttingen, 2003, pp. 193–246.

Le Goff, J. *The Birth of Purgatory*, trans. A. Goldhammer, Chicago, 1984.

Lévi-Provençal, E. 'La "Description de l'Espagne" d'Ahmad al-Rāzī: essai de reconstitution de l'original arabe et traduction française', *Al-Aandalus* 18 (1953), 51–108.

Link, E. *Sozialer Wandel in Klösterlichen Grundherrschaft der 11 bis 13 Jahrhunderts. Studien zu den familiae von Gembloux, Stablo-Malmedy und Saint Trond*, Göttingen, 1979.

MacCormack, S. *Art and Ceremony in Late Antiquity*, Berkeley, 1995.

McCormick, M. *Origins of the European Economy. Communications and Commerce AD 300–900*, Cambridge, 2001.

# Bibliography

Magnou-Nortier, E. 'Étude sur le privilege d'immunité du IVe au IXe siècle', *Revue Mabillon*, 60 (1984), 465–512.
Manzano Moreno, E. *La frontera de al-Andalus en la época de los Omeyas*, Madrid, 1991.
Marshall, P. *Heretics and Believers. A History of the English Reformation*, New Haven and London, 2018.
Matheus, M. 'Forms of social mobility: the example of the *Zensualität*', in A. Haverkampf and H. Vollrath (eds), *England and Germany in the High Middle Ages*, Oxford, 1996, pp. 357–69.
Meersseman, G. *Ordo Fraternitas. Confraternite e Pieta del Laici nel Medieovo*, 3 vols, Italia Sacra. Studi e documenti di storia ecclesiastica 24–6, Rome, 1977.
Miramon, C. de. *Les donnés au Moyen Age. Une forme de vie religieuse laïque v. 1180 – v. 1500*, Paris, 1999.
Morimoto, Y. 'Problèmes autour du polyptyque de Saint-Bertin (844–859)', in Y. Morimoto, *Études sur l'économie rurale du haut Moyen Age. Historiographie, regime domanial, polyptyques carolingiennes*, Brussels, 2008, pp. 399–424.
Morimoto, Y. 'Aspects of the early medieval peasant economy as revealed in the polyptych of Prüm', in P. Linehan, J. Nelson and M. Costambeys (eds), *The Medieval World*, 2nd edn, London, 2017, pp. 705–19.
Mukund, K. *The Trading World of the Tamil Merchant*, Hyderabad and London, 1999.
Musset, L. 'Quelques notes sur les baleiniers Normands du Xe au XIIIe siècle', *Revue d'Histoire Économique et Social* 42 (1964), 147–61.
Naismith, R. 'Guilds, States and Societies in the Early Middle Ages', *Early Medieval Europe* (forthcoming).
Naismith, R., and Tinti, F. 'The Origins of Peter's Pence', *English Historical Review* 134 (2019), 521–52.
Nelson, J. 'Peers in the early Middle Ages', in P. Stafford, J. Nelson and J. Martindale (eds), *Law, Laity and Solidarities. Essays in Honour of Susan Reynolds*, Manchester, 2001, pp. 27–46.
Nelson, J. *Charles the Bald*, Harlow, 1992.
Nelson, J. 'The settings of the gift in the reign of Charlemagne', in W. Davies and P. Fouracre (eds), *The Languages of Gift in the Early Middle Ages* (Cambridge, 2010), pp. 116–48.
Nelson, J. 'Alcuin's letter to Meginfrid', in A. Dierkens (ed.), *Penser la paysannerie medieval, un défi impossible? Recueil d'études offert à J.-P. Devroey*, Paris, 2017, pp. 111–25.
Nelson, J. *King and Emperor. A New Life of Charlemagne*, London, 2019.
Niermeyer, J.-F. *Mediae Latinitatis Lexicon Minus*, Leiden, 1984.
Noble, T. F. X. *The Republic of Saint Peter. The Birth of the Papal State 680–825*, Philadelphia, 1984.
Noonan, T. S., and Kovalev, R. K. 'Wine and Oil for All the Rus! The Importation of Byzantine Wine and Olive Oil to Kievan Rus', *Byzantium and the North (Acta Byzantina Fennica)* 9 (1999), 118–52.

# Bibliography

Noonan, T. S., and Kovalev, R. K. 'Prayer, Illumination and Good Times: the Export of Byzantine Wine and Oil to the North of Russia in pre-Mongol times', *Byzantium and the North (Acta Byzantina Fennica)* 8 (1997), 73–96.

O'Carraragáin, E. *The City of Rome and the World of Bede*, Jarrow Lecture, 1994.

Oexle, O. G. '"Conjuratio" et "ghilde" dans l'Antiquité et dans le Haut Moyen Age. Remarques sur la continuité des forms de la vie sociale', *Francia* 19 (1982), 1–19.

Pelteret, D. *Slavery in Early Medieval England*, Woodbridge, 1995.

Petke, W. 'Die Pfarrei in Mitteleuropa im Wandel vom Früh- zum Hochmittelalter', in E. Bünz and G. Fouquet (eds), *Die Pfarrei im späten Mittelalter, Vorträge und Forschungen 77* (Ostfildern, 2013), pp. 21–60.

Pini, A. I. 'Vite et olivo nell'alto Medioevo', in *L'Ambiente Vegetale nell'alto Medioevo*, Settimane di Spoleto 37 (1990), 329–70.

Pini, A. I. 'La vite e olivo nell'Italia padana. Due collture specialistiche del Medioevo', in V. Fumigalli and G. Rosetti (eds), *Medioevo rurale. Sulle trace della civiltà Contadina*, Bologna, 1980, pp. 119–38.

Postles, D. 'Lamps, Lights and Layfolk: Popular Devotion before the Black Death', *Journal of Medieval History* 25.2 (1999), 97–114.

Pracy, S. 'Social Mobility and Manumissions in Early Medieval England', *Haskins Society Journal* 31 (forthcoming, 2020).

Prinz, F. *Frühes Mönchtum im Frankenreich*, Munich, 1965.

Reuter, T. 'Debate. The "Feudal Revolution" III', *Past and Present* 155 (1997), 177–95.

Reuter, T. *Germany in the Early Middle Ages 800–1056*, London, 1991.

Reynolds, A., and Webster, L. (eds), *Early Medieval Art and Archaeology in the Northern World. Studies in Honour of James Graham-Campbell*, Leiden and Boston, 2013.

Reynolds, S. *Kingdoms and Communities in Western Europe 900–1300*, Oxford, 1984.

Reynolds, S. *Fiefs and Vassals. The Medieval Evidence Reconsidered*, Oxford, 1996.

Rhijn, van, C. *Shepherds of the Lord. Priests and Episcopal Statutes in the Carolingian Period*, Turnhout, 2007.

Rio, A. 'Charters, law codes and formulae: the Franks between theory and practice', in P. Fouracre and D. Ganz (eds), *Frankland. The Franks and the World of the Early Middle Ages*, Manchester, 2008, pp. 7–27.

Rio, A. *Legal Practice and the Written Word in the Early Middle Ages. Frankish Formulae c. 500–1000*, Cambridge, 2009.

Rio, A. *Slavery after Rome 500–1100*, Oxford, 2017.

Rosenwein, B. *Negotiating Space: Power, Restraint and Privileges of Immunity in Early Medieval Europe*, Manchester, 1999.

Rosser, G. 'The Anglo-Saxon gilds', in J. Blair (ed.), *Minsters and Parish Churches. The Local Church in Transition 950–1200*, Oxford, 1988, pp. 31–4.

Rössner, P. 'Luther – ein tüchtiger Ökonom? Über die monetären Ursprünge der Deutschen Reformation', *Zeitschrift für Historische Forschung* 42 (2015), 37–74.

Sánchez Albornoz, C. *Despoblación y Repoblación del Valle del Duero*, Buenos Aires, 1966.

Sani, E. 'Renaissance Light: a Glass *Cesendello* (Hanging Lamp) Rediscovered', *Journal of Glass Studies* 59 (2017), 193–205.
Sapoznik, A. 'Bees in the Medieval Economy: Religious Observance and the Production, Trade, and Consumption of Wax in England c. 1300–1500', *Economic History Review* 72.4 (2019), 1152–74.
Sato, S. 'The Merovingian accounting documents of Tours', *Early Medieval Europe* 9 (2000), 143–61.
Schmieder, F. 'Die Pfarrei in der deutschen städtischen Kirchenlandschaft', in E. Bünz and G. Fouquet (eds), *Die Pfarrei im späten Mittelalter, Vorträge und Forschungen 77* (Ostfildern, 2013), pp. 131–56.
Schroeder, N. *Les hommes et la terre de Saint Remacle. Histoire sociale et économique de l'abbaye de Stavelot-Malmedy VIIe–XIVe siècles*, Brussels, 2015.
Schrott, G. *Mönche, Bienen, Bücher. Ein ertragreiche Symbiose*, Amberg, 2011.
Schulz, K. 'Stadtrecht und Zensualität am Niederrhein (12–14 Jahrhundert)', in E. Ennen and K. Flink (eds), *Soziale und wirtschaftliche Bindungen in Mittelalter der Niederrhein, Klever Archiv* 3, Cleves, 1981.
Schulz, K. *Die Freiheit des Bürgers. Städtische Gesellschaft in Hoch- und Spätmittelalter*, Darmstadt, 2008.
Schulz, K. 'Zensualität und Stadtentwicklung im 11/12 Jahrhundert', in K. Schulz, *Die Freiheit des Bürgers. Städtische Gesellschaft in Hoch- und Spätmittelalter* (Darmstadt, 2008), pp. 106–30.
Schulz, K. 'Zum Problem der Zensualität im Hochmittelalter', in K. Schulz, *Die Freiheit des Bürgers. Städtische Gesellschaft in Hoch- und Spätmittelalter* (Darmstadt, 2008), pp. 69–105.
Scribner, R. 'Civic Unity and the Reformation in Erfurt', *Past and Present* 66 (1975), 29–60.
Smith, J. M. H. *Europe after Rome. A New Cultural History 500–1000*, Oxford, 2005.
Stasolla, M. G. *Italia euro-mediterranea nel medioevo: testimonianze de scrittore arabi*, Bologna, 1983.
Stoclet, A. *Immunes ab omni teloneo. Étude de diplomatique, de philologie et d'histoire sur l'exemption de tonlieux au haut Moyen Age et spécialement sur la 'Praeceptio de navibus'*, Brussels and Rome, 1999.
Story, J. 'Land and lights in early medieval Rome', in R. Balzaretti, J. Barrow and P. Skinner (eds) *Italy and Early Medieval Europe* (Oxford, 2018), pp. 315–38.
Swanson, R. *Religion and Devotion* in *Europe c. 1215–1515*, Cambridge, 1995.
Taylor, H. M. 'The Architectural Interest of Æthelwulf's De Abbatibus', *Anglo-Saxon England* 3 (1974), 163–7.
Thacker, A. 'Memorialising Gregory the Great: the Origins and Transmission of a Papal Cult in the Seventh and Early Eighth Centuries', *Early Medieval Europe* 7 (1998), 59–85.
Thomás-Faci, G. and Martín-Iglesias, J. C. 'Cuatro documentos inéditos de San Martín de Asán (522–586)', *Mittellateinisches Jahrbuch* 52 (2017), 261–86.

# Bibliography

To Figueras, L. *Família i hereu a la Catalunya nord-oriental (segles X–XI)*, Montserrat, 1997.
Toubert, P. 'The Carolingian moment (eighth century)' in A. Burguière (ed.), *L'histoire de la famille*, trans. S. Hanbury-Tenison, *The History of the Family*, Cambridge, 1996, pp. 379–406.
Trout, D. E. *Paulinus of Nola. Life, Letters and Poems*, Berkeley, Los Angeles and London, 1999.
Varani, G., and Brugnoli, A. 'Olivi e olio nel patrimonio della famiglia di Totone di Campione', in S. Gasparri and C. La Rocca (eds), *Carte di famiglia. Strategie, rappresentazione e memoria del gruppo familiar di Totone di Campione (721–877)*, Rome, 2005, pp. 141–56.
Vauchez, A. *The Laity in the Middle Ages*, trans. B. Schneider, Notre Dame, Ind., 1993.
Verhulst, A. *The Carolingian Economy*, Cambridge, 2002.
Vesteinsson, O. *The Christianization of Iceland*, Oxford, 2000.
Vincent, C. *Fiat Lux. Lumière et luminaires dans la vie religieuse du XIIe au XVIe siècle*, Paris, 2004.
Wandel, L. *Voracious Idols and Violent Hands. Iconoclasm in Reformation Zurich, Strasbourg and Basel*, Cambridge, 1995.
Weidmann, M. *Das Testament des Bischofs Bertramn von Le Mans von 27 März 616*, Mainz, 1986.
Weiner, A. *Inalienable Possessions: the Paradox of Keeping-While-Giving*, Oxford, 1992.
West, C. *Reframing the Feudal Revolution. Political and Social Transformation between Marne and Moselle c. 800 – c. 1100*, Cambridge, 2013.
White, S. 'Tenth-century courts at Mâcon and the perils of structuralist history: re-reading Burgundian judicial institutions', in W. Brown and P. Górecki (eds), *Conflict in Medieval Europe: Changing Perspectives on Society and Culture*, Aldershot, 2003, pp. 37–68.
Wickham, C. 'Lawyers' time: history and memory in tenth- and eleventh-century Italy', in H. Mayr-Harting and R. Moore (eds), *Studies in Medieval History Presented to R. H. C. Davis*, London, 1985, pp. 53–71.
Wickham, C. *Framing the Early Middle Ages. Europe and the Mediterranean, 400–800*, Oxford, 2005.
Wickham, C. *The Inheritance of Rome*, London, 2009.
Wickham, C. *Sleepwalking into a New World. The Emergence of Italian City Communes in the Twelfth Century (The Lawrence Stone Lectures)*, Oxford, 2015.
Wild, J. 'Libri censualium', in G. Hetzer and B. Uhl (eds), *Festschrift Hermann Rumschöttel zum 65. Geburtstag*, 2 vols, Cologne, Weimar and Vienna, 2006, pp. 1105–21.
Wilson, S. 'Annotated bibliography', in S. Wilson (ed.), *Saints and Their Cults: Studies in Religious Sociology Folklore and History*, Cambridge, 1983, pp. 309–417.
Wood, I. 'A prelude to Columbanus: the monastic achievement in the Burgundian territories', in H. Clarke and M. Brennan (eds), *Columbanus and Merovingian*

*Monasticism*, British Archaeological Reports, International series 113, Oxford, 1981, pp. 3–32.
Wood, I. 'Teutsind, Witlaic and the history of Merovingian *precaria*' in W. Davies and P. Fouracre (eds), *Property and Power in the Early Middle Ages* (Cambridge, 1995), pp. 31–52.
Wood, I. *The Transformation of the Roman West*, Leeds, 2018.
Wood, I. 'Creating a Temple Society in the Early Medieval West', Annual *Early Medieval Europe* Lecture', Leeds International Medieval Congress, 2019, *Early Medieval Europe* (forthcoming).
Wood, S. *The Proprietary Church in the Medieval West*, Oxford, 2006.
Wormald, P. '*Lex Scripta* and *Verbum Regis*: legislation and Germanic kingship from Euric to Cnut', in P. Sawyer and I. Wood (eds), *Early Medieval Kingship*, Leeds, 1977, pp. 105–38.
Xanthopoulou, M. 'Lampes en metal, lampes en terre cuite: vies parallèles', *Lychonological Acts* 1 (2005), 303–6.
Young, F. M. *Biblical Exegesis and the Formation of Christian Culture*, Cambridge, 1997.

# Index

Aaron, brother of Moses 20
    sons of Aaron and priesthood 19, 20, 21, 96, 196, 204, 207
    *see also* Nadat and Abiu
Abbotsbury guild statutes 120
Ahmad al-Rāzi, geographer 79, 139
Albert Bisschop, merchant of Lübeck 193
Aleman law 164
Alemannia 93
Alfonso, king of Pamplona, brother of Peter 137
*ancilla* (female slave or maidservant) 161, 165
Anglo-Saxon charters 118
Anglo-Saxons in Rome 37
*Annals of Saint Bertin* 96
Ansa, Lombard queen 80, 81, 82
Ansbert, bishop of Rouen 61
arabic formulary 139, 152n.124
Aragon, kingdom 133, 138
Arascués (Huesca), charters concerning 137–8, 139
Asturias, kingdom 132, 133
Augsburg, Germany 193–4
'auto-dedition' (gift of self) 160–4, 167–8
'auto-tradition' (gift of *se et sua* in the later Middle Ages) 186–7
    contrasts with earlier gifts of self 187

Balzaretti, Ross 125, 127, 128
Barthélemy, Dominique 166, 167, 168, 169
Basel, Switzerland 196
Bavaria 93, 161, 170
Bavarian law 164
Bede 37, 118
beekeepers 33, 46n.72, 136
bees 38–9, 185, 200n.10, 213
    bees in Zoroastrian culture 39
Bellagio peninsula, Lake Como 125–6, 128
*beneficia* 90, 92, 97, 111, 121, 137
Bertramn bishop of Le Mans 50–1
    will of 51, 67, 86, 162
Bloch, Marc 10, 157, 164
Bobbio, monastery 80, 128
    income of 81, 86
Boleyn, Anne, queen 197
Boncampagno, author of *Cedrus* 129
Bonnassie, Pierre 138, 157
'book-keeping for the beyond' 182, 199n.3
*bunuaria*, unit of land 109, 145n.7

Candlemas 120, 181
Canterbury, charters of 119
    shrine of Beckett at 197
Capitulary of Frankfurt (794) 94
Capitulary of Herstal (779) 92, 117
Carey, George, archbishop of Canterbury 212

# Index

Carolingian legislation 94, 117, 159, 174, 207
cash 26, 30, 31, 34, 51, 56, 57, 61, 110
  raised from immunities and tolls 52, 55, 57
  spent on oil 60, 61, 64
Catalonia 130, 131, 133, 134
  immunities from 134
Celanova, monastery 136
*censuales* 9, 52, 93, 116, 156, 158, 160, 175
  conditions and privileges of 158, 169–75, 186
  in towns 171–2
  *see also Zensualität*
census 71, 115, 125, 135, 154, 159, 161, 173, 208
  census paid for *precaria* or *beneficia* 91–2, 97, 111
  census payers 154, 158
  *see also censuales*
*cerarii* 113
*cerocensuales* (payers of *census* in wax) 92, 113, 158, 159, 172
Charlemagne, Frankish king and emperor, conquest of Italy 80–2, 86, 159
  grants to Frankish monasteries 82
  capitularies of 94
Charles 'the Simple', Frankish king, charters of 88
Charles Martel, ruler of Francia 62
Charles the Bald, Frankish king and emperor, charters of 108–10
  legislation of 95, 111, 207
Charles the Fat, Frankish king 127
Chaucer, Geoffrey 195
Chelsfield, Kent 184
chirograph 138
chrism 1–2, 38, 94–5, 121
church buildings 79, 89, 94, 98, 211
  architectural changes in the seventeenth century 189
  dedication of ('the significance of the twelve candles') 98
  roofs of 34, 98, 171
*colliberti* 10, 156, 164, 174, 209
  compared to *servi* and *censuales* 166, 174
commemoration 4, 5, 12, 21, 24, 69, 107, 111, 120, 134, 137, 171, 181, 188, 206
commemorative lighting 24, 53, 67, 69–70, 86–7, 110
commodifying eternity 211–12
confraternities 6, 8, 13, 99, 117, 123, 141, 143, 182, 184, 189
  in Augsburg 194
  in England 192
  in Italy 123, 128, 129
Confraternity of Notre Dame des Ardents at Arras 184–5
Confraternity of Saint Martin of Canigou 143–6, 184
*coniurationes* (sworn associations) 117
Conrad II, king of Germany 160, 169, 172
  grant to the church of Speyer 169
Constantine emperor, gifts of 25–8, 78, 162, 205
  'Donation' of 78, 86, 108
Corbie, monastery, exemption from toll 57, 60, 62, 68
Cordoba, mosque at 140
Council of Aachen (836) 20, 21, 95, 207
  letter from 95–6
Council of Chalons (813) 95
Council of Elvira 22, 23, 196
Council of Estinnes (743) 90–2
Council of Rome (826) 95
Council of Soissons (853) 97
Council of Tours (813) 94
Council of Worms (868) 97
Councils of Braga 36, 64, 89, 90, 97, 130, 188
Councils of Toledo 34, 41, 89, 129, 130, 162, 169

Dagobert I, Frankish king 51, 59, 86
Davies, Wendy 135
Desiderius, Lombard king 80, 81
*Devotio Moderna* 187
Diana, Princess of Wales 212
Duero valley, 133
Duffy, Eamon 198, 199

232

## Index

Eberhard, count, in conflict with Stavelot-Malmedy 170–1
Edict of Pîtres (864) 111
Eizabeth I, queen of England 197–8
Engelric, serf of Marmoutier 165, 166, 175
Episcopal Statutes (*Capitula Episcoporum*) 97–8, 107, 183
  Statutes of Hincmar of Reims 99
  Hincmar on guilds 99, 106n.103
Erbio, client of Wissembourg 91
Ermenegild, donor 135
Esders, Stefan 163, 175
eucharist 1, 63
*ewige Rindern* (eternal cattle) 183
*ewiges Licht* (eternal light) 4, 183
*exenium* (gift of supplies) 124
Exeter guild regulations 120

Farfa monastery 65, 87
  charters of 6, 7, 67
'feudal crisis'/'feudal revolution' 54, 72n.9, 138, 141, 142, 145, 157–8, 165
fisc 56–8, 60, 163, 205
Flanders 117, 156, 164, 168, 170
Florence, confraternities in 189
formularies 7, 50, 71n.1
*Formulary of Bourges* 163
*Formulary of Marculf* 52–3, 162
Fourth Lateran Council of 1215 182
Frederick I, 'Barbarossa', emperor 171, 172, 208
friars 182
Fulda, monastery 83, 87

Galicia 133, 136
Gallicanism 190
*geneats* 114, 119
Gorze, monastery 116, 160
Gratian, *Decretum* 188
Gregorian Reform 142
Gregory 'the Great', Pope 29, 37
Gregory Bishop of Tours, works of 32, 33, 35, 51
guilds 5, 6, 8, 13, 99, 107, 116–18, 142, 182, 210
  guilds and drinking 117, 120, 123

guilds in England 119–21, 192–3
  *see also* confraternities
Gundebert, holder of the church of Saint Salvator 108–9, 112

*haistaldi* 114, 119, 155
Henry III, king of England, expenditure on wax 187–8
Henry VIII, king of England 197
*heriscarii* 113
Hildegard, queen, wife of Charlemagne 81, 82
  commemorative light for 24, 86
Hilduin, abbot of Saint Bertin 109
Hilton, Rodney 125, 128
Hinduism and lights 18–19
*hubs*, pious endowment in Muslim Spain 140, 208
Hugh son of King Lothar II 84, 85, 88

Iceland 1–3
immunities, privileges of 51, 52, 54–5, 57, 60, 163
indulgences 183, 186, 195, 210
Irmina, donor to Gorze 116, 160
Islam and lights 20, 79, 140
Italian charters 64, 65, 67, 69
Italian communes 122, 187, 189

Jacob's dream 89
Judaism and lights 19–20
Jumièges, monastery 59, 62–3

Kappenberg, convent, privileges for *cerocensuales* 172
Kiessling, Rolf 194
Koziol, Geoffrey 87–8
Kuchenbuch, Ludwig 115, 119

Lake Como, Italy 69, 82, 83, 87, 125
Lake Garda, Italy 67, 79, 81–2, 128
lamps 3, 12, 19, 20, 28, 29, 32, 37, 50, 68, 110–11, 190, 196
  glass lamps of the Renaissance 190
  lamps donated by Constantine 26
  lamps in mosques 140
leases in Italy 123, 125

# Index

Leire, Navarre, charters from 137–8
*leohtgesceot* (light-scot) in England 120–1, 192
León, antiphony from 136–7
documents from 133, 134, 135
*Liber Pontificalis* 25, 28–9, 78
*libri censualium* (books of *censuales*) 161
Limonta, charters from 125
'the Limonta dispute' 125–8
Lobbes, monastery, polyptych of 112, 114, 115
Lombard law 63, 64–5
Lothar I, emperor 82, 83
Lothar II, Frankish king divorce case of 83–5
Louis IV, Frankish king, charters of 88
Louis the Pious, emperor, legislation of 94–5
Lübeck, Germany 193
wills from Lübeck 193, 202n.45
*luminarii* 113, 115, 116, 131, 141, 155
*lunarii* 114, 119, 141
Luther, Martin 195

'maiden lights' 193
Mālikī tradition of jurisprudence 139–40
*mancipia* (un-free people or slaves) 35, 84, 91, 109, 113, 114, 116, 125, 131, 135, 160, 165, 169, 171
*see also servi*
*mansi* 91, 92, 95, 110
free and servile *mansi* 115
size of *mansi* 114, 127–8
manumission 116, 159, 161, 162, 166, 169, 172
Bodmin manumissions 119
documents of manumission 116, 162, 163
Marmoutier, monastery 165–9, 175, 183
'Book of Serfs' of Marmoutier 165, 169, 179
Marseilles 31, 33, 57–8, 59, 61–2, 81
mass, cost of 183
'middling sort' 116, 123, 141, 142
minster churches in England 121, 122

Morebath, Devonshire 198–9, 210
parish stores in 198
mosques 20, 42n.8, 140
*mu'aqqab*, family endowment in Islam 140
compared to inheritance strategies in the North 140
Muslim Spain 79, 139–40

Nadat and Abiu, sons of Aaron 21, 96, 204
Norman Conquest of England 192
Northern Spain 132, 133, 135

Odalburg, *ancilla* 161
Old Testament 20, 21, 204
Ölgötzen (oil-guzzling idols) 6, 196
olive oil 1–2, 11, 19, 20, 26, 38, 185, 205
consumption of in the Roman Empire 26
oil as fuel 185
production of and trade in 21, 28, 30–1, 139
olives 1, 7, 19, 29, 30, 35, 63, 65, 80, 124–5, 139
cultivation of 44nn.44, 45, 82–3, 128
number and value of olive trees 11, 26, 35, 65, 67
Oresme, Nicholas 195
Origen 21
Otho de Grandison, of Chelsfield, Kent, bequest of 184
Otto I, king and emperor of Germany 128

Pamplona, kingdom 133, 137, 138
papacy 1, 25, 30–1, 63–4, 78, 80, 142, 195
parishes 3, 89, 130, 131, 186, 190, 193
in Augsburg, Germany 194
Parliamentary inquiry into guilds 193
Paschal candle, ceremony of 136–7
Paulinus of Nola, poems of 23–4
Peace Movement 142
Peter, king of Pamplona 137
Pippin, king of Aquitaine 95
Pistoia, Tuscany 66, 69, 124
charters from 124

# Index

*pizzaras*, slate charters from Spain 35, 46n.82
polyptychs 5, 108, 111, 115
  polyptych of Saint Bertin 112–13
*precaria/e* 70–1, 77n.82, 90, 91, 93, 208
  *precaria* and *census* 92, 93, 125
Provence 28, 58, 60, 61–2, 79, 85
Prüm, monastery, polyptych of 111, 112, 114, 115
Purgatory 182, 183, 189, 192, 195, 210
  challenges to the concept of 197, 199
  confraternities dedicated to 183, 195
  Confraternity of Purgatory of Lavaur (France) 183

Qur'ān 20, 140

*radcnits* 114, 119
Ravenna, leases from the church 124–5
Reformation, the 13, 142, 181, 183, 193, 195, 198, 210
  in Augsburg 194–5
Reichenau, monastery, claiming Limonta 127
*Rentenlandschaft* 115, 119
Ripuarian law 164
Roman law 36, 52, 130, 140, 162, 163
Russia 2–3

Sahagun, monastery, documents from 134, 137
Saint Arnulf's, church in Metz 86
Saint Bertin, monastery 59, 108–9
Saint Denis, monastery of 53, 57
  charters of 59, 60, 61, 82, 84–5, 110
Saint Germain-des-Prés, monastery 59, 60, 62
  polyptych of 113, 160
Saint Martin's at Tours, monastery and shrine 31–2, 34, 59, 60, 81–2
Saint Peter's at Ghent, monastery 156–7, 167, 168, 175
  cartulary of 157
  *tributarii* in 157
Saint Vaast, 184
Saint Wandrille, monastery 58, 59, 61
  clients of 91

San Sepolcro, confraternity of San Bartolomeo 189–90
Sant' Ambrogia, monastery 125, 126, 127, 128
Schulz, Knut 156, 157, 158
*servi* (serfs or slaves) 32, 64, 115, 127, 165, 166, 171, 174
  see also *mancipia*
sheep, income from for the lights 183–4, 198
Speyer, privileges granted by King Henry V 172
  inscription celebrating privileges of 172
Stavelot-Malmedy, twin monasteries 9, 10, 59, 62, 159, 175, 208, 209
  *censuales* of 171
  income from *familia* of 170
Stenetland, inventory of 108–9
Strasbourg, France 196

*ta'ifa* kingdoms in Spain 137
Tertullian 21–2
Theutberga, wife of King Lothar II 84, 85
tithes 94, 131, 186
  abuse of 95, 99, 107
  payment for lights from 95, 125, 154, 159
tolls, exemption from 50, 51, 53, 54, 57, 60, 61, 62, 79, 82
Toto of Campione, gifts of 67–8

un-freedom 115, 119, 127, 135
Urgell, church consecrations in the diocese of 136, 138, 157

Valpuesta, monastery, charters from 134, 135
Vermudo, donor to Celanova 136
Vincent, Catherine 13, 14, 156
Visigothic Spain 133, 135
  charters of 35–6, 130
  hagiography from 35
  formula for donation for the lights 7, 39, 40, 130, 131, 133
  see also *pizzaras*

*Visio Baronti* 63
*Vita Ansberti* 58, 61

Waldrada, wife of King Lothar II 84, 85, 88
*waqf* pious endowment in Islam 140, 208
wax 2, 4, 32–3, 38, 39, 119, 136, 189
   amount consumed in the fifteenth century 185
   hallowing of 38, 136–7, 185
   imports of 185, 188
   tributes paid in 10, 66, 92, 113, 135, 158–9, 170
whale oil 2, 63
Wissembourg, monastery 91, 116, 159, 170

Worms, Germany, privileges of 172, 173–4

Xanten, monastery, *cerocensuales* of 161–2

*yardland* 114, 119

Zacharias, Pope 30
*Zeche(n)* 14, 73, 186, 194
   *Zechen* of Saint Moritz, Augsburg 194
*Zensualität* 5, 9, 52, 135, 156, 209
   see also *censuales* and *cerocenusales*
Zürich, lamp smashing in 196, 199
Zwingli, Ulrich 196

EU authorised representative for GPSR:
Easy Access System Europe, Mustamäe tee 50,
10621 Tallinn, Estonia
gpsr.requests@easproject.com

www.ingramcontent.com/pod-product-compliance
Ingram Content Group UK Ltd.
Pitfield, Milton Keynes, MK11 3LW, UK
UKHW021840140426
5217IPUK00022B/1532